Introduction to Intercultural Studies

Introduction to Intercultural Studies

Ríoghnat Crotty

Gill & Macmillan

Gill & Macmillan
Hume Avenue
Park West
Dublin 12
with associated companies throughout the world
www.gillmacmillan.ie

© Ríoghnat Crotty 2013

978 07171 5630 6

Index compiled by Adam Pozner
Print origination by Carole Lynch
Printed by GraphyCems, Spain

Lyrics from 'The Great Hunger' with kind permission of John Gibbs.
Lyrics from 'The Fields of Athenry' with kind permission of Peter St John.

For permission to reproduce photographs, the author and publisher
gratefully acknowledge the following:
© Alamy: 57, 58, 94, 105, 136; © Getty Images: 19, 108, 168; © Kobal/
Picture Desk: 150B; © Rex Features: 150T; Courtesy of Jane Elliott: 29.

The paper used in this book comes from the wood pulp of managed
forests. For every tree felled, at least one tree is planted, thereby renewing
natural resources.

A CIP catalogue record is available for this book from the British Library.

In memory of my mother, Sheelagh

Thanks to Bernadette McDonald for the use of her books, her kitchen table and, most of all, her ears.

Contents

Chapter 7 The Print Media, Attitudes and Objectivity 123

Chapter 8 Ethnicity and Culture in Television,   138
Cinema and Music

Chapter 9 Legislation, the United Nations and   157
Human Rights

Overview of Learning Outcomes and Learner Record Tips

Learning Outcomes

This book has been designed to match the learning outcomes specified by FETAC for the Level 5 Intercultural Studies module (5N0765). While some of the learning outcomes are represented in distinct chapters, learning outcomes 1 and 12 are more reflective and analytical and so are interspersed throughout the chapters in the form of activities and project ideas. Learning outcomes 2 to 11 are more content-based and are dealt with in specific chapters. The learning outcomes are as follows.

1. Demonstrate a critical understanding of intercultural issues by developing a respect for self, others and for diversity and exploring a variety of ways of dealing with issues arising from cultural differences.

2. Discuss the key elements of 'culture', 'society', 'stereotyping', 'cultural myths', 'racism', 'xenophobia', 'nationalism', 'assimilation' and 'integration' (see Chapter 1).

3. Discuss the manner in which a variety of cultures mark significant life milestones, i.e. marriage, death, and compare the role of religious belief in two contrasting societies (see Chapter 3).

4. Examine the influence of culture on personal identity and recognise prejudice and stereotyping in other people and in themselves (see Chapter 2).

5. Discuss the links between aid, colonialism, trade, slavery and racism (see Chapter 6) and explore possible reasons why groups such as emigrants, migrants and immigrants may experience prejudice and discrimination from members of a dominant culture (see Chapter 5).

6. Explore the contribution of the media to attitude formation, cultural identity and popular opinion and critically evaluate the portrayal of cultural diversity in a variety of popular magazines (see Chapter 7).

7. Analyse and evaluate various aspects of interculturalism using a range of methods and sources, i.e. investigating the cultural origins of current popular music and cinema (see Chapter 8).

8. Design appropriate survey methods, e.g. questionnaires, interview, to explore key choices and challenges posed by living in a new cultural environment and examine some ways societies promote and foster a sense of belonging and cultural identity (see Chapter 4).

9. Explore and discuss the key legislation governing interpersonal relationships in Irish society, for example the Equality Act, Equal Status Act, Employment Equality Act, and examine the role of peace-making and peace-keeping organisations (see Chapter 9).

10. Exercise initiative and independence by exploring attitudes that contribute to racist behaviour by identifying and exploring incidences and reason for some current intercultural conflicts (see Chapter 5).

11. Critically examine and evaluate her/his values in relation to intercultural issues, for example refugees, aid, work permits (see Chapter 5).

12. Process and present findings from research and outline key principles for guidelines to promote inclusive behaviour in, for example, the workplace, clubs, societies, schools, training centres.

The Learner Record

As part of this module, you will be required to keep a learner record. The learner record is described by FETAC as 'The learner's self-reported and self-reflective record in which he/she describes specific learning experiences, activities, responses and skills acquired.' This should be an ongoing record of your own responses to the material covered, showing how your self-awareness and analytical skills progress throughout the year.

Learner Record Tips

The purpose of the learner record is to chart your own progress, so make sure you write about your own personal experience and thoughts. It is not a repetition or revision exercise but involves your own reaction and reflection.

- However, don't be too personal – it's not your diary. Make sure you stay on topic and be clear in what you are saying.
- Examining reasons for mistakes made on work experience is a useful exercise – it should help you improve. Elaborating and dwelling on the mistake itself is no use. Instead, focus on what you have learned and what you would do differently in future.

- Don't forget to update your learner record regularly – we forget very quickly. If you don't keep it updated regularly, you will find it harder to catch up and you will learn less.

- The learner record should show change. Make sure to include any changes. For example, if you change your opinion or something you were unsure of becomes clearer, ensure that you put this in your account.

- Where a topic leads to more questions than answers, don't worry. You are not necessarily supposed to come up with answers, just show engagement with the material.

- You don't have to agree with other people – this is *your* learning experience. Even if you are outnumbered, learning to defend a view is an excellent learning experience.

- Use your learner record to make links between new topics and earlier material. Don't regard any section of the course as 'finished'. Something that comes up later may make you want to rethink earlier opinions.

- If you are unsure about what you have to do, ask. Don't waste your time working on something that you are unsure about.

- Try not to confine your learning to the classroom, but keep a curious mind in the rest of your life. Television, the internet, magazines and newspapers can complement some of your learning.

- Focus on self-knowledge. Don't just state your opinion, but explain why you think this way. Be aware of where your opinions come from.

- All reactions are worthy of note, including annoyance or disagreement as well as surprise. You can disagree, but be respectful. Again, it can be a useful experience to see how you handle disagreement.

- If you are shy and not always willing to take part in discussions, your learner journal is a chance to air your opinions. Also, getting into the habit of expressing your opinions on paper might help you feel confident enough to speak in public.

CHAPTER 1

An Intercultural Society

By the end of this chapter, students should:

- Be able to describe and discuss multicultural and intercultural approaches and understand the terms *assimilation* and *integration*.
- Be able to define culture and society and list the five components of culture in society.
- Be aware of Ireland's historic pattern of emigration.
- Be able to define *nationalism* and explore how it can be a barrier to accepting other cultures.
- Be able to discuss, using statistical examples, how culture changes over time.
- Be able to define *racism*, *race*, *ethnicity* and *xenophobia*.
- Understand the term *segregation* and discuss the effects of segregation under the apartheid regime in South Africa.

Multicultural and Intercultural Societies

The terms *multicultural* and *intercultural* both relate to approaches to how to build a society where there is a diversity of cultures. The key difference lies in the words themselves. *Multi* means 'many', so the term *multicultural* simply acknowledges the existence of more than one culture. *Inter* means 'between', so the word *intercultural* signifies communication and shared responsibility.

Until the 1940s, much of Europe was involved in global exploration and conquest, and there was little immigration to Europe itself. During this time 'it was widely assumed that all those who lived within a state boundary should assimilate to its predominant ethos, into which successive generations were socialised' (Council of Europe 2008:18). People of other cultures were expected to assimilate; that is, to forsake their own culture and become like the majority. Assimilation is defined as 'the blending of the culture and structure of one racial or ethnic group with the culture and structure of society' (Curry *et al.* 2005:199). Assimilation will be discussed in more detail in Chapter 5.

After 1945, in a post-war Europe, immigration became more common and government policy was often based on the concept of multiculturalism. This meant that recognition was given to the values of minority communities along with those of the 'host' majority, but little thought was given to integration.

Integration has been described as 'a two-sided process and as the capacity of people to live together with full respect for the dignity of each individual, the common good, pluralism and diversity, non-violence and solidarity, as well as their ability to participate in social, cultural, economic and political life' (Council of Europe 2008:11), while Jandt states that 'True integration is maintaining important parts of one's original culture as well as becoming an integral part of the new culture. Integration ensures a continuity of culture' (Jandt 2004:337).

Multiculturalism did encourage equality and tolerance for other cultures, but it emphasised lines of separation of minority and majority cultures, rather than promoting contact and understanding. People of other cultures were seen as separate communities and well-meaning but faulty attempts were made to cater for them as separate groups. Immigrants were often seen as having no cross-over with the majority and assumptions were made about their needs without consulting them. The majority 'host' society was encouraged to tolerate difference, but no efforts were made at finding common ground between the two. Lack of communication often resulted in stereotyping and discrimination. 'Whilst driven by benign intentions, multiculturalism is now seen by many as having fostered communal segregation and mutual incomprehension' (Council of Europe 2008:19). Thompson states that multiculturalism is insufficient, that cultural and religious pluralism are not enough, and calls for 'the state to be more actively involved in promoting a common citizenship and greater civic participation' (Thompson 2008:56). This point of view argues that racial and religious tolerance are not enough and that integration needs to be promoted through better educational and employment opportunities and greater civic engagement.

The policy of multiculturalism was increasingly seen as outdated, contributing to dividing people into rigid categories. A 2008 Council of Europe report, *Living Together as Equals in Dignity*, found that 'old approaches to the management of cultural diversity were no longer adequate to societies' (Council of Europe 2008:9). A new approach was needed for the twenty-first century and intercultural dialogue was seen to be the way forward. Intercultural societies involve people of different cultures not only living together but interacting and exchanging ideas. Through conversation, we can 'see where they are coming from' and develop respect for views other than our own. Recognition of the equal value of different cultures comes about by education and consultation. It is recommended that intercultural dialogue must not only be a policy at government level, but must take place in every area of life, 'be it the neighbourhood, the workplace, the education system and associated institutions, civil society and particularly the youth sector, the media, the arts world or the political arena' (Council of Europe 2008:10).

An intercultural approach is concerned with the exchange of views between those of different cultures, in an effort to build trust, understanding and respect. Participation by all in society is a key aim – newcomers must feel able to participate in every area of society and not be 'boxed off' into special areas of interest. For example, many schools dedicate one day to celebrating the different nationalities of pupils, but efforts should be made to include them across the entire school year.

The ultimate aim of intercultural dialogue is for people 'to learn to live together peacefully and constructively in a multicultural world and to develop a sense of community and belonging' (Council of Europe website: 'The concept of intercultural dialogue'). Intercultural dialogue can also prevent or resolve conflict and promote respect for human rights and democracy. Some of the goals of intercultural dialogue are:

- To share different perspectives of the world and try to understand and learn from those with different views.
- To recognise similarities as well as differences between different cultures.
- To reach agreement that disputes should be resolved peacefully.
- To ensure that all cultures participate equally.
- To reassure those who view diversity as a threat.

Summarised from Council of Europe website: 'The concept of intercultural dialogue'.

Some conditions that favour intercultural dialogue are that people bring open and curious minds to the process, are aware of the basic features of their own and other cultures and are willing to see similarities as well as differences between their own and other cultures.

Finding shared areas of concern results in increased integration. Rotimi Adebari, a former asylum seeker, was elected as a local government councillor in Portlaoise in 2004, became Ireland's first black mayor in 2007 and was re-elected in 2009. His success was based on focusing on local issues shared by all, such as childcare, hospital closures, public transport and employment initiatives, winning support not just among immigrants but in the wider society.

Summarised from Council of Europe (1995, 2008, website: 'The concept of intercultural dialogue'); Fanning (2012).

Activities

1 A local community centre offers mother and toddler groups for Polish women. Consider whether this is good intercultural practice. What arguments could be made for and against providing separate groups for different nationalities?

2 An Irish person moving to live in another country would probably be surprised if the locals assumed they ate only bacon, cabbage and potatoes, listened only to Irish music and followed only Gaelic games. What assumptions do you make about other cultures' interests?

3 What areas that are of interest and importance to you do you think immigrants might also think important?

4 Discuss what qualities and interests you would look for in a friend or colleague. Are these qualities and interests likely to be shared across cultures?

5 Discuss which of the following are most important in forming bonds with people: shared age group; shared taste in music, films, books; shared religion; shared personal circumstances (e.g. losing a loved one, having a toddler in the house, being divorced); shared heritage; shared hobbies; shared workplace or place of study; shared standard of living.

Culture

What is culture? We all use and hear the term regularly, but what do we mean by it? It has been defined as 'the values, customs and acceptable modes of behaviour that characterise a society or social groups within a society' (Marsh & Keating 2000:24). Simply put, culture involves the set of unwritten rules guiding how we live. We all live in a society and without being aware of it, we operate in a similar pattern to those about us.

'A society is a system of structured social relationships connecting people together according to a shared culture' (Giddens 2001:699). Society is dependent on culture and culture is dependent on society – neither can exist without the other.

We are individuals, but we share certain common beliefs and ways of behaving. This is more than a matter of choice: we must share a common code in order for society to function. This common code is our culture. For instance, we all know that it is bad manners for a guest to wear white at a wedding, we know what words are appropriate at a funeral, we recognise the difference between the distance required in a bank queue and a supermarket queue.

One of the things that culture reminds us of is that home is much more than a name we give to a dwelling place. It is also a whole set of connections and affections, the web of mutual recognition that we spin around ourselves and that gives us a place in the world. (O'Toole 1997:136)

Culture is a very broad term, so in order to examine it closely, sociologists have divided culture into five components: symbols, language, values, norms and material culture. These five components are common to all cultures and it is the variety of these components that makes each culture unique and distinct.

Symbols

Symbols are 'anything that carries a particular meaning recognised by people who share culture' (Macionis & Plummer 2002:100). Symbols are instantly recognisable. If we see a picture of a harp, Ireland immediately comes to mind. The colour red has become symbolic of danger or warning in our culture, for example the red card in football or a red light for 'stop'. Symbols can vary from one culture to another. In Arab culture, showing the sole of your shoe to a person is considered highly insulting, while in Ireland such an action would be merely puzzling.

Language

In order for us to communicate with each other we need a shared language. Apart from being the practical means of communication, language can have an emotional appeal. Also, apart from the actual language used, such as French or English, the variety of expression and even the use of slang will pinpoint a person's particular culture – words and phrases used in Ireland will differ from those in other English-speaking countries. Use of language also varies from generation to generation – for example, teenagers in Ireland often use Americanisms and abbreviations in texting and internet use that would be incomprehensible to an older person.

Values

'Fundamental to all cultures are the ideas which define what is considered important, worthwhile and desirable. These abstract ideas, or values, give meaning and provide guidance to humans as they interact with the social world' (Giddens 2001:22). We may think of our own values as being universal, but on closer inspection we can see that they are particular to a certain culture. For instance, a shared value in western society is monogamy within marriage, but other cultures allow a man to have many wives.

The values of Irish society were in the past often tied in with the Catholic faith. For example, sex outside marriage was not acceptable and any display of sexuality was frowned upon: 'Even students in Dublin would not dare to be seen holding hands, and in the country to make love before marriage was to risk banishment' (David Thomson, quoted in Somerville-Large 2000:131).

Norms

Norms are the 'rules and expectations by which a society guides the behaviour of its members' (Macionis & Plummer 2002:107). Norms consist of what we should and shouldn't do to fit into society. Again, what is forbidden or rude in one culture may be completely acceptable in another. 'In China, people curious about how much money colleagues are paid readily ask about their salaries. In Europe, people consider such a question rude' (Macionis & Plummer 2002:107). In the extreme heat of Australia, women may go shopping in their bikinis without anyone being shocked, yet to do so in Ireland would probably result in a mention on the news.

The consequences of disobeying norms vary from mild disapproval to being cut off from society. Because of the wide range of norms, they can be divided into four sub-groups: mores; folkways; taboos; and laws. The terms 'mores' and 'folkways' were devised by the American sociologist William Graham Sumner.

Mores

Sumner used the term 'mores' to refer to a society's standards of proper moral behaviour. Because of their importance in maintaining a society's way of life, people develop an emotional attachment to mores and breaking them results in a strong reaction. Disobeying mores threatens the welfare of society and can cause serious offence. For example, public nudity and drug use go against the mores of society and carry heavy social punishment.

Folkways

'Sumner used the term folkways to designate *a society's customs for routine, casual interaction* . . . In short, while mores distinguish between right and wrong, folkways draw a line between right and *rude*' (Macionis & Plummer 2002:108). Folkways involve less serious matters than mores, such as everyday courtesy and appropriate dress. Because they are less serious, there is more leeway around folkways and breaking them will result in mild disapproval rather than punishment. For example, a guest who turns up at a wedding wearing jeans will probably evoke disapproving comments or laughter but will not be punished or excluded in any way. A person who bumps into us and makes no apology will probably cause annoyance, but this will not be seen as a serious matter.

Taboos

These are rules that are so serious it is almost unthinkable to break them. A person who violates a taboo puts themselves outside society altogether and is regarded with horror.

The consequence of breaking a taboo is to be excluded from society altogether. 'Taboos are norms about things that are so serious as to be almost beyond comprehension . . . violating taboos typically will result in extreme punishment and ostracism' (Curry *et al.* 2005:36). Examples of taboos are incest, cannibalism and bestiality.

Laws

These are rules written and enforced by the state. Breaking taboos often involves breaking the law, but not every crime is taboo. Breaking laws results in more than disapproval: penalties, such as imprisonment or fines, result in most people complying with them.

Material culture

While symbols, values, language and norms are non-material concepts, material culture refers to the actual objects that surround us. The physical environment, which includes infrastructure, along with the range of objects we use and are familiar with, has an enormous impact on our culture. For example, mobile phones and the internet influence the way we interact with each other, creating huge changes in modern society. Material culture often changes at a faster pace than our ideas and values. 'William Ogburn (1964) observed that technology moves quickly, generating new elements of material culture (such as "test tube babies") faster than non-material culture (such as ideas about parenthood) can keep up with them.' (Macionis & Plummer 2002:110).

Culture sources: Curry *et al.* (2005); Giddens (2001); Macionis & Plummer (2002); Marsh *et al.* (2000); O'Toole (1997); Somerville-Large 2000.

Activities

1 Make a list of what makes Irish culture distinct. Try to include all five components of culture.

2 Compare your list with other classmates' and discuss what items you have in common. How many of the items listed do you believe in or practise yourself?

3 Working in pairs, take a country. Try to list what you know of this country's culture under each of the five headings.

4 Although in Ireland English is spoken more often than Irish, there is still a distinct difference in how the language is used. Make a list of certain words and phrases that are used only in Ireland or even only in your own locality. Discuss what other factors – for example speed, number and length of pauses, filler words – make Irish conversation unique.

Nationalism

Nationalism can be defined as 'a set of beliefs and symbols expressing identification with a given national community' (Giddens 2001:694).

These shared beliefs and symbols provide a sense of being part of a shared community, often giving people a sense of being connected to a larger group. Feelings of shared identity in a social group are very powerful because the need for identity is a central part of being human. However, although this sense of unity is largely a positive force, it can also create barriers to accepting other cultures.

National identity is often linked to political struggle, so Irish identity is often linked with the antagonistic relationship with Britain. Share, Tovey and Corcoran argue that Irish nationalism largely focused on what made us different from the English. 'The nation in Ireland was defined by prioritising those elements of culture where the contrast with the emerging English nation was greatest' (Share *et al.* 2007:349). We attach importance to elements in our culture that emphasise our difference and distinctiveness, so as the Irish language declined, other aspects such as religion became central to national identity.

Being Irish was often associated with being Catholic, and many famous figures of nationalism, such as Roger Casement, Maud Gonne and Constance Markiewicz, converted to Catholicism because 'to be Irish was to be Catholic' (Somerville-Large 2000:100). Seán O'Casey, the famous Irish playwright, was told as a child that his religion meant he was not Irish: 'One day, an' us playin', Kelly told me that us Catholics were really Irish; an' as we were Protestants, we couldn't anyway be near Irish' (O'Casey, quoted in Somerville-Large 2000:102).

Outside influences have often been seen as a threat to nationalism:

> The Gaelic League, launching a renewed anti-jazz campaign in 1934 declared that 'It is this music and verse that the Gaelic League is determined to crush . . . Its influence is denationalising in that its references are to things foreign to Irishmen.' (O'Toole 1997:133)

Douglas Hyde, the first president of Ireland, 'argued that Irish men should stop wearing trousers (an English dress custom) and return to the "traditional" dress of knee-breeches' (Share *et al.* 2007:350).

In this way, nationalism can become dependent on ideas of 'them' and 'us'. The danger is that in being over-protective of our own identity, we may be unwelcoming towards anyone from another culture. If we regard our culture as being fragile, immigrants will be regarded as a threat. 'Those for whom a nation is defined by a shared and distinctive culture often argue that maintenance of national difference depends on a degree of isolation from, or a barrier against, intercultural contact' (Share *et al.* 2007:343–4). However, trying to protect traditional ways of life through a policy of isolation is impossible in today's world. Modern trends towards internationalism and globalisation already change society; they 'ultimately give rise to a shared "world culture" in which nationalism and national cultural barriers are no longer significant' (Share *et al.* 2007:344). It has been argued that forces of globalisation create a new 'borderless world' in which national identity is less important than previously (Kenichi Ohmae, quoted in Giddens 2001:446).

We do not have to regard immigration as a threat to our national identity, but instead can choose to allow new experiences to enrich us and help create new identities. Intercultural dialogue can be important in holding on to the important aspects of our identity while being open to new ideas and new voices. Such an approach is:

. . . a mechanism to constantly achieve a new identity balance, responding to new openings and experiences and adding new layers to identity without relinquishing one's roots. . . . Identities that partly overlap are no contradiction: they are a source of strength and point to the possibility of common ground. (Council of Europe 2008:19)

Nationalism summarised from: Council of Europe 2008; Giddens 2002; Somerville-Large 2000; Share *et al.* 2007.

Activities

1   Consider this statement: 'In imagining it as a community, nationalists assert that those within the nation share a deep sense of solidarity with even those fellow-nationals they never meet and with past generations' (Share *et al.* 2007:349).

Discuss whether a shared nationality gives a sense of oneness that crosses all boundaries. For instance, would an Irish farmer have more in common with an Irish factory worker than a Greek farmer? Would a teenage Irish student have more in common with an Irish pensioner than a Polish student who is studying the same subject and has a similar family background?

2   Has technology, such as mobile phones and the internet, had a significant impact on the idea of a national identity? Split the class into two halves: half the class will argue for and half against this notion. Vote on which reasons are the most convincing.

3   'Daniel Corkery's famous definition of Irishness as characterised by Land, Nationality and Catholicism remained ideologically potent well into the 1970s. The idea that authentic Irishness was both rural and Catholic was perhaps a way of making the best of a bad job' (O'Toole 1997:15).

Do you consider the above traits as being central to Irish identity today? What other core beliefs do you have about being Irish – e.g. being born here, being white, etc. – and do they exclude anyone? Can a person from another country ever become Irish? How many generations would it take, in your opinion, for a person of foreign ancestry to become Irish? Reflect on these things in private and then discuss them in class.

4   There are some aspects of Irish culture that are relatively new or did not originate in Ireland, although we think of them as core symbols of identity. Research the Irish flag, the national anthem, the harp as a symbol of Ireland and the first St Patrick's Day parade. Share your results and discuss whether you found any them surprising.
    Try the following websites:
    www.askaboutireland.ie/learning-zone/secondary-students/music/special%20study-turlough-ocarolan/the-harp-a-symbol-of-irel/
    www.history.com/topics/st-patricks-day-facts
    www.historyireland.com/volumes/volume4/issue1/features/?id=113150
    www.taoiseach.gov.ie/upload/publications/1104.pdf

5   Education is an important tool for building a shared national identity. 'In a national education system, new generations of students can be socialised into a common culture, language and values and thus increase their sense of national belonging' (Share et al. 2007:351). How much impact did your school have on your sense of nationality?

Ireland Past and Present

Ireland has historically been a land of emigrants. During the famine of 1845 to 1849, one and a half million people are estimated to have emigrated, largely to the USA, Canada, Australia and Britain (Ruckenstein & O'Malley 2004:129). By 1851, the population was reduced to 6.1 million and this fell again to 4.4 million by 1911 (Ruckenstein & O'Malley 2004:130). After World War I, immigration restrictions to the USA ruled out that destination, but the outward flow continued, mainly to Britain. 'Between 1924 and 1928 130,000 emigrated, of whom eighty per cent were aged between fifteen and thirty-five. Whole hurling teams would leave' (Somerville-Large 2000:124). In the decade from 1951 to 1961, the population fell by 142,252 (CSO 2011b:9). Money sent from abroad was essential to keep those at home afloat: 'As late as 1958 American money constituted approximately two and a half per cent of the national income' (Somerville-Large 2000:125). From the 1960s onwards, emigration slowed and the population at last began to climb, with births outnumbering emigration and deaths. The trend has continued upwards, except for the late 1980s, when the population dipped by just under 15,000 (www.cso.ie).

The Census of 2011 lists 4,588,252 as the latest population figure (CSO 2011b). Results from the 2011 Census show that 12 per cent (544,357) of the current population is of non-Irish nationality. The top ten non-Irish nationalities represented are Polish, British, Lithuanian, Latvian, Nigerian, Romanian, Indian, Filipino, German and American (USA) (CSO 2011b:33). Immigration to Ireland is a new experience and, to some people, not a welcome one:

> One of the great paradoxes of Irish history after the foundation of the State is the complete contradiction between the expectation, on the one hand, that Irish people had a right to emigrate to wherever they could, and on the other, the great reluctance to allow immigration into Ireland. (O'Toole 1997:131)

People are comfortable with the familiar and may feel threatened by change. Many people view immigrants with suspicion, afraid that these newcomers will alter the familiar culture. 'Some of the concern currently being expressed about immigration to Ireland springs from a fear that this will dilute Irish cultural distinctiveness' (Share et al. 2007:344).

However, no culture remains the same, even without newcomers. Change is inevitable, but not without resistance; there is 'an endless cultural war between tradition and change' (O'Toole 1997:233). The term 'generation gap' highlights the changes that take place in a society over time.

In Ireland, we have seen massive changes in our culture in the last century. Material culture has altered hugely, our rates of wealth have gone from recession to boom and back to recession again, but despite our current economic woes we still take for granted material comforts that were once unthinkable. In 1932 barely eight per cent of children received a secondary education; and 'In 1938 there were over 60,000 tenements in Dublin, "human piggeries", rat infested and without basic amenities' (Somerville-Large 2000:171, 124). The census of 1946 revealed that 310,265 houses had no toilet, and there were 55,052 houses in Dublin alone with no bath (Somerville-Large 2000:247). The Rural Electrification Scheme started in 1946 but uptake was slow due to the cost, so it was not until the late 1970s that 98% of homes had electricity (Delaney n.d.).

In contrast, the 2011 Census showed that 1.36 million Irish households had at least one car, and 28 per cent of third-level students had their own car; 65.3 per cent of households had broadband (CSO 2011c); and fewer than one household in every 50 had no central heating (CSO 2011b:46).

Society has also seen a massive shift from rural to urban, with the number of farms declining: in 1961, 46.4 per cent of the population lived in urban areas; by 2011, this figure had increased to 62 per cent (CSO 2011b:13).

The average family has also changed hugely. In the past, most families were very large, which was an indicator of social values. Mothers did not go out to work and religious beliefs prevented family planning. In 2011 there were only 1,592 families with seven or more children (CSO 2011b:26), while statistics from 1911 show a pattern of very large families –147,407 women had between seven and 15 children (National Archives).

Attitudes have changed massively in the last century. A good example is the attitude to having children outside marriage. In the recent past, giving birth to a child outside marriage was a great scandal. Unmarried mothers could be sent to Magdalene laundries, and even if this was not the outcome, society would frown on not only the parent but the child itself:

> An illegitimate child . . . could not be a priest . . . That rule reflected a wider prejudice in an overwhelmingly Catholic society obsessed with sexual purity. The playwright Hugh Leonard, who grew up illegitimate in the Dublin of the 1930s and 1940s, 'knew that to be what they called illegitimate was an occasion for deep shame. There had been a sin of some kind and because of it you were not the same as children who had parents' . . . Even in the early 1960s, an American Jesuit researching attitudes in Ireland found that the general belief was that 'Illegitimate babies are bad, bad, bad.' (O'Toole 1997:37)

This cultural attitude was reflected in the law. Under the Legitimacy Act of 1931 an illegitimate child could have no claim on its father's estate. Not until 1964 did Irish law recognise the right of an unmarried mother to be the guardian of her own child. 'As late as 1985, the Irish Supreme Court ruled that children born out of wedlock had no rights of succession to their father's estate. Not until 1987 was the legal concept of illegitimacy abolished in Ireland' (O'Toole 1997:38). Nowadays children born outside marriage have the same rights as those born within marriage. Apart from the law, attitudes have also seen a dramatic shift. In 2010 33.7 per cent of births were outside marriage (CSO 2011d:64). This percentage indicates a huge cultural change.

Summarised from CSO (2011b,c,d); Delaney; National Archives; O'Toole (1997); Ruckenstein & O'Malley (2004); Somerville-Large (2000).

Activities

1 A famous quote from L. P. Hartley's novel *The Go Between* is, 'The past is a foreign country, they do things differently there.' Discuss what he means by this.

2 Talk to a person at least 20 years older than yourself and note differences between the society they grew up in and the society of today. Areas of interest would include living standards, education, moral attitudes, family life, work, religion and socialising.

3 Statistics show that in the past we were poorer, less urban, more religious and more likely to emigrate. What problems do we face today that previous generations did not have to cope with?

4 One example of cultural change is the change in gender roles. Ireland has had two female presidents and a female Olympic boxer. What other examples of changing cultural attitudes regarding gender can you think of?

5 Reflect on your attitude to change in society. Why do you think people are frightened of change?

Race

Race is defined as 'A socially constructed term used to refer to the division of human beings into distinct "types" recognisable through reference to physical characteristics (e.g. skin colour)' (Marsh & Keating 2000:785). The belief that humans are separated into biologically distinct races was often used to justify colonialism. Soldiers, slavers and settlers did not have to feel guilty when they regarded natives as beings entirely different from themselves.

Count Joseph Arthur de Gobineau (1816–1882) divided people into three races: white (Caucasian); black (Negroid); and yellow (Mongoloid). He believed white people to be highly intelligent, yellow people to be cunning and black people to be stupid and animal-like. 'The ideas of de Gobineau and fellow proponents of scientific racism later influenced Adolf Hitler, who transformed them into the ideology of the Nazi party, and other white supremacist groups such as the Ku Klux Klan in the United States and the architects of apartheid in South Africa' (Giddens 2001:245–6).

Dividing the human race into categories often leads to associating certain qualities with certain groups. The belief that biology, rather than socialisation, moulds a person's character is outdated. Modern genetic science shows the lack of basis for assuming major differences in people of different backgrounds. 'The overall genetic differences between "races" – Africans and Europeans, say – is no greater than that between different countries within Europe or within Africa' (Jones (1991), cited in Marsh & Keating 2000:381).

Some sociologists argue that the term 'race' should only be used with inverted commas to show its lack of scientific basis. Yet, because of its everyday usage and social meaning, others see the term as important in any attempt to examine society: 'Others . . . argue that the term "race" has a social relevance, with very real consequences, and therefore should be retained without commas' (Marsh & Keating 2000:785).

Giddens argues that although race has no biological foundation, it is important to examine it and question why and how certain differences – such as eye colour – hold no importance for society, yet other differences are of major importance. This arbitrary choice of what differences are meaningful have to do with maintaining command of wealth and power resources:

Differences in skin colour for example are treated as significant, whereas
differences in colour of hair are not . . . Racial distinctions are more than
ways of describing human differences – they are also important factors in the
reproduction of patterns of power and inequality within society. (Giddens
2001:246)

Having a different skin colour from that of the majority population may also mean that
children or even grandchildren of immigrants may be permanently excluded from majority
society, because the belief that they are of a different race dominates perception of them.
Studies of the Chinese population in Ireland show that recent Chinese immigrants and
second-generation Chinese, whose parents came to Ireland in the 1980s, are two distinct
groups but are often lumped together. 'Even though second-generation Chinese are Irish
Born Chinese (IBC), they are still limited in their abilities to claim "Irishness" because
of race' (King-O'Riain 2008:77). Irish-born Chinese may feel an Irish national identity
but remain branded 'other' – 'The Irish label equated with white and the uncertainty of
accepting an Irish identity was further communicated' (Yau (2007), cited in King-O'Riain
2008:77).

   Summarised from Giddens (2001); King-O'Riain (2008); Marsh & Keating (2007).

Ethnicity

The notion of race assumes biological differences, while the notion of ethnicity is
completely based on a shared culture. Ethnicity may often be defined by a nation, but
it is also a fluid identity that can be recreated, given new circumstances: 'Black slaves in
the USA developed a common identity as black people despite coming from different
parts of Africa, where there were different cultures and languages' (Haralambos &
Holborn 2004:181).

   As discussed earlier in the section on nationalism, groups or even whole nations
define themselves by their shared cultural identity and their differences from others.
'Ethnicity refers to the cultural practices and outlooks of a given community of people
that set them apart from others . . . Different characteristics may serve to distinguish
ethnic groups . . . [the] most usual are language, history or ancestry, religion, style of
dress' (Giddens 2001:246–7).

   However, in the modern world, where globalisation ensures a blurring of obvious
differences, more subtle markers of ethnicity come into play:

Membership in the 'Irish Nation' . . . may relate to quite minor aspects of
interaction, such as how close a person stands to another, how they pitch their
voice or the sort of jokes they make . . . a 'real Irish person' ought to recognise
Cromwell's phrase 'to hell or to Connaught' or know who Seán Óg Ó hAilpín is.
(Share *et al.* 2007:343)

The term 'ethnic' applies to all cultures, but has come to be regarded as applying mainly to minority groups. For example, 'Chinatown' in New York would be perceived as ethnic, because it is surrounded by a different culture. However, we would probably not think of the surrounding American society as being ethnic. Ethnicity has come to be seen as signifying difference from the norm.

Every society has its own cultural values, but there may be smaller groups within the society who do not share the same identity. Those of the dominant ethnic group may feel threatened by those who do not share their way of life. Being too attached to our own culture can cause problems. 'Issues of common identity and cultural difference are mobilised to account for the fear and hostility of the host population towards the ethnic other' (Marsh & Keating 2000:391). Feeling threatened in this way often results in excluding and isolating those who are different. Exclusion does not just take place on a social level but results in disadvantage on a wider scale. 'In virtually all societies, ethnic differences are associated with variations in power and material wealth' (Giddens 2001:688).

Summarised from Giddens (2001); Haralambos & Holborn (2004); Marsh & Keating (2000); Share *et al.* (2007).

Xenophobia

Xenophobia literally means 'a fear of strangers'. 'It is generally used to denote negative attitudes towards immigrant groups on account of their cultural differences' (Marsh & Keating 2000:790).

Activities

1   Discuss as a class what ideas you hold about race and where those ideas come from.

2   Research the way in which theories of race have been used to justify unfair treatment. Present your findings to the class.

3   Irish people speak English, wear similar clothes and share a similar lifestyle to people in the UK. Discuss ways in which you think our ethnicity differs from theirs.

4   Reflect on reasons why a society might feel threatened by another ethnicity.

5   King-O'Riain's research found that 'The Irish label equated with white.' Reflect on your own beliefs about skin colour and nationality.

6   Seán Óg Ó hAilpín, the GAA star, was born in Fiji. He has an Irish father and Fijian mother but his status of 'Irish' is never in question. Discuss why barriers to being accepted remain for some but are not a problem for others.

> 7   The New Zealand All Blacks, a team composed of both Maoris and players of
>   European descent, perform the Haka before each match. The Haka was originally a
>   Maori ceremonial dance but now has a new meaning beyond one ethnicity. Discuss
>   how something that was traditional for one group only can fuse with another culture
>   in a way that benefits both groups.

Stereotypes and Cultural Myths

Stereotypes are 'rigid and inaccurate images that summarise a belief' (Curry *et al.*
2005:198). They categorise people in a very narrow and limited way, not allowing for
the huge variety of behaviour and ability in people. Examples of stereotypes are 'dizzy
blonde', 'drunken Irish' and 'loud American'. Stereotypes are mental 'shortcuts' that we
often use to try to simplify the world.

> A bewildering array of identity role models are offered by the global media.
> Faced with such complexity, applying to 'the other' a simplifying stereotype – on
> to which all the ills of the world can be projected – can be insidiously seductive.
> (Council of Europe 2008:34)

Stereotypes will be dealt with in more detail in Chapter 2.

Cultural myths are everyday shared ideas that often support stereotyping, such as
'women are bad drivers' and 'boys don't cry'. 'Cultural myths gain such enormous power
over us by insinuating themselves into our thinking before we're aware of them. Most
are learned at a deep, even unconscious level' (Colombo *et al.* 2001:4). These commonly
held beliefs reflect and uphold the standards of society. They are so ingrained that we
think of them as 'common sense' and natural truths. However, when we consider some
of these 'truths' from the past, such as 'children should be seen and not heard', 'spare
the rod and spoil the child' and 'a woman's place is in the home', we may not be so sure
of our own assumptions.

Summarised from Colombo *et al.* (2001); Curry *et al.* (2005);
Council of Europe (2008).

Labelling

'Labelling is a process by which individuals or groups categorize certain types of
behaviour and certain individuals' (Marsh & Keating 2000:663). Society may fix labels
on certain groups and then treat them in such a way as to produce the type of behaviour
they have been labelled with. Thus, if a group is labelled as 'troublemakers', society
will react to them in a way that confirms this behaviour. The education system, social
services, police and legal system will be more likely to come down heavily on groups

that are labelled in a negative way: 'Rules tend to be applied more to some persons than others . . . The middle class boy is less likely, when picked up by the police, to be taken to the station; less likely when taken to the station to be booked; and it is extremely unlikely that he will be convicted and sentenced' (Becker (1963), cited in Marsh & Keating 2000:664–5). Labelling children in the classroom as 'disruptive' or 'difficult' may result in them being treated differently from other pupils. Similarly, labelling ethnic groups in a negative way causes people to react to them unfavourably and may even produce the very behaviour they were labelled with.

Summarised from Bilton *et al.* (2002); Marsh & Keating (2000).

Activities

1   Have you ever been labelled? Discuss how difficult it is to break free from a label once it has been applied.

2   Consider the old sayings, 'Give a dog a bad name and hang him' and 'Get the name of an early riser and you can sleep all day.' Discuss ways in which they may apply to labelling.

3   If all students agree, they can investigate the process of labelling. Ten students can be the 'guinea pigs'. The rest of the class will be told that five of them are labelled negatively as 'unco-operative', 'lazy', 'stupid', 'aggressive', etc. while the other five are given positive labels such as 'willing', 'positive attitude', 'diligent', etc. The 'guinea pigs' will not know which labels they have been given and will behave as normal. Over a week, the class will try to find evidence to support these labels and will present this 'evidence' at the end of the week. The purpose of this activity is to demonstrate how once a label has been applied, people will often find proof to justify it. (Note: make an effort to respect the sensitivities of the 'guinea pigs'!)

Racism

Racism has been defined as 'The attributing of characteristics of superiority or inferiority to a population sharing certain physically inherited characteristics. Racism is one specific form of prejudice, focusing on physical variations between people' (Giddens 2001:696). Racist beliefs hold that all the members of one particular group are either superior or inferior. No regard is given to individuality – a decision has already been made based on a person's origin. A racist view sees a person defined only by their race and destined to act only in stereotypical ways – 'to display genetically determined patterns of social, cultural, political and economic behaviour' (Marsh & Keating 2000:790).

The Irish have often been victims of racism. In 1860 Charles Kingsley described the Irish as 'human chimpanzees' (quoted by Fanning 2012:13). Fanning also states that in

2000, the Report of the Commission on the Future of Multi-Ethnic Britain (the 'Parekh Report') included Irish people, along with Jews, Muslims and black people, as being targets of racism, and 'argued that anti-Irish racism has many of the same features as most racisms' (Fanning 2012:13).

Institutional Racism

The idea of institutional racism 'was developed in the United States in the late 1960s by civil rights campaigners who believed that racism underpins the very fabric of society, rather than merely representing the opinions of a small minority' (Giddens 2001:252). The belief is that racism exists not only in individuals but also within key powerful institutions, such as the courts, the police force, government bodies, the health service and schools. A study done on 'stop and search' police practice in the UK found that black people were 7.5 times more likely to be stopped than white people (Statewatch (1999) cited in Bilton *et al.* 2002:390).

The television and film industry, along with the print media, are also seen as guilty of institutional racism because of their negative or limited portrayal of ethnicities.

Biological racism is now outdated, but a more subtle and sophisticated version has replaced it, a version that 'uses the idea of cultural differences to exclude certain groups' (Giddens 2001:252). Ethnicity, not only skin colour, is often a target for racist beliefs. The most obvious displays of racism are those that involve violence, taunts and discrimination, but more subtle forms of racism exist. People who are different from mainstream culture 'have to cope with a society in which they are portrayed as "other", as inferior, different, threatening' (Marsh & Keating 2000:382).

Summarised from Bilton *et al.* (2002),Fanning (2012); Giddens (2001); Marsh & Keating (2000).

Project ideas

1   One of the most famous examples of institutional racism is the Tuskegee Study. Research this case and present your findings.

2   Marsh and Keating point out how European history focuses only on the achievements of white people, and they compare the fame of Florence Nightingale with the relative obscurity of Mary Seacole, who also nursed in the Crimea. Research the life of Mary Seacole and discuss why she is not well known.

3   'As Miles (1993) has reminded us, racism against black people has long coexisted with racism against Irish and Jewish people' (Marsh & Keating 2000:384). Research racist attitudes towards Irish people.

Segregation

Segregation is defined as 'the physical and social separation of categories of people' (Macionis & Plummer 2002:678). Under such a system, groups of people remain entirely separate and are treated differently instead of being treated as equals. The apartheid regime in South Africa was an example of a segregated society. Sadly, there are still many examples of segregated societies, for example the caste system in India.

Case study: Apartheid in South Africa

Apartheid is defined as 'The official system of racial segregation established in South Africa in 1948 and practised until 1994' (Giddens 2001:688).

During the colonial era, Africa was largely under European control, but many African states gained independence during the 1960s. An exception to this was South Africa, whose population included three million South Africans of English and Dutch descent. The white minority adopted a policy of forced racial segregation known as apartheid.

People were divided into four categories – white, coloured (mixed race), Asian and black – and the social system was organised to favour the whites.

The non-white majority (15 million people) wanted independence and change but the white South Africans were determined not to let go, for three reasons:

1 South Africa was a very wealthy country, and 'whites owned all the best farm land, and the fabulous gold and diamond mines that made South Africa one of the world's richest countries' (Neill 1975:176).

2 White South Africans had no homeland to return to – having been settled for so long, they now looked on South Africa as their home. 'The Dutch settlers had no desire to return to Holland; they had developed a separate language, Afrikaans, and a separate racial identity' (Neill 1975:170).

3 They were unwilling to surrender the advantages that they had ensured for themselves, such as top jobs being given only to whites, while white and black workers were paid

different wages for doing exactly the same job. 'The average weekly wage of a white miner in 1961 was £115, but the wage of his black counterpart was only £9' (Neill 1975:170).

The system of separation called 'apartheid' had been encoded in law in 1948 and was enforced brutally. Non-whites had no vote, no representatives at government level, and segregation existed at every level of society: separate schools, hospitals, neighbourhoods, public transport and even different sides of the street were designated for whites and non-whites. Brutal force was used to keep this system in place and any opposition parties, such as the African National Congress (ANC) were banned and their leaders imprisoned. For example, Nelson Mandela was imprisoned in 1962. Torture during imprisonment was common.

Any resistance, such as protest marches, was brutally supressed. In the Sharpeville massacre in 1960, protesters were shot at by police and 70 people died.

Over the years, resistance continued and much international pressure was put on the South African government. Economic sanctions were used, foreign investments were withdrawn and trade restrictions put in place. Global campaigns encouraged boycotts of South Africa, South African athletes were banned from competing at the Olympics, the South African football team was suspended from FIFA, and many musicians would not tour there.

In 1990, President F. W. de Klerk lifted the ban on the ANC and Nelson Mandela was freed after 27 years of imprisonment. In 1994, the first election was held in which non-whites could vote. The ANC got 62 per cent of the vote, Mandela became president and remained in office until 1999.

The new constitution outlawed all forms of discrimination, but much damage had been done during the apartheid regime. Of a population of 38 million, nine million lived in poverty, 20 million were without electricity, half the black population was illiterate and infant mortality rates were ten times higher among blacks than whites. There was also massive political and racial tension.

During his term as president, Mandela sought to reconcile and unite black and white under the common goal of improving South Africa; he aimed to address the past and move forward. An effort was made to bring dissenters, such as the Zulu-based Inkatha Freedom Party, into parliament in order to promote unity and ease tension.

From 1996 to 1998, the Truth and Reconciliation Commission (TRC), headed by Desmond Tutu, heard and examined cases of human rights abuses under the apartheid system. The sessions were open to the public and were widely covered in the media. These sessions were not trials, no punishments were given; instead the commission focused on uncovering the results of living under such a system. They hoped to deal with the past and start afresh. Those who had been in charge — government officials and policemen – were given amnesty from prosecution for their crimes in return for openness and truth.

The TRC published a 3,500-page report in 1998. Some criticised it for simply cataloguing events, while others argued that the testimonials from both abused and abusers served to highlight the massive injustices of such a system. 'The TRC forced attention to be paid to the dangerous consequences of racial hatred and ... demonstrated the power of communication and dialogue in the process of reconciliation' (Giddens 2001:243).

South Africa today still struggles with its past, yet there is huge effort being made in overcoming racial divisions.

Summarised from Giddens (2001); Neill (1975).

Project ideas

1   In Ireland in the mid-1980s, 12 Dunnes workers went on strike after a cashier was suspended for refusing to check out South African goods (RTÉ 2005). Find out what happened and what the outcomes were. A useful web link to start with is www.historyireland.com/volumes/volume14/issue4/features/?id=330.

2   'A caste society is a closed society, with no social mobility possible from one caste to another' (Browne 1992:12). Research the caste system in India.

Revision questions

1   Compare multicultural and intercultural approaches to diversity.
2   Describe what integration means.
3   List the five components of culture.
4   Describe how nationalism can be a barrier to accepting other cultures.
5   Outline briefly some ways in which Ireland has changed in the last century.
6   Explain how the concept of 'race' is different from 'ethnicity'.
7   Explain the term 'institutional racism'.
8   Describe the effects of 'labelling'.
9   Describe what segregation means.
10 Outline how outside pressure helped end the apartheid regime.

CHAPTER 2

Socialisation and Attitudes to Difference

By the end of this chapter, students should:

- Be able to define *prejudice* and *stereotyping*, recognise the impact of both and distinguish between discrimination and prejudice.
- Be able to discuss and explore how prejudice and stereotyping may take positive and negative forms, which can affect a person's life, attitude and chances.
- Understand how culture influences identity.
- Understand how sociology aids the study of cultures.
- Be able to list the four major agents of socialisation, identify whether they are primary or secondary groups and understand how the values of a culture are transmitted through some of these agents.
- Understand how cultures differ in their socialisation methods and aims.
- Be able to discuss prejudice in the classroom and understand the significance of positive and negative expectations.
- Be able to define globalisation and understand its impact on world culture.

Sociology and Culture

Sociology is a valuable tool for helping to understand why people act in certain ways. Sociology can be defined as 'the systematic study of human society' (Macionis & Plummer 1997:4). If we want to understand ourselves and other cultures, the first step is to realise that we often act and respond according to the dictates of our society without realising why. 'Observing sociologically requires giving up the familiar idea that human behaviour is simply a matter of what people *decide* to do and accepting instead the initially strange notion that society guides our thoughts and deeds' (Macionis & Plummer 1997:4). Many of us may believe we are individuals who choose our own way of life, but our surrounding culture may influence us more than we realise. Sociology examines ways in which people 'fit in' or are outside the dominant culture. Some groups and individuals may seek to be outside the mainstream, for example biker or punk culture, but immigrants may have no choice in the matter: 'For some categories of people . . . being an outsider is part of daily living. . . . No Turkish guest worker in Germany or Pakistani in England lives for long without learning how much race affects personal experience' (Macionis & Plummer 1997:12).

Sociologists often study inequality in society and seek to explain why that inequality exists. It may be a common belief that those who do not do well in life have only themselves to blame, but sociologists perceive imbalances in power that keep certain groups of people in place.

> Everybody knows that the fight is fixed
> The poor stay poor, the rich get rich. . .
> Everybody knows the deal is rotten
> Old Black Joe's still pickin' cotton
> For your ribbons and bows.
>
> (From 'Everybody Knows', a song by Leonard Cohen)

For those who are outside the dominant culture, it can be difficult to live life believing that you are an individual, who will be judged on your own merits. Being of the majority means being able to blend in with the crowd and avoid being judged. Being different from the majority may result in prejudice, stereotyping and discrimination.

Prejudice

Prejudice has been defined as 'an attitude that predisposes an individual to prejudge entire categories of people unfairly' (Curry et al. 2005:196).

While prejudice may have multiple forms – sexism, ageism, racism, etc. – it has certain key features:

- Prejudice is emotional, not logical, so it is difficult to defeat with argument.
- Prejudice is resistant to change and selective in what it chooses to see: 'only these facts and beliefs that fit the prejudice are given credence' (Curry et al. 2005:196).
- Prejudice may *lead* to discrimination, but it is not the same as discrimination.
- Prejudice can be positive or negative and serves to reassure people of their superiority: 'Our positive prejudices tend to exaggerate the virtues of people like ourselves, while our negative prejudices condemn those who differ from us' (summarised from Macionis & Plummer 1997:328).

Negative prejudices can influence a group's entire life chances and can lead to a vicious circle in which those who suffer prejudice become disheartened and angry, sometimes leading to behaviour such as crime and drug addiction, which is then used to justify the initial prejudice.

> Negative attitudes will inevitably lead to negative behaviour, which in turn results in a deterioration of the conditions of those against whom the negative attitudes are directed. The worsening of the social and living conditions of those prejudiced against will reinforce and rationalise the negative attitudes. (MacGreil 1996:28)

Hope lies in the fact that, 'The great thing about the vicious-circle theory is that it works in the positive direction also' (MacGreil 1996:28). If the dominant group changed their attitude towards minorities, aspirations would increase as those minorities felt less hopeless, and conditions such as housing, education and job opportunities would improve. These new circumstances 'would challenge the racialist attitudes and further strengthen positive behaviour' (MacGreil 1996:28).

While negative prejudices are obviously damaging, positive prejudices can also be harmful as they can serve to limit the supposed ability of a group to one area alone. Positive prejudices such as 'black people are excellent athletes and dancers' can come to imply that their physical abilities outshine their intellectual gifts. 'White racists are quite prepared to concede a degree of superiority in areas of physique and physical prowess to Black people, while denying them equality or superiority in intellectual and spiritual (i.e., the more exclusively human) traits. The racist literature of the Deep South in the United States of America in the past would highlight sexual prowess, athletic skill and natural rhythms of the "negro slaves"' (MacGreil 1996:135). Positive prejudices imply that the person is simply lucky and talented rather than acknowledging the hard work and sacrifice that usually accompany achievement. Jandt (2004) has noted how television sports commentators describe black athletes as 'natural' and 'gifted', while white athletes are described as smart, disciplined and hard working.

Summarised from Macionis & Plummer (1997); MacGreil (1996).

Activities

1   List some common prejudices that you know of. Compare your list with others in the class.

2   Discuss how positive prejudice can be as harmful as negative prejudice.

Prejudice and Discrimination

There is a distinction between prejudice and discrimination. Discrimination is defined as 'the unfair and harmful treatment of people based on their group membership' (Curry *et al.* 2005:197). While a prejudiced person may dislike a certain group of people, they might not go so far as to treat them differently, or may not be in a position where they are able to discriminate.

Social scientist Richard LaPiere (1899–1986) conducted an experiment to test the distinction between prejudice and discrimination. In the 1930s he spent two years travelling around the USA with a Chinese couple, staying at many hotels and eating at various restaurants. Six months after his return, LaPiere wrote to each hotel and restaurant and asked whether they would serve Chinese people. The majority (90 per cent) replied that they did not welcome Chinese people, but only one restaurant had actually refused to serve the couple. The experiment proved that while many people may be prejudiced, few will go so far as to discriminate. 'Perhaps this behaviour was due to the upper-class appearance of the couple, who arrived at the hotel well dressed, in their own car, accompanied by a white male' (LaPiere, quoted in Curry *et al.* 2005:196).

Unfortunately, prejudice often does lead to discrimination. Studies in Britain show that: '(1) White applicants are more than four times as successful as black applicants when answering job advertisements. (2) It was three times as difficult to get an interview for a job if you were Asian, and five times as hard if you were black. (3) Black and Asian employees are having to wait longer than whites for promotion' (Commission for Racial Equality report, quoted by Webb & Tossell 1999:98). McIntosh (1994) writes that while prejudice puts some at a disadvantage, it simultaneously ensures privilege for others, and describes privilege as 'an invisible package of unearned assets which I can count on cashing in on each and every day. . . . If I make any grammatical or spelling errors, no one will attribute my mistakes to my race or my ethnic group. If I have a responsible job, no one thinks I got it because of "quotas". No one assumes that when I give my opinion on something that I am speaking on behalf of my race' (cited in Jandt 2004:455–7).

Irish sociologist and psychologist Michael MacGreil gathered data on prejudiced attitudes in Ireland, initially in 1972–73 and again in 1988–89. The following table shows some of the data he collected: the percentages in brackets are from the 1972–73 research.

Prejudiced attitudes in Ireland 1988–89 (1972–73)

STATEMENT	YES	DON'T KNOW	NO
1. If you had a boarding house would you refuse digs to Black people?	14.7 (27.6)	5.8 (5.7)	79.6 (66.7)
2. Do you think that because of their basic make-up Black people could never become as good Irish people as others?	16.7 (26.5)	10.0 (4.8)	73.3 (68.7)
3. Do you believe that there should be a stricter control on Black people who enter this country than on Whites?	26.8 (39.2)	8.7 (4.6)	64.5 (56.3)
4. Do you believe that the Black person is basically or inherently inferior to the White person?	10.8 (13.4)	5.9 (3.8)	83.3 (82.8)
5. Would you stay in a hotel or guest house that had Black guests also?	90.9 (93.3)	2.9 (0.9)	6.2 (5.8)
6. Do you believe that the Black person deserves exactly the same social privileges as the White person?	92.9 (93.5)	3.5 (2.0)	3.6 (4.5)
7. Do you hold that by nature the Black and the White person are equal?	86.8 (88.2)	5.7 (3.2)	7.5 (8.6)
8. Do you believe that Black people are naturally more highly sexed than White people?	17.4 (24.6)	50.0 (37.5)	32.6 (37.8)
9. Would you hold that Black people should be sent back to Africa and Asia where they belong and kept there?	8.9 (14.8)	6.8 (4.4)	84.3 (80.8)
10. Do you agree that it is a good thing for Whites and Blacks to get married where there are no cultural or religious barriers?	52.4 (36.6)	16.2 (5.8)	31.4 (57.6)

Source: MacGreil 1996:133
Summarised from Curry *et al.* (2005); MacGreil (1996); Webb & Tossell (1999).

Activities

1   Consider the above data from MacGreil's research and discuss whether prejudice or discrimination is shown by the responses.

2   Answer MacGreil's questions as a class and discuss the results.

3   In MacGreil's second survey, nearly 93 per cent of respondents agreed that black people deserve the same social privileges as white people but only 52 per cent thought mixed marriages a good thing. Discuss reasons why some people believe in equality yet do not agree with mixed marriages.

Stereotypes

Stereotypes were defined in the previous chapter as 'rigid and inaccurate images that summarise a belief' (Curry *et al.* 2005:198). Stereotypes, like prejudice, may be positive or negative. 'Blondes have more fun', 'Redheads are passionate' are examples of everyday positive stereotypes. Unfortunately, even positive stereotypes have a flipside and often carry a negative implication – blondes may be seen as stupid and redheads as having no self-control. Stereotypes imply that an entire group carries the same trait, but the language we use may have a positive or negative connotation, depending on our opinion of the group described. For example, the same person may be described by two different people as confident or full of themselves, assertive or pushy, obliging or a push-over, carefree or irresponsible. 'When Chinese people congregate with their families, they may be described as "clannish", but when Swedes engage in the same behaviour, they may be described as "showing strong family solidarity". Scots are stereotyped as "stingy", but the same behaviour by the British [*sic*] is described as "thrifty"' (Katz & Braley (1968), cited in Curry *et al.* 2005:198). Irish people may enjoy being stereotyped as fun-loving, friendly and hospitable, while others may see us as irresponsible and lacking in seriousness. We may value attributes that we think we possess and ridicule other cultures for their qualities.

Stereotyping can serve as a comfort to those unhappy with their lot – 'Stereotyping elevates the status of the group that engages in it. A poor white racist might take comfort in believing that he or she is superior, simply because of skin colour, to any member of another racial or ethnic group' (Hacker (1995), cited in Curry *et al.* 2005:198).

Preconceived Ideas

Preconceived ideas often arise from stereotypes. The person may not have harmful intent, may even mean to be helpful, but an assumption of another's needs may be wrong and have harmful consequences.

> Girls in general tend to receive less attention from teachers than boys. In the case of Asian girls, the prevailing stereotype of them as 'passive' can lead some teachers to pay an even lesser degree of attention to this category of girls. Teachers, who may assume Asian parents to be opposed to their daughters going into further or higher education, may discourage these girls from studying subjects at O and A levels, and from pursuing academic careers, yet many Asian parents are very keen for their daughters to gain higher level qualifications. (Brah 1999:74)

Activities

1   Make a list of words that mean the same thing but have positive or negative qualities attached, for example fun-loving/irresponsible, stingy/thrifty, careful/unspontaneous, strong/bossy.

2   List and discuss the stereotypical views of your nationality. How do they relate to you and your lifestyle?

3   Do you think stereotypes/preconceived ideas have been influential on your own life experiences?

4   What stereotypical ideas and beliefs do you hold? Think of a nationality with which you have had no contact and list what you believe about them. Examine where these beliefs came from.

Case study: Jane Elliott and the blue eyes/brown eyes exercise

In 1968, Jane Elliott was a third grade teacher in Riceville, Iowa, a small, all-white farming town in the USA. On hearing of Martin Luther King's assassination, she wondered how to teach her eight-year-old students about discrimination and its negative effects. In her own words, she felt that:

> There had to be a way to do more as a teacher than simply tell children that racial prejudice is irrational, that racial prejudice is wrong. We've all been told those things. . . . Yet we continue to discriminate, or to tolerate it in others, or to do nothing to stop it. What I had racked my brain to think of the night before was a way of letting my children find out for themselves, personally, deeply, what discrimination was really like, how it felt, what it could do to you. (Elliott, quoted in Peters 1987:17)

She decided to divide her class into two groups on the basis of whether they had blue eyes or brown eyes. For the first day (Friday) the brown-eyed group would be superior and the blue-eyed children inferior; the following Monday the position of the groups would be reversed. She started with a class discussion, asking the children what they knew about black people. The answers developed into a pattern – black people 'weren't as smart as white people. They weren't as clean. They fought a lot. Sometimes they rioted. They weren't as civilised. They smelled bad' (Peters 1987:15). Elliott asked the class if they could imagine how it felt to be a black child and then suggested that they find out for themselves what discrimination felt like.

She divided up the groups and outlined the rules for the day. Brown-eyed children would have five minutes' extra break, would go first to lunch and could drink from the water fountain as usual, while blue-eyed children had to use paper cups. Blue-eyed children could not play with brown-eyed children unless invited and could not play on the big playground equipment. The brown-eyed children could invite a blue-eyed child to play, but Elliott warned them to be careful what others would think of them for doing so.

Throughout the day she helped brown-eyed children patiently and praised every success, while criticising the efforts of the blue-eyed group and pointing their mistakes out to the class as typical of this group. When a child was belittled or praised, she or he was not treated as an individual, but always held up as an example of the overall inferiority or superiority of the group.

The effect on the children was swift. The 'superior' group were happy, alert and working extremely well, while the 'inferior' group were nervous, withdrawn, slumped in their desks with their eyes downcast and could not perform tasks that they were usually well able for. The behaviour of the children towards each other changed, too; the brown-eyed group quickly believed that they were superior and turned on the other group.

The following week the positions of the children were reversed. The results of discrimination against the 'inferior' group were the same, but Elliott did note that the blue-eyed children – having already experienced discrimination – were less vicious in their treatment of their classmates. A group discussion closed the exercise and the class concluded that 'Discrimination could change the kind of person you were if it went on long enough' (Peters 1987:36). Quotes from the children revealed how even one day of discrimination had opened their eyes:

- 'I didn't want to work. I didn't feel like I was very big. Discrimination is no fun at all.'
- 'I have blue eyes. I felt like slapping a brown-eyed person. It made me mad. Then I felt like kicking a brown-eyed person. I felt like quitting school.'
- 'I do not like discrimination. It makes me sad. I would not like to be angry all my life.' (Peters 1987:32–3)

Elliott noted how the anger and demotivation expressed shed new light on the children's previous comments about black people being more aggressive and less clever than whites.

The results of discrimination tend to create and confirm prejudice. It's a simple enough equation: choose a group, discriminate against it, force it by your discrimination to look and act inferior, and then point to the way it looks and acts as proof of its inferiority. . . . A child who has been denied a decent education will become an uneducated adult. To those who didn't see – or refuse to recognize – the denial, he will seem simply stupid. (Elliott, quoted in Peters 1987:101)

Elliott continued to do the exercise each year with each new class and noted that test scores went up for a 'superior' group and down for an 'inferior' group. In 1970 the exercise was filmed by an ABC news crew and broadcast as *The Eye of the Storm*. In 1984 a school reunion of the class who had taken part in *The Eye of the Storm* was filmed and shown as *A Class Divided*. The young adults described the experience of both discriminating and being discriminated against and how it had affected their current views.

- 'It felt tremendously evil. . . . All your inhibitions were gone. And no matter if they were my friends or not, any pent-up hostilities or aggressions . . . you had a chance to get it all out . . . I knew I had support. I had the power.'
- 'You could do anything. You could read. You could spell. You could do math. The next day . . . I felt, gee, this stuff was easier yesterday. . . . When people say you're dumb, you feel dumb, you act dumb . . . but when you're on top and you're told you can do no wrong, you can't.'
- 'You hear people talking about, you know, different people – how they're different, and they'd like to have them out of the country . . . and sometimes I just wish I had that collar in my pocket. ['Inferior' children had to wear collars.] I could whip it out and put it on them and say "Wear this and put yourself in their place." I wish they would go through what I went through.'
- 'I still find myself sometimes, when I see some blacks together, and I see how they act, I think, well, that's black. . . . And right in the next second . . . I'm saying, well I've seen whites do it. I've seen other people do it. It's not just the blacks. It's just that the different colour is what hits you first.'
- 'Our children won't learn how to be prejudiced from us.' (Peters 1987:119–24)

Soon after the documentary was aired, Jane Elliott began a new career of diversity training with adults – along the same pattern as the original exercise – and she continues to this day. She intends it to target not only racism, but discrimination on any basis, and states: 'The problem is majority group reaction to differentness. As long as members of the majority group see differences as negative and respond in negative ways to those who possess them, the problems of racism and sexism and ageism will persist.' (Elliott, quoted in Peters 1987:167)

Summarised from Peters (1987).

Activities

1   Divide the class into two. One half will take on the role of parents who are supportive of the experiment, while the other half will represent parents who are outraged. Make notes and debate the issue.

2   Why did the children in the 'superior' group turn so quickly on the others? Reflect on why being a member of a powerful group can change behaviour.

3   How well do you think this type of exercise would work on adults? Would you resent this type of training day in your college or workplace?

4   Recall a time when you were treated unfairly and how it made you feel. Did it make you feel that you wanted revenge or that you wanted to stop the same thing happening to others?

Culture and Identity

In Chapter 1 culture was defined as 'the values, customs and acceptable modes of behaviour that characterise a society or social groups within a society' (Marsh & Keating 2000:24).

But how do we become members of one culture or another? Animals are genetically programmed to behave in certain ways and a French dog will act in the same ways as an Irish dog, but humans are unable to learn things from instinct alone. A child must learn to fit the particular culture it is born into, and the expectations and rules of cultures vary widely. 'No cultural trait is inherently "natural" to humanity, even though most people around the world view their own way of life that way. What is natural to our species is the capacity to create culture in our collective lives' (Macionis & Plummer 1997:101).

The process of moulding us to fit into our society begins when we are born. Absorbing the customs and behaviours approved by our culture is called *socialisation*, which can be defined as 'the process by which people learn the skills, knowledge, norms and values of their society, and by which they develop their social identity' (Curry *et al.* 2005:66). The future of any culture depends on a society's successful organisation of this process. Socialisation begins at birth and will continue through adult life.

Agents of Socialisation

There are four major agents of socialisation: the *family*, *school*, *peer groups* and the *mass media*. These agents of socialisation are further divided into primary groups and secondary groups.

Primary groups include the family, the extended family and close friends. 'Primary groups are based on intimate relationships and face to face interaction; they are crucial in establishing early codes of conduct as well as self-perception. . . . The family is the clearest example of a primary group and it is here that the most basic rules of culturally acceptable behaviour are found' (Marsh & Keating 2000:30).

Secondary groups are more distant and impersonal: examples are school and mass media. 'Secondary groups are less intimate and more formal organisations, which do not provide the personal interaction of primary groups. These groups are often our first contact with society in general; as such, they not only reinforce the lessons learned within primary groups but also introduce us to new standards of behaviour which are universally agreed upon by society at large' (Marsh & Keating 2000:30).

The Family

No parent wants their child to grow up unable to 'fit in', an outcast who cannot make their way in the world. So every parent, as well as taking care of the physical needs of the child, will also begin the process of socialisation. The child will learn not only how to behave within the family but will begin to learn what is expected of it in the outside world. Families will aid their child in developing physical and intellectual skills, but as well as this, the family 'gives the child a social location within society. A child born to an upper class family will be socialised into wealth, power and social acceptance, whereas a child born to an impoverished family will learn about day to day survival, low pay and social rejection' (Curry *et al.* 2005:73).

The family meets the needs of the child and also 'shoulders the task of teaching children cultural values, attitudes and prejudices about themselves and others' (Macionis & Plummer 1997:139).

The child absorbs parental attitudes, not only towards others, but also about themselves and how they are regarded by society. Gender, class and ethnic socialisation will take place and children may learn that boys don't cry or wear pink; they may learn that their class or culture is less favoured than others. 'The family also confers on children a social position; that is, parents not only bring children into the physical world, they also place them in society in terms of race, ethnicity, religion and class' (Macionis & Plummer 1997:140).

Children will learn attitudes from their family – the attitude the family has towards the wider world and also the attitude the wider world has towards themselves and various groups of people. So a child will learn from a young age whether it is of a favoured or less favoured group in the eyes of the world. Children will learn to look down on certain groups of people; they will pick up their parents' prejudices or be on the receiving end of prejudice. 'We know from research evidence that by the time they enter primary school, white children may well be on the road to believing that they are superior to black people. Black children may believe that society is not going to show them the same respect and esteem that white people receive' (Commission for Racial Equality, *From Cradle to School* (1989), cited by Webb & Tossell 1999:91).

School

School is an important agent of socialisation in the secondary group. School attendance is compulsory until the age of 16. The child will move from the enclosure of family and friends and begin to experience a wider society. 'Schooling enlarges children's social world to include people with social backgrounds that differ from their own. As children confront social diversity, they learn the significance society attaches to people's race and sex and often act accordingly' (Macionis & Plummer 1997:140).

While families differ in the amount of flexibility and freedom offered to the child, schools will adhere to rigid and basic rules. As well as learning skills such as reading and writing, the children will also learn to put their hand up for permission to speak or go to the toilet, to sit still for long periods, to queue and wait their turn. The teacher is there to impart knowledge, but unless the children behave in an ordered way and obey certain behaviour rules they will be punished – despite what they know or do not know. 'Although the formal curriculum of the school emphasises the development of cognitive skills, the informal life of the school subtly reinforces values that are central to the society' (Curry *et al.* 2005:74).

The *hidden curriculum* is a term used to describe the messages promoted within the school that are not formally part of any lesson – 'the "unstated agenda" involved in schooling – conveying, for example, aspects of gender difference' (Giddens 2001:690). For example, school uniform policy may demand that girls wear skirts, while certain hairstyles and jewellery may be forbidden. Children will learn what is good or bad in the eyes of the teacher, what is approved of and what is frowned upon, although it may not break a specific rule. 'Teachers were involved in the "surveillance" of students, by constantly monitoring them in the hallways, instructing them to "look at me when I'm talking to you" and "walk properly down the corridor"' (Giddens 2001:15). Prejudice and stereotypes may influence teachers' expectations and pupils' performance at school and any questioning of the social order is not encouraged. 'The hidden curriculum teaches children that their role in life is "to know their place and to sit still in it"' (Illich (1973), cited in Giddens 2001:512).

Peer Group

The peer group is another agent of socialisation. It is made up of a group of friends who are close in age and social status. The peer group provides informal socialisation, and 'The influence of the peer group increases with age, peaking during adolescence' (Curry *et al.* 2005:74). The peer group may be seen by its members as being the place where they can be themselves, free from parental and educational pressure. But the demands of the peer group, although subtle (because all members are equal), nevertheless exist. Members of the peer group will have the same interests and attitudes, and a certain level of conformity will be expected. According to Macionis and Plummer, peer groups unite by discrediting other peer groups. Students who are different, or from a minority, may find themselves judged and sidelined by dominant peer groups.

Mass Media

Mass media can be defined as 'Impersonal communications directed to a vast audience' (Macionis & Plummer 1997:141). They include books, newspapers, radio, television and cinema, but television is 'the dominant medium, by far' (Curry *et al.* 2005:74) and is hugely influential in forming a child's picture of the world. Television dominates because the child must become literate before having access to books, and cinema trips involve an excursion from the home and so are rare. Radio is as present in the house as television, but because it offers sound without vision, it cannot compete.

'Average households' may well keep a television on for seven hours or more each day. Years before children learn to read, watching television has become a regular routine and, as they grow up, young girls and boys spend as much time in front of a television as they do in school. Indeed, television consumes as much of children's time as interacting with parents. (Macionis & Plummer 1997:41)

Summarised from Curry *et al.* (2005); Giddens (2001); Macionis & Plummer (1997); Marsh & Keating (2000); Webb & Tossell (1999).

Activities

1 Describe the importance of your family in making you who you are. What were the most important messages and values you learned and would like to keep through your life? What messages and values are no longer important to you?

2 Describe how education and mass media help build an identity that is shared by all your generation.

3 How important is your peer group to you? Reflect on similarities between members of your peer group and how much difference and disagreement are tolerated.

4 What images of other cultures do you have? Try to identify which you learned from your family, and which from your school, peer group or from mass media.

Case study: The Six Cultures study of child rearing – socialisation in the family

People often talk about a 'mother's instinct', but rather than instinct, mothers the world over follow definite cultural patterns in their socialisation of children. Child-rearing style will reflect the surrounding culture.

> Children born in diverse cultures appear to enter the world with similar endowments ... cultural forces do modulate social development and lead to increasing differences in the kinds of behaviour which adults expect in children, which they give children the most opportunity to practice, and which they make meaningful to them in terms of central cultural goals and values. (Whiting & Edwards 1988:266)

In 1963, John and Beatrice Whiting instigated a study of these differences. Teams of social scientists were sent to six destinations – Mexico, India, the Philippines, the USA, Okinawa (an island off Japan) and Kenya in Africa – to observe different methods of child rearing. The major differences in child-rearing practices were between the US and the non-western cultures, but the non-western societies were not uniform in their approach.

- In poorer countries, mothers had less time to spend with their children and it was important that the children became independent and useful quickly. From a young age they were expected to mind siblings and animals, carry food and water, sweep and wash; and even children as young as three would be sent on errands. Children were eager to help and saw work as associated with advanced status in the family. Young Kenyan women believed that 'to be assigned a chore was to be part of the family, to be important in the mother's eyes. To be overlooked when work was handed out was interpreted as disapproval' (Whiting & Edwards 1988:185) However, in India families tried not to give girls too many chores because 'a girl is considered a guest in her own home ... a girl must work so hard in the house of her husband, she should not have to work at her parents' house' (Whiting 1963:335).

- American children remained without responsibility and were encouraged in activities, such as colouring, counting and playing with building blocks, that would prepare them for school rather than work. 'In all of the communities, parents appear concerned with ... teaching them the skills and behaviours that they consider necessary for maturation. The Kenyan parents ... stress the socialisation of work habits and the skills required of an agricultural economy, while the Orchard Town [USA] mothers emphasise the skills needed in a society where literacy and verbal facility are essential' (Whiting & Edwards 1988:212).

- American children were frequently asked if such and such an experience was enjoyable, and praise was frequent. In Kenya, 'praise is extremely rare, as mothers believe it can make even a good child rude and disobedient' (Whiting 1963:165). Like the Kenyans, Indian mothers regarded praise as making a child disobedient, so insults and punishments rather than praise and rewards were used to control behaviour.

- In the USA, parents were totally responsible for rearing and children tended to stay in their own homes, while in other cultures, the extended family and community had a greater input into the child's upbringing, and children had more freedom to roam in groups around their homestead or locality. In the USA, notions of fair play and equality dominated, so adults often interfered in and adjudicated children's squabbles. The parents in non-western cultures were busy with work and other children were often in charge, so 'children learn the pecking order based on size and age' (Whiting & Edwards 1988:219). As a result children were eager to grow up, as power increased with size and age.

- American children owned many games and toys, while children in the other cultures had few, if any, toys, and the announcement 'Mine' was rare. The games children in non-western cultures played were often unstructured, with no rules or turn-taking, because they might be interrupted at any moment to run an errand for parents. The games they played often imitated their parents' work and were divided strictly along gender lines, as their future work would be.

- In the USA, sibling jealousy was considered normal. 'Mothers tried not to be punitive of the experience of hostility toward the new baby; rather they attempted to placate the older child' (Whiting & Edwards 1988:188). Children in the non-western countries did not display as much sibling rivalry, due to the child being eager to grow up and also because a baby did not command as much attention. In Kenya any jealousy shown by a toddler towards a new baby was punished severely, as the villagers believed in the evil eye and the child's jealousy was seen as a death wish against the new baby.

- American toddlers received more attention from parents, but spent more time alone in cribs and play pens, while non-western toddlers received less individual attention but were seldom alone – they were either in groups of children or watching their parents at work. Babies were entertained not with rattles and such, but by being in constant company.

- Tolerance of a child's bad behaviour differed. In Okinawa, obedience from a young child was not expected – 'play and fight are children's work', and a child who had a tantrum was left on the ground to cry it out while the carer walked away. In Kenya, if the child had a tantrum and was disrespectful, no leeway was given because of its age. 'Mothers overwhelmingly reported severe punishment, beating and depriving of food, as their response to being struck or insulted by a child, and some regarded it as inconceivable that a child would do such things' (Whiting 1963:165).

Summarised from Whiting (1963); Whiting and Edwards (1988).

Activities

1   Discuss the different methods of child rearing described. What are the benefits and disadvantages of each of these childhoods?

2   Some of the attitudes towards children may seem very harsh. Consider why some mothers had such strict attitudes.

3   Describe your own childhood in relation to the following: punishments and rewards; responsibilities and expectations about helping out with chores; attitudes to discipline; amount of alone time and group time; freedom to wander from home; amount of praise, and what behaviour was praised; amount of time spent indoors and outdoors. Compare with other classmates and see what similarities and differences there are. If there are different age groups and cultures in the class, evaluate what differences there are in upbringing.

4   'Material culture is a key component of overall culture.' Discuss how child-rearing practices differ according to the wealth of a country. What cultural changes will come about in families as a result of moving from boom to recession?

5   How does cultural change affect families? Consider the changing roles of fathers and how fathers' roles today compare with previous generations.

Project idea

Two recent books, *French Children Don't Throw Food* (Pamela Druckerman) and *Battle Hymn of the Tiger Mother* (Amy Chua) argue that certain cultural practices concerning child rearing are better than others. Research the main ideas put forward in the books and present them to your classmates. Discuss how cultural approaches differ and whether you agree with the ideas in these books.

Case study: The Pygmalion effect – positive and negative expectations in the classroom

In Greek myth, Pygmalion was a sculptor who fell in love with a statue, which then became alive in answer to his wishes. The *Pygmalion effect* concerns self-fulfilling prophecies in the education system – the effect that the teacher's own positive or negative expectations have on students' performance and growth. Those labelled positively often succeed, while those labelled negatively respond accordingly.

The effect was studied in 1966 by Rosenthal and Jacobsen in the Oak School Experiment. A group of first- to sixth-graders were given an intelligence test. Individual students were randomly selected and teachers were told that these students had huge potential. Eight months later the students were re-tested and it was found that those labelled as gifted had showed greater improvement than the rest of the group. The approved students were also reported as being more curious, happier and better socially adjusted than the others. Just as high expectations increase success, low teacher expectations will have a negative result. The implications for people who are the victims of stereotyping or prejudice are obvious. 'Teachers expected [black boys] to achieve little at school. Asian pupils, meanwhile, were seen as quiet and compliant. Not surprisingly both groups of pupils tended to live up to their stereotypes' (Ofsted report (1996), cited by Webb & Tossell 1999:100). While some groups suffer, other favoured groups benefit from the negative expectations towards others. 'White students may actually experience what they call "stereotype lift" – that is, a relative boost in performance due to … negative academic stereotypes about their black classmates' (Walton & Cohen (2003), cited by Earp 2010:10). Teaching styles may also be influenced by expectations: if the teacher thinks certain students are not particularly able, they may not give of their best. 'If you think your students can't achieve very much, are perhaps not too bright, you may be inclined to teach simple stuff, do a lot of drills, read from your lecture notes, give simple assignments calling for simplistic factual answers' (Rosenthal, quoted by Rhem 1999:2).

Summarised from Earp (2010); Webb & Tossell (1999).

Activities

1   Compare the Oak School Experiment with Jane Elliott's brown eyes/blue eyes exercise.

2   What attitude did your teachers have towards you and how did it affect you?

3   From your own experience, describe how both positive and negative treatment has affected you.

Globalisation and Cultural Identity

Globalisation may be defined as 'Growing interdependence between different peoples, regions and countries in the world as social and economic relationships come to stretch worldwide' (Giddens 2001:690). The internet, cheap travel, world brands and worldwide export of music and film may mean that wherever we go we see more of the same. Because of this, cultures may begin to seem similar, for example national forms of dress are replaced the world over by T-shirts and jeans, national foods and drink are replaced by global brands, and chain restaurants appear in multiple cities. 'Today, more than ever before, we can observe many of the same cultural patterns the world over . . . we find familiar forms of dress, hear well known pop music and see advertising for many of the same products we use at home' (Macionis & Plummer 1997:116).

There are three arguments for a positive view of global culture:

1 The global economy ensures an international flow of goods. We can find many of the big name consumer goods and brands worldwide.
2 Global communications have revolutionised how quickly we receive information. The flow of information and images is instantaneous.
3 Global migration has increased. Travel is cheaper and the flow of people has increased; most countries host large numbers of people who were not born there. (Summarised from Macionis & Plummer 1997:118.)

Yet, despite these three arguments, there are limitations to the global culture theory:

• The flow of goods, information and people has been uneven. Urban areas are the major target, but rural areas remain isolated. Nations of greater power (economic and military) such as North America and Western Europe exercise the greatest influence but are not influenced in a similar vein.

• Many goods and services may be available internationally, but the poverty in which much of the world lives means there is not equal access to goods and services.

• 'Glocalisation' is the term given to the different ways a culture will respond to the same phenomenon. For example, karaoke originated in Japan, but it takes on different meanings when performed elsewhere – in Ireland, for example, karaoke is often performed in a joking way, often by young women and usually with drink taken; but in Japan, participants are of any age and sex and perform with utmost seriousness. (Summarised from Macionis & Plummer 1997:118.)

Summarised from Giddens (2001); Macionis & Plummer (1997).

Activity

If you have spent time abroad, note what elements of culture were exactly the same as at home. Were you disappointed or pleased?

Project ideas

1 Choose a country and research it with a view to comparing its culture today with that of the past – a century ago or more. Some areas to include are language, dress, customs, religion, music, urban living.

2 Macionis and Plummer state that the effects of globalisation are limited in very poor countries. Research a third world country and see what evidence you can find that traditional customs have changed less there than in richer countries.

Revision questions

1 Briefly explain what sociology is.
2 Describe what prejudice involves and how it impacts on a person.
3 Explain how prejudice differs from discrimination.
4 State what a stereotype is.
5 Describe the experiment Jane Elliott performed with her class.
6 List the four agents of socialisation and state whether each is from a primary or secondary group.
7 Explain the term 'hidden curriculum'.
8 Describe how cultures have different methods and aims of socialisation.
9 Explain the 'Pygmalion effect'.
10 List some ways in which globalisation changes cultures.

CHAPTER 3

Religious Belief, Difference, Conflict and Change

By the end of this chapter, students should:

- Be able to list some functions of religion in society.
- Understand the history and core beliefs of three world religions – Christianity, Islam and Judaism.
- Be able to recognise the similarities shared by different religions.
- Be aware of current statistics on religious affiliation in Ireland.
- Recognise some key features of marriage and death rituals in three cultures.
- Be able to define and discuss religious intolerance, fundamentalism and sectarianism.
- Be aware of examples of sectarian conflict.
- Understand the term *secularism* and discuss conflict between religious and secular views in society.

Introduction

Religion plays an important part in culture, and it influences people's values and behaviours. In some societies, religion is so central that it can be said to dominate culture. Religion can have a unifying role in society and encourage a sense of solidarity and community.

O'Donnell (2002) lists the main functions of religion in society as:

1 *Social cohesion* – religion provides a common ground for a wide variety of people.
2 *Rites of passage* – religious ceremonies mark important milestones in life.
3 *Integration* – religion gives people a feeling of belonging.
4 *Supportive* – religion gives comfort at difficult times.
5 *Moral direction* – religion gives clear directions on how to live a good life.
6 *Explanation* – religion gives meaning to life.
7 *Reintegration* – religion accepts those who do wrong back into society.

Summarised from O'Donnell (2002).

Christianity

According to Macionis and Plummer, in 2002 Christianity had two billion followers, amounting to one-third of humanity. Most Christians live in the western world – Europe and the Americas. This dominance is reflected in many ways in western culture; for instance the western calendar is divided into the years before the birth of Jesus (BC) and after it (AD).

Christianity originated in the Middle East, beginning as a small movement led by Jesus of Nazareth, but over time it grew to become a world religion. Jesus preached at a time of Roman occupation, and his teachings made those in power so uncomfortable that he was arrested and sentenced to death. Followers believe that he was resurrected after death, and the image of the cross that he died on has become a symbol of death and rebirth.

Christianity retained some elements of its predecessor, Judaism, such as the teachings of the Old Testament, but places more emphasis on the New Testament, which deals with the life and death of Jesus. The distant God of the Old Testament becomes closer and more personal in the teachings of the New Testament.

Christianity is a monotheistic religion, which means its followers believe in one God rather than many (polytheism). A key Christian belief is the Holy Trinity, a concept which holds that God the father, his son Jesus and the Holy Spirit exist as separate beings, yet are one God. Each is distinct from the other, but all are God – not three gods but one. St Patrick is said to have used the shamrock to help explain this concept – the shamrock has three distinct leaves, yet remains one plant.

The followers of Jesus, the apostles, spread the message of Christianity widely. Early Christians were at first persecuted under the Roman Empire but they refused to give up their faith. In AD 313, Emperor Constantine of Rome announced Christianity as the official faith of the Roman Empire. Early Christians shared one faith, but two traditions developed: an Eastern tradition centred on Constantinople (now Istanbul); and a Western tradition centred on Rome. In AD 320 the capital of the Roman Empire was moved from Rome to Constantinople, which led to a split. Many shared traditions of worship remained, but gradually differences and disputes developed. In AD 1054, the Great Schism split the Church into the Catholic Church (West) and the Orthodox Church (East).

The Catholic Church increased in power but became corrupt, leading disillusioned people such as Catholic monk Martin Luther to protest against its many wrongs. Martin Luther was excommunicated by the Pope for his criticisms. He then established his own church, triggering a new divide known as the Reformation. His ideas spread rapidly and Protestant Churches proliferated, eventually splitting into six chief branches – Lutheran, Anglican, Presbyterian, Baptist, Methodist and Quaker.

The Catholic Church continued with the Pope at its head; the Orthodox Church is governed by patriarchs; while Anglicans are governed by the General Synod. Although Catholicism, Protestantism and Orthodoxy remain one religion – Christianity – much conflict has arisen from these divisions throughout history and to the present day.

The seven sacraments – baptism, communion (eucharist), confirmation, reconciliation (confession), matrimony, holy orders and anointing of the sick (last rites) – are shared by both Catholic and Orthodox churches, while most Protestants acknowledge only baptism and the eucharist as sacraments. Shared Christian festivals include Christmas, Easter and Lent.

Summarised from Boyle & Boyle (2001); Macionis & Plummer (2002).

Islam

In 2002 Islam had 1.1 billion followers (Muslims), or 19 per cent of the world's population. The majority of Middle Eastern people are Muslims and Islam is strongly associated with the Arab world, yet the majority of Muslims are not Arabs but live in North Africa and Western Asia. Islam is also the second largest faith in Europe.

Islam originated in Arabia in the sixth century. The prophet Muhammad – a married businessman who lived in Mecca – disliked the corruption he saw about him. At this time, Arabs worshipped many gods. After much thought, praying and fasting, Muhammad came to believe that there was only one God, Allah. In AD 610 Muhammad received a revelation (a vision from god containing a message) in which he was told he was to be a prophet. His wife and cousin became his first converts to the new religion, Islam.

After another revelation, he began to preach to the people of Mecca, telling them to worship only Allah and saying that after death people would be held accountable for their good and evil actions. Gradually he won more converts, but not without opposition. Eventually threats to his life and to his followers forced him to depart to the city of Medina – this departure is known as the Hegira and the Muslim calendar is dated from this event, just as the Christian calendar is dated from the birth of Jesus.

His teachings were honoured in Medina but he was determined also to convert the people of Mecca to Islam. He waged a jihad (holy war) against Mecca and was victorious. Following this victory, he had all idols removed from the city and Mecca became the centre of Islam. Arabs from all over Arabia became united under Islam, they pledged allegiance to Allah and Muhammad, and raised a powerful army to wage holy war. Muhammad died at Medina two years after the victory at Mecca, but a series of caliphs continued the campaign to win territory and converts.

Over the course of history, Christians and Muslims have often been in opposition and involved in wars against each other. Like Christianity, Islam has split into different denominations, such as Shias and Sunnis. The majority of the world's Muslims are Sunnis, but Shias are in the majority in Pakistan, Iran, Iraq and the Lebanon. Sunni and Shia Muslims disagree over leadership issues. Shias believe that parts of the Qur'an were changed by enemies of Islam and so are suspicious of traditional meanings and interpretations of the Qur'an; but both denominations share practices such as the Five Pillars of Islam. These two denominations have a history marred by fighting among themselves.

Muslims believe that the word of God was revealed to Mohammed, but Mohammed himself is not regarded as a divine being (in contrast to the Christian belief in Jesus as both divine and human). Like Christians, they believe that God will punish and reward deeds when a person has died. The word 'Islam' means both 'submission' and 'peace' and they believe that the path to inner peace is through submission to Allah.

All branches of Islam accept the Five Pillars of Islam:

1 First pillar: *Shahadah* – a prayer acknowledging Allah as the one true God and Muhammad as his prophet.

2 Second pillar: *Salat* – the duty to pray five times a day and attend at mosque on Friday. Imams lead the people in prayer, while mullahs explain beliefs and rituals.

3 Third pillar: *Zakat* – giving to charity.

4 Fourth pillar: *Saum* – requires fasting during Ramadan, which is the ninth month of the Muslim year.

5 Fifth pillar: *Hajj* (pilgrimage) – every Muslim must journey to Mecca once in their lifetime.

The Qur'an (Koran) is the sacred book of Islam and it is said to have been dictated by God's messenger to Muhammad. The Qur'an contains Islam's basic beliefs and restrictions on behaviour (such as not consuming pork or alcohol), and advice on marriage, divorce and business. Muslims may only eat meat that is 'halal' – meat that has been killed in a specific way.

Allah is seen as separate and remote from people, a being of such greatness and goodness that no human being can be compared to him, neither can he be compared to anything – therefore it is forbidden to draw or paint an image of Allah.

Mosques (Muslim places of worship) contain no human images (statues or paintings) and are decorated with geometric patterns. Before entering a mosque, shoes must be removed and heads covered. There are no seats, and worshippers must bring their own prayer mat. They kneel on their mats in the direction of Mecca and bow in a sequence, praying.

There are three major festivals in the Muslim calendar:

- *Hijrah* marks the beginning of the Muslim year and celebrates Muhammad's journey from Mecca to Medina.
- *Eid-ul-Fitr* takes place after Ramadan. A celebratory meal is shared, friends visit, new clothes are bought, children get sweets and food is sent to the poor.
- *Eid-ul-Adha* is held in the final month of the Muslim year and celebrates the completion of the annual pilgrimage to Mecca. There is a celebratory meal and an exchange of gifts.

Births and marriages are not celebrated in the religious sense. Babies have a naming ceremony – *Aquiqa* – but do not become Muslim until the age of ten, when they are seen as old enough to tell right from wrong. This is when their religious instruction begins.

Condensed from Boyle & Boyle (2001); Macionis & Plummer (2002).

Judaism

In 2002 Judaism had 15 million followers worldwide, making it the smallest of the major world religions. The majority of Jews live in Israel (in the Middle East), which they believe is their promised homeland. A large population also live in Europe and the USA, compensating for small numbers worldwide by their location in powerful and highly influential countries.

Judaism is the world's oldest monotheistic faith and it originated in the Middle East. The Jewish nation was ruled by a series of kings, including David and Solomon, but after splitting into two rival kingdoms, it was weakened, then conquered, and exiled to Babylon. They returned to their homeland half a century after exile to Babylon, only to be conquered by the Romans and exiled again, losing their homeland and becoming dispersed worldwide.

Jewish people share a strong sense of history, a history often of persecution. They have endured persecution through most of Europe over centuries. The Christian Church regarded them with enmity in the past and they were often separated from Christians and forced to live in ghettos outside the city walls. An attempt at total elimination in Germany during World War II (the Holocaust) resulted in the setting up of a Jewish state in Israel.

Like Christianity and Islam, Judaism is monotheistic: Jews believe in one God. Jews believe they are God's 'chosen people' and that they have a covenant (special relationship) with God. This covenant requires a duty to observe God's laws, recorded as the Ten Commandments, which were delivered to Moses after he led his people from slavery in Egypt. A series of prophets have appeared through their history to remind them of their duties. The Jewish God (known by a number of different names) is a rather strict God.

The holy book of Judaism is the Tanakh, which Christians know as the Old Testament of the Bible. The Tanakh is both scripture and a record of Jewish history. Rabbis (holy men) serve to help people understand the Tanakh, which is divided into three sections.

1 The *Torah* (meaning 'teaching' and 'law') is regarded as the holiest part of the Tenakh. It comprises Genesis, Exodus, Leviticus, Numbers and Deuteronomy.

2 *Nevi'im*: the prophets' writings.

3 *Ketuvim*: the psalms and proverbs.

Judaism is split into three main denominations: Orthodox, Hasidic and Conservative. Orthodox is the strictest denomination. Orthodox Jews hold separate services for men and women and practise strict kosher laws relating to food; Hasidic Jews are very spiritual; and the Conservatives occupy the middle ground.

The term 'kosher' refers to restrictions regarding preparation methods and choice of food. Pork and shellfish are not permitted and animals must be slaughtered and prepared in a special way. The 'shochet' – slaughterer – is trained and licensed to perform his task. He must drain blood quickly from the animal and then soak the meat in salted cold water to remove all traces of blood. Meat and dairy products must not be eaten at the same meal and a separate set of dishes should be used for each – there may even be separate washing-up bowls and tea towels for each set of crockery. Some denominations practice kosher more strictly than others.

Festivals

There are three pilgrim festivals, of which the most important is *Pesach* (Passover), which celebrates the release of the Jewish people from slavery in Egypt. The highlight of the festival is the Seder meal, in which all of the food and drink is symbolic: for example, matzo (unleavened bread) is served in recollection of the bread eaten by Israelites when fleeing in haste from Egypt and bitter herbs are served to recall the bitterness of slavery.

Rosh Hashanah is a new year festival in which people make resolutions for the future. The feast on New Year's Eve follows 40 days of penitence. Symbolic food is served, such as bread dipped in honey to symbolise a sweet year ahead. A prayer service, which can last up to six hours, takes place in the synagogue (place of worship) the following day.

Condensed from Boyle & Boyle (2001); Harley (2005); Macionis & Plummer (2002).

Similarities between Christianity, Islam and Judaism

Religion can be a positive force in society, but it can also be divisive. Much blood has been shed in religious wars throughout history. Despite their differences, there are many similarities between Christianity, Islam and Judaism. Perhaps the most important similarity is what is known as 'the golden rule', which instructs followers that the correct way to live is to treat others as you would wish to be treated. Quotes from various holy books emphasise this shared belief:

- Judaism: 'What is hateful to you, do not to your fellow men' (Talmud, Shabbat 31a).
- Christianity: 'In everything do to others as you would have them do to you' (Matthew 7:12).
- Islam: 'No one of you is a believer until he desires for his brother that which he desires for himself' (Hadith al-Nawawi 13).

There are also five shared characteristics: creed, code, scriptures, community and ritual.

1 *Creed*: 'A shared set of beliefs about God and the meaning of life' (Boyle & Boyle 2001:26), for example the belief that God will punish or reward after death.
2 *Code*: 'Guidelines for living' (Boyle & Boyle 2001:29). A code contains instructions on how to tell right from wrong, such as the Ten Commandments (which are common to Judaism, Christianity and Islam). A code may include dietary restrictions.
3 *Scriptures*: holy books/sacred texts that contain essential teachings, stories and histories. Examples are the Jewish Tanakh; the Christian Bible (both Old and New Testaments); and, in Islam, the Qur'an.
4 *Community*: a community of faithful, like-minded people who share beliefs and support each other in difficult times. Religious communities often gather at a shared place of worship, such as a church for Christians, a mosque for Muslims or a synagogue for Jewish people. Religious communities also have spiritual leaders (priests, ministers, rabbis and imams).
5 *Ritual*: ceremonies that mark important moments, such as birth or death, remind the faithful of important past events, teach about God and bolster faith. Ritual can be private or a public event in a place of worship.

Summarised from Boyle & Boyle (2001).

Activities

1   How important is religion to you? Do you consider difference in religion to be a barrier to friendship? Write a short reflective piece on this theme.

2   Discuss your awareness of other religions' beliefs and practices and where this information came from. Conduct a quick class survey on how often members of the class come into contact with those of other beliefs.

3   In Ireland, Protestants and Catholics often live very separate lives. Is it surprising that members of one religion have difficult relations with each other?

4   How is awareness of others' beliefs important in the following settings? School, college, the workplace, institutions such as hospitals and care homes.

5   Discuss the importance of being aware of similarities as well as differences between various faiths.

6   How important is the 'golden rule' in building tolerance and understanding?

Project ideas

1   Research a religion not mentioned above. Look into its history, festivals, main beliefs and practices and present your findings to your class.

2   Research in more detail the various branches of the Christian religion.

Religion in Ireland

Ireland has a long tradition of Catholicism and according to the Census of 2011 Catholics are still in the majority. However, there are a range of other faiths in Ireland today, as demonstrated by the table below.

Population by Religion: Census Year 2011

Roman Catholic	3,861,335	Atheist	3,905
Church of Ireland, England, Anglican, Episcopalian	129,039	Baptist	3,531
Muslim (Islamic)	49,204	Agnostic	3,521
Orthodox (Greek, Coptic, Russian)	45,223	Jewish	1,984
Other Christian religion, n.e.s.	41,161	Pagan, Pantheist	1,940
Presbyterian	24,600	Mormon	1,284
Apostolic or Pentecostal	14,043	Lapsed (Roman) Catholic	1,279
Hindu	10,688	Society of Friends	925
Buddhist	8,703	Baha'i	520
Methodist, Wesleyan	6,842	Brethren	336
Jehovah's Witness	6,149	Other stated religions (3)	14,118
Lutheran	5,683	No religion	269,811
Protestant	5,326	Not stated	72,914
Evangelical	4,188		

Source: CSO 2011e

Marriage and Death Rituals

There are important milestones in people's lives, both sad and happy, and cultures mark the importance of these events with rituals. The ceremonies vary across cultures, and over time some traditions disappear. Marriage and death are important life events in every society and each culture has its own unique customs to mark the occasion.

Marriage Customs

Chinese Traditions

In China, it was traditional for the parents to arrange the marriage. They would consult an astrologer to determine if the couple were a good match. A ceremony was held for the engagement and a lucky wedding day was set. The bride's family presented a dowry to the groom's parents. These days, people choose their own partners and a dowry is not paid. However, many traditional customs are still followed.

- Wedding guests give money in a red envelope – red is considered a lucky colour.
- The bride will change her clothes many times throughout the day, 'a traditional custom thought to provide the opportunity for the bride to show off her wealth' (Cherrytree 2007a:11).
- The wedding banquet used to be held at the groom's family home but nowadays is often held at a hotel or restaurant. The banquet consists of up to 12 courses 'including roast pig, shark fin soup, rice, noodles and dessert' (Cherrytree 2007a:11).
- The couple may still follow the traditional custom of calling on the bride's family three days after the ceremony.
- The traditional wedding ceremony was very simple. The bride and groom would pray to their ancestors at a family altar, and the ceremony was completed by the bride and groom bowing to each other, while 'in some regions, they both drank wine from the same goblet and ate a lump of sugar shaped like a rooster. Roosters were believed to ward off evil and bad luck' (Cherrytree 2007a:11).
- Traditionally the bride would have been carried to the wedding in a sedan chair (a chair carried on poles). She would have been hidden behind curtains 'to protect her from evil spirits and to prevent her from seeing anything unlucky' (Cherrytree 2007a:10).
- In the past fruit and nuts would have been placed on the bridal bed the day before the wedding. 'Children, a symbol of fertility, were invited to scramble around the bed for the food' (Cherrytree 2007a:10).

Indian Weddings

In India ceremonies are usually Muslim or Hindu. Hindu weddings are still very traditional and are often arranged by the couple's parents. Because of the importance of caste, marriage is seen as too serious a business to be left to romance. The marriage would often have been arranged between very young children without their consent, 'But now, children are included in marriage discussions and they must be at least fourteen years old' (Cherrytree 2007a:19).

A formal engagement ceremony will take place, with prayers to the gods, and the couple exchange garlands (made of flowers, fruits, ribbons and beads) and gold rings. The future bride is given gifts by her intended's family to show their acceptance. There may be ceremonies starting several days before the wedding.

- The bride wears a silk sari, often embroidered with gold or silver thread and decorated with jewels. Different regions of India have their own traditional colours for a bride. 'Southern brides wear a yellow silk sari with a wide, gold belt and flowers in their hair. In the west, they wear green and decorate their hair with pearls. Northern brides wear red, while in the northeast they wear red and white' (Cherrytree 2007a:17).

- Preparations for the day are important. Mehndi is a ritual celebrated by the bride on the day before the wedding. Female relations and friends come to her house to paint designs on her hands and feet. A henna paste is mixed to paint the intricate designs, which may take many hours. When the paste is removed, the design will remain for many days.

- On the wedding day the bride will be ritually cleansed before dressing in her wedding sari. Her father will apply a bindi or tika (dot) of red paste to her forehead, a symbol of the third eye of the god Shiva.

- The ceremony itself takes place under a canopy known as a mandap. The groom will arrive on horseback in procession with musicians, family and friends. 'A partition is held in front of the groom and not removed until he says he accepts the bride' (Cherrytree 2007a:18). The bride is brought in and the couple's feet are cleansed with milk and water by the bride's parents, who also place garlands of coloured threads on the couple. They clasp the right hands of the couple together and fasten them with thread to symbolise their bond. A priest lights a ceremonial fire and the couple make their vows. They are then led around the fire by the bride's brothers, throwing offerings into it. 'Then the bride and groom take seven steps together while chanting seven oaths, which symbolise seven blessings for their future journey together' (Cherrytree 2007a:18).

- Only after the ceremony is complete are the relations and friends allowed to enter the mandap to offer their congratulations.

Muslim Weddings in Central and Southern Asia – Pakistan, Uzbekistan and Afghanistan

Muslim weddings vary depending on the region. However, certain features are common to all Muslim weddings. The marriage contract is signed at the Nikah ceremony and a gift called a mahr will be given from the groom to the bride. There is a religious and a non-religious (civil) element to the marriage. The ceremony itself is civil: a contract (the nikah) is signed in front of witnesses. The religious element is contained in the Qur'an, which details what is expected of a husband and wife. 'The husband is responsible for looking after his wife and ensuring she has food, clothing and a comfortable home. He is to respect her and treat her with kindness . . . a wife is instructed to be faithful and attend to the comfort of her husband' (Cherrytree 2007a:21).

- In Pakistan, there are four days of celebration of a marriage: Mienu, which is a party held by the separate families; Mehndi, where the bride-to-be has her hands and feet decorated with henna; Shadi, the wedding day itself; and Valima, when the groom's family serve dinner.

- In Uzbekistan, the tradition is to hold weddings in early autumn, and the wedding always takes place on a Friday.

- In Afghanistan, a wedding contract is signed privately, but then a celebration is held. Musicians play to family and friends. The wedding party stand up as the couple enter with the Qur'an held above their heads. Feasting, singing and dancing follow, and the traditional attan circle dance is performed at the end of the evening. Buzkashi – the Afghan national sport, which is played on horseback – is often played for spectators to enjoy.

Summarised from Cherrytree (2007a).

End of Life Customs

China

These days, traditional funerals are mainly held in rural areas. Burial is generally preferred to cremation, although Chinese Buddhists prefer to cremate their dead.

- Mourners and cemetery workers wear white, the colour of mourning in China. The hearse that brings the coffin and the coffin itself will be highly decorated. As the coffin is lowered, mourners will turn away as it is considered bad luck to watch.

- 'Most Chinese believe that after death a person's soul descends to hell where there are ten courts and ten judges' (Cherrytree 2007b:13). Each judge will punish any evil actions before the soul passes on to the next court. Relations often burn paper money as an offering to the judges in the hope that they will be lenient towards their loved ones.

- White banners are hung outside a house to announce a death and people send flowers of either white or yellow (the colour of dignity). 'Red flowers, symbolising happiness and good luck, are acceptable for those who have lived a long life of at least eighty years' (Cherrytree 2007b:13).

- The traditional mourning period is 100 days.

- Chinese people celebrate a festival of the dead known as 'the feast of the hungry ghosts', which is celebrated on the fifteenth day of the seventh month of the Chinese calendar. It is thought that the ghosts are the restless souls of those who died in an accident, were not properly buried or have no relations or descendants to honour them. These spirits roam about during the seventh month and so must be fed and entertained to appease them and prevent them doing harm. Paper money is burned and food placed outside homes as offerings for the hungry ghosts, while children are urged to be home before dark. It is also important to entertain the ghosts as well as feed them. 'Performers attempt to please the ghosts with singing, dancing and theatrical performance. These productions are very serious affairs that often take place at dusk' (Cherrytree Books 2007b:14).

India: Hindu Death Rituals

- Hindus have many gods, and Yama is the god of death. The funeral rite is called Antyeshti and this ceremony ensures that the soul travels on to the next world.

- The corpse is ritually washed and dressed in new white clothes, before being placed on a bier (wooden platform) with the head pointing south. The eldest son drapes the body in white cloth and it is then carried in procession to the cremation area, which is often close to water.

- On arrival at the cremation area, gold for purity is placed on the lips of the dead, the body is bathed again and the hair and nails are trimmed. Chanting takes place to scare off evil spirits and the body is then placed on a pyre of logs. The eldest son walks three times around the pyre sprinkling water before lighting the fire.

- After the cremation, mourners must bathe in the river to purify themselves and must touch stone, oil, fire and water before entering their houses. Mourners are considered polluted for a period of 12 days and so cannot cook for themselves. Neighbours and friends are responsible for feeding them.

- The ashes are collected after three days and must be thrown into the River Ganges. Hindus believe in reincarnation and believe that if they are cremated in the city of Varanasi on the banks of the Ganges this 'will liberate them from the endless cycle of birth, death and rebirth. Many go to Varanasi with the intention of dying there' (Cherrytree 2007b:21).

- In the past, Hindu widows would often practice a custom called suttee: the widow would throw herself on to her husband's funeral pyre, dying so that she could follow him to the next life. 'Although the practice of suttee was voluntary, many women felt pressured to do it and tried to escape. Women who practised suttee were highly respected. In some instances when a man's death was expected or imminent, his wife was often sacrificed before he died' (Cherrytree 2007a:21). Another reason for suttee being so widespread was that the widow would often be left in poverty. However, in 1829 during the period of British colonisation of India, Lord William Bentinck abolished suttee, penalising those who stood by and did not intervene. The tradition died out, although there have been occasional incidents, even to the present day.

Muslim End of Life Rituals in the Middle East: Iran, Iraq, Sudan, Syria

Muslims are never cremated because of the belief that the dead will be raised on the day of judgement, when those who have lived badly will be punished in hell, while those who have done good will be rewarded in paradise.

- A dying person will be surrounded by family and friends until the end. After death, the body will be washed by a close relation of the same sex and then wrapped in a white shroud. Men's shrouds are of three sheets, while women are wrapped in five or seven sheets.

- The body is traditionally not placed in a coffin but carried openly to the cemetery. These days, the body is often placed in a simple wooden coffin for the journey but is removed from the coffin for burial. The funeral procession is quiet and dignified and mourners take turns carrying the body.
- The body is placed on its right side in the grave with the face turned towards Mecca. The body rests on earth, but a barrier is placed on top of the body to stop earth touching the body when the grave is filled in. 'Muslims believe the body should rest on the earth, instead of the earth resting on the body' (Cherrytree 2007b:27).
- The grave is marked with a simple headstone. A husband or a wife is mourned by their spouse for four months and ten days. Other deaths are mourned for three days and nights.

Summarised from Cherrytree (2007b).

Activities

1   Discuss the importance of marriage and death rituals to a culture.
2   Consider how knowledge of a different culture's rituals is important in building an intercultural society.

Project idea

Research traditional Irish marriage and death rituals. How many old traditions are still in use today?

Fundamentalism

Fundamentalism is a religious attitude that will not tolerate other faiths and beliefs. It is defined as 'a conservative religious doctrine that opposes intellectualism and worldly accommodation in favour of restoring traditional, other-worldly spirituality' (Macionis & Plummer 2002:478). Fundamentalism is a particular version of religion and not to be confused with the religion itself. For example, in Islam some societies practice a very strict interpretation of their religion, but Islamic fundamentalists are not representative of every Muslim believer. Fundamental Christianity has experienced a resurgence in the USA in recent times.

Common features of fundamentalism include the following.

- Sacred texts are taken literally and not interpreted in modern ways.
- Religious pluralism is rejected; other faiths are not tolerated.

- All areas of life are sacred; there is no separation of ordinary life from religious life.
- Modern secular life is viewed as corrupting.
- Traditional beliefs and rules are held to be correct, e.g. that the man should rule the family.
- Fundamentalism often emerges in times of crisis, e.g. during wars or conditions of desperate poverty.

Summarised from Macionis & Plummer (2002:478–9).

Activity

Extreme events make news. How much of your knowledge of Islam comes from events relating to fundamental extremism? Discuss how fair it is to judge an entire religion by such cases.

Project ideas

1 Despite being banned, the practice of suttee still occurs in modern India. Research the reasons why it still continues and why the ban is difficult to enforce. A useful article to start with is available online at www.guardian.co.uk/world/2002/aug/23/gender.uk1.

2 Research fundamentalist movements in two religions.

Sectarianism

Sectarianism is discrimination or hatred arising from attaching importance to differences within a group, such as between different denominations of a religion: 'the process . . . whereby religious differences are noted . . . then evaluated and sometimes acted upon in a way that is discriminatory' (Share *et al.* 2007:408).

When a religious group splits into different denominations, the result is often that the different groups fight about their differences rather than recognising their common ground. There have been numerous conflicts through history between those who share a common religion, such as Christianity, but who cannot accept the differences between them. Sadly, sectarian conflict is alive and well in the twenty-first century.

Religious Intolerance and Persecution

Ideally, religion should be a source of personal comfort and each individual should be free to practise their own faith. However, some groups refuse to respect different beliefs and religious intolerance has been the cause of persecution and wars throughout history. In the first century AD, early Christians were persecuted by the Romans for refusing to worship the Roman emperor as a god. 'The Christians, who believed in just one God, were refusing to scatter incense before images of the emperor . . . Nero had them arrested wherever he found them and they were brutally put to death. Some were torn to pieces by wild beasts in the arena, while others were burned alive as torches' (Gombrich 2005:94–5).

As well as being victims, Christians have been hugely intolerant of other faiths or even of differences within their own religion. In 1096 the first crusade took place, when a Christian army decided to take Jerusalem from Muslim control. They did this for religious, not political reasons. 'Their aim was to liberate the land in which Christ's cross had once stood . . . Once inside Jerusalem . . . they massacred all the Muslims and committed horrible atrocities. Then they did penance, and, singing psalms, proceeded barefoot to Christ's tomb' (Gombrich 2005:142).

After the Reformation, sectarian conflict between Catholic and Protestant became common. 'The most ferocious wars were fought in France, where Protestants were known as Huguenots. In 1572 the French queen invited all the Huguenot nobility to a wedding at court, and on the eve of St Bartholomew, she had them assassinated' (Gombrich 2005:189).

The Thirty Years War between Catholics and Protestants started in 1618 when 'discontented Protestants threw three of the emperor's Catholic councillors out of a window at Prague castle' (Gombrich 2005:193). Apparently the three councillors were unharmed by their fall, but this event triggered fighting that spread throughout Europe.

Conflicts over religious differences are not confined to the past but remain a feature of modern life.

Summarised from Gombrich (2005).

Activities

1   Gombrich describes how Christian knights led a massacre and followed this by a display of religious devotion. Discuss whether you think this was a hypocritical action.

2   The 'golden rule', common to many religions, preaches respect for all other people. Reflect on why people find it difficult to follow this rule.

Project idea

Research the penal laws and Catholic emancipation in Ireland.

Case study: Sectarianism in Northern Ireland

Ireland fought for independence from Britain from 1919 to 1921. A truce was declared in 1921, but a treaty (the Anglo-Irish Treaty) then had to be ironed out. One difficulty was the situation of a majority of Protestants in Northern Ireland, who were determined to remain linked to Britain. Unionists had their own identity and wanted to preserve their way of life. This problem had existed before the War of Independence when the system of home rule was being considered for Ireland. Protestants were a majority in the North but would be a minority in a 32-county Ireland. They were convinced that 'Home rule might mean Rome rule' (Neill 1975:192) and were also afraid that their businesses would suffer under an Irish government. This fear increased after the War of Independence and Unionists determined they would never accept Irish Catholic rule.

Partition of Ireland seemed the only solution and this became a central condition of the Treaty. The 26 counties gained independence, but the counties of Antrim, Derry, Down, Fermanagh, Tyrone and Armagh remained a part of the United Kingdom. Disagreement over the Treaty led to an Irish civil war from 1922 to 1923. At the end of this war, partition remained in place.

Northern Ireland had its own parliament at Stormont but retained its links with Britain. The six counties held a Protestant majority, who treated the Catholic minority unfairly. They were discriminated against in employment – many factories were owned by Unionists who refused to employ Catholics. Sir Basil Brooke, who was Prime Minister of Northern Ireland from 1943 to 1963, openly stated, 'Many in this audience employ Catholics, but I have not one about my place. Catholics are out to destroy Ulster with all their might and power ... I would appeal to Loyalists, therefore, whenever possible, to employ good Protestant lads and lassies' (quoted in Neill 1975:195).

The voting system was also unfair. Votes were allocated on the basis of property ownership. Catholics were generally poorer and often did not own their own houses, so they had no vote, while Protestant businessmen who owned many properties had many votes. This system allowed control even in Catholic majority areas such as Derry. Power at every level – from parliament to local councils – was dominated by Protestants. Local councils administered corporation housing for poor people, but Protestants got most council houses, just as council jobs were not for Catholics.

Social life was also segregated:

Protestants joined the Orange order, while Catholics belonged to the Ancient Order of Hibernians, there were Catholic pubs and Protestant pubs, Catholic dances and Protestant dances. Catholic youths usually played Gaelic football, while their Protestant counterparts went in for the more 'English' games of soccer and rugby. (Neill 1975:195)

Protestants and Catholics also lived in separate neighbourhoods and had their own schools.

This way of life continued for decades, but it could not continue unchallenged. 'Matters reached a head in 1968 in Co. Tyrone, where a Catholic family which had been awarded a Council house saw their plans fizzle when a young Protestant girl who happened to be the secretary of a local Unionist leader was given their house instead' (Neill 1975:196). A demonstration was staged as a result of this decision and the Northern Ireland Civil Rights Association was formed. More demonstrations followed and Unionists often reacted with violence against the marchers.

In 1969, the Social Democratic and Labour Party (SDLP) was formed from an amalgamation of civil rights groups. The party's main aim was to improve conditions for Catholics. The IRA had existed since the end of the Civil War and had vowed never to accept the border. There had been little support for them, but their popularity surged in 1969 as people became impatient that their demands were unmet. 'As the Unionists seemed so unwilling to make changes, many people began to listen to what the Provisional IRA had to say. Marches, demonstrations and peaceful protests had not changed the unionist's minds – perhaps bullets might' (Neill 1975:197). Bombings and riots became frequent in Ulster and Unionists also took up illegal arms. 'The Ulster Volunteer Force (UVF), for decades as weak as the IRA, got increased support from a protestant community increasingly afraid of being "bombed into the Republic"' (Neill 1975:198).

In 1969, Prime Minister Terence O'Neill was seen as too soft in trying to meet the demonstrators' needs, and was forced to resign by those who wanted firmer measures. He was succeeded by a more traditional Unionist, James Chichester-Clarke. In 1970, extreme rioting led to Chichester-Clarke asking Britain to send troops. By the end of 1970 there were 10,000 troops in Northern Ireland. In 1971 the new Prime Minister, Brian Faulkner, introduced 'internment' – imprisonment without trial. It was an unfair system as 'The men judged most dangerous by the Unionist-controlled police were usually Catholics' (Neill 1975:198). By the end of 1971, 500 men, mostly Catholics, were in prison. The policy of internment backfired as it led to even more support for the IRA and even the moderate SDLP protested by withdrawing from parliament. Mass demonstrations were organised to protest against internment, despite such demonstrations being banned.

On 30 January 1972, a large march took place in Derry. British soldiers fired on the crowd and 14 people died. Soldiers claimed that they had been fired on first and were acting in self-defence, but this was denied by those involved in the march. Following the events of that day, which became known as Bloody Sunday, peaceful protest gave way to an upsurge in violent action.

In 1972 Stormont was abolished and Ulster was then ruled directly from Britain. The British government attempted to resolve the difficulties by 'power-sharing': under the Sunningdale Agreement a new government would be set up, which would include Unionists and the SDLP. However, extremists on both the Protestant and Catholic sides were not happy with this and the agreement collapsed. Loyalist Protestant groups – the Ulster Defence Association (UDA) and Ulster Volunteer Force (UVF) – and the nationalist Catholic IRA engaged in a campaign of violence that would last for decades. By 2004, 3,600 people had died in the conflict.

Attempts at peace-making were made and ceasefires announced over the years but they did not last. However, in 1997, the IRA declared a new ceasefire and its political wing, Sinn Féin, became involved in negotiations. The Good Friday Agreement of 1998 signalled a turning point towards a more peaceful time. 'Power-sharing' between Catholic nationalists and Protestant Unionists in a Northern Irish Assembly was introduced. Violence did not stop overnight, with dissidents on each side continuing attacks. However, despite many difficulties and disagreements, efforts have been made to overcome the bitterness and forge a lasting peace.

Summarised from Neill (1975); Ruckenstein & O'Malley (2004).

Case study: Sectarian fighting in Syria

The majority of people in Syria, about three-quarters of the population, are Sunni Muslims, yet government members are mainly Alawites – a minority Shia sect. Since 1963, the Alawi-controlled Ba'ath Arab Socialist Party has ruled Syria. The party allows no opposition, and any resistance to the established power structure is not tolerated. 'The Alawites comprised perhaps 12 per cent of Syria's 15 million people. So under Assad's rule, any questioning of the apparent disproportion of Alawites to the majority Sunnis in positions of power could cost you your freedom or your job' (Fisk 2005:1012–13).

Conflict between the al-Assad regime and the Sunnis has led to terrible bloodshed on both sides. In 1979, the Sunnis attacked an artillery school in Aleppo, and 'more than fifty Alawite officer cadets were massacred' (Fisk 2005:1013). Car bomb attacks by Sunnis in Damascus followed and in 1982 a Sunni uprising took place in which many government officials were targeted. The military crushed the uprising brutally, by shelling the city of Hama, and thousands of mostly civilian Syrians were killed. 'Up to 20,000, it was said, died in the underground tunnels and detonated buildings' (Fisk 2005:1005). The Hama massacre succeeded in crushing the rebellion, but discontent remained.

Hafez al-Assad was President of Syria from 1971 to his death in 2000. His son, Bashar al-Assad, became president after him, but any hopes for a fairer regime were soon crushed. Even the election of Bashar was an unfair process as there was no opposition candidate. Also, the law was changed specifically to suit Bashar, who was 34 when his father died, while the presidential minimum age was set at 40: 'The Syrian parliament lowered the age of future presidents to thirty-four to accommodate Bashar' (Fisk 2005:1013). Bashar initially allowed more freedoms – some political prisoners were released and restrictions on the media and freedom of speech were relaxed. However, these new freedoms were soon withdrawn and protests in 2011 were reacted to with extreme force. Syrian security forces failed to crush the uprising and an all-out civil war followed, with the Shia-dominated government and army fighting against Sunni rebels.

The UN refugee agency (UNHCR) reported that 100,000 people fled from Syria during August 2012 alone. The total number of Syrian refugees was given as 235,300 in September 2011. The UN responded by sending a supervision mission to Syria, which was withdrawn on 19 August 2012. UN observers ended their mission because efforts at peacemaking, including an agreed ceasefire, had failed.

Summarised from BBC (2011); Fisk (2005); Whitaker (2012); www.un.org/en/ peacekeeping.

Ireland: Tradition and Secularism

Ireland has traditionally been a Catholic country and religion has been central to Irish history and identity. The Catholic Church has long enjoyed enormous power in Ireland, which fuelled the belief amongst Ulster Protestants that 'Home Rule is Rome Rule'.

The Catholic Church enjoyed unique authority in Ireland during the twentieth century; Church and State were completely intertwined. 'The power of the church reached its peak during Éamon de Valera's first term of office as head of the Irish government (1932–1948), when he famously consulted Catholic Archbishop John Charles McQuaid for help in drafting the 1937 Constitution' (Bacik 2004:29).

The 1937 Constitution made reference to the special position of the Catholic Church in Ireland, and outlawed divorce and abortion. Religious orders dominated the health and education system, while religious values were enforced by law. 'Catholic morality was enshrined in law . . . under 1935 legislation, the sale, import and advertising of contraception were all criminalised' (Bacik 2004:101). Unmarried mothers were often shut up in Magdalene laundries, which were run by nuns: 'Those institutions had originally been established in the eighteenth century as homes for prostitutes, but gradually they became used to house those girls and women who had children while unmarried . . . or who were regarded as "wild" or uncontrollable, or who had intellectual or learning disabilities' (Bacik 2004:52).

Secularisation has been defined as 'The process in which religious beliefs and sanctions become less important as guides to behaviour and decisions' (O'Donnell 2002:324). The functions of the Church are changing: education and charity, for instance, were once the responsibility of the Church alone, but are now taken on by governments. Church and State are now separated, while on an individual level people see religion as being just one area of their lives, rather than letting it dominate their choices and attitudes. Ireland, for so long a Catholic state, has begun to become more secular.

Many factors have combined to weaken the authority of the Catholic Church in recent years. 'Industrialisation and urbanisation, the spread of education, the effects of television – all made a degree of secularisation and scepticism inevitable' (O'Toole 1997:94). Legislation that reflected traditional Catholic values has gradually changed. Campaigns in the 1970s forced the enactment of new legislation to allow limited use of contraception. Initially, contraception could be prescribed by a doctor for married couples; in 1992 contraceptives were deregulated so that condoms could be sold in shops and in vending machines, and health boards were also obliged to provide family planning services.

Recent scandals about child abuse have also lessened traditional respect for the church. Revelations of mass abuse in Church-run institutions led to the setting up of the Commission to Inquire into Child Abuse (CICA) in 1999. The investigation focused largely on the period 1936 to 1970. The findings were that abuse had been widespread and that the State had failed to intervene because of the dominant position of the Church in society. 'Physical and emotional abuse and neglect were features of the institutions. Sexual abuse occurred in many of them. . . . The deferential and submissive attitude of the Department of Education towards the Congregations compromised its ability to carry out its statutory duty of inspection and monitoring of the schools' (CICA 2009). Some religious congregations subsequently issued apologies, but others did not.

In 2009, another commission investigated the Diocese of Cloyne, with regard to the Church and State handling of reports of sexual abuse from 1996 to 2009. The Cloyne Report concluded that even in recent years, the Church had not reported sexual abuse to the Gardaí and had proved unco-operative with the inquiry. In 2011, Taoiseach Enda Kenny made a statement to the Dáil regarding the findings of the Cloyne Report, in which he strongly criticised the Catholic Church for attempting to retain its own reputation at the expense of children:

> A report into child sexual abuse exposes an attempt by the Holy See to frustrate an inquiry in a sovereign, democratic republic as little as three years ago, not three decades ago. . . . The rape and torture of children were downplayed or 'managed' to uphold instead, the primacy of the institution, its power, standing and 'reputation'. . . . This report tells us a tale of a frankly brazen disregard for protecting children. . . . Cardinal Josef Ratzinger said: 'Standards of conduct appropriate to civil society or the workings of a democracy cannot be purely and simply applied to the Church.' As the Holy See prepares its considered response to the Cloyne Report, as Taoiseach, I am making it absolutely clear, that when it comes to the protection of the children of this State, the standards of conduct which the Church deems appropriate to itself cannot and will not be applied to the workings of democracy and civil society in this republic. (RTÉ News 2011)

The traditional links between Church and State in Ireland seem finally broken.

Religion is no longer as central in the lives of individuals in Ireland as it once was. Many couples are now choosing a civil marriage ceremony instead of a traditional church wedding. Statistics from the CSO show that in 1970 only half a per cent of couples opted for a civil marriage; this increased to 1.8 % in 1980; to 3.7% in 1990; and to 23% in 2007 (www.cso.ie). Multidenominational schools such as those run by the Educate Together group provide an alternative to religious schools, as so many schools in Ireland still retain a Catholic ethos. A secular ethos aims to keep religion outside the school gate – 'The ethos of such a system is "in school, you teach, and in church, you preach, you shouldn't mix the two"' (Bacik 2004:46).

Divorce had been banned in the 1937 Constitution, but 'The last specifically Catholic clause' (O'Toole 1997:219) was removed in the 1995 divorce referendum. Despite Church warnings that divorced people would not be entitled to the sacraments, the constitutional amendment was passed. In 1997, there were 95 divorces granted; 1,421 in 1998; 3,684 in 2007; 3,630 in 2008; 3,341 in 2009; and 3,113 in 2010 (www.cso.ie).

In the 2011 Census 269,800 people stated that they had no religion, an increase of 64.4% since the previous census in 2006 (CSO 2011a:43). A recent poll showed that only 47% of people viewed themselves as a religious person, compared with 69% in 2005 (*Irish Independent* 2012).

Summarised from Bacik (2004), CICA (2009), CSO (website); Cloyne Report (2010), *Irish Independent* (2012), O'Donnell (2002); O'Toole (1997); RTÉ News (2011).

Activities

1 Reflect on whether you believe an increasingly secular society to be a good or bad thing. Write a short piece on this topic and then compare and discuss with other classmates.

2 Talk to an older person about how religious influence in Irish society affected their life, for good or for ill.

3 'The Red C global poll also found that the richer you got, the less religious you defined yourself. Religiosity was higher among the poor, with people in the bottom-income groups 17pc more religious than those in the top-earning groups' (*Irish Independent* 2012). Discuss why wealth might have an effect on religious belief.

Case study: Secularism and religion – the hijab in France

In 1989, three girls were suspended from school in France for wearing their hijabs (Islamic scarves) in class. Unlike the niqab, which partly covers the face, and the burqa, which covers the entire face, the hijab covers the head alone. This religious display was seen as being inappropriate in a secular place such as a school. The principle of secularism is important in France and a law separating Church and State had been passed in 1905. In response to the suspension of the girls, the minister for education stated that it was up to each individual school to decide if the hijab could be worn or not.

In early 1990, three more girls were suspended from another school for wearing the hijab. After various protests and legal cases, in 1993 a memorandum was issued that outlined the differences between 'discreet' religious symbols, which were allowed to be worn in public establishments, and 'ostentatious' religious symbols, including the hijab, which were not. Many students protested and between 1994 and 2003 around a hundred girls were suspended or even expelled from school for continuing to wear the hijab.

In 2004, the French parliament passed a law forbidding the wearing of 'ostentatious' religious symbols such as the Islamic veil, large Christian crosses and the Jewish kippa in public institutions; but small crosses, stars of David (Jewish) and hands of Fatima (Islamic) could be worn. There was strong reaction to the law at first, but extremist protest action led protesters to back down: 'French Muslims marched against a move that many condemned as intolerant. The first blow to the anti-ban campaign came in August last year – ironically at the hand of militants who abducted two French reporters in Iraq, demanding the law should be withdrawn. Protests died down, as French Muslims refused to be associated with the hostage-takers' (Astier 2005).

Writing in 2005, Astier observed the situation in schools. 'Every morning headteacher Genevieve Piniau stands guard at the gate.... She is there to ensure no rules are broken, including a ban on Muslim headscarves and other "conspicuous" religious symbols in French state schools. Dozens of girls duly take off their hijabs as they approach the gate.' Piniau stated that most of the girls were compliant after she explained the situation. 'I said I had the deepest respect for their faith, but did not want to know what their religion was any more than I wanted them to know what mine was.' Some students the reporter spoke to remained resentful, and one teenage girl is quoted as saying she felt targeted as a Muslim – 'Christians have crucifixes, why can't we have headscarves?' Another student agreed: 'It is a war of religion. Islam is targeted through the headscarf.' Other Muslim girls had accepted the ban and agreed that their religion does not need to be advertised. '"Some teachers would not see beyond the scarf and judge us – it's best if we have to take it off" ... "Faith is in the heart"' (Astier 2005).

Wearing the hijab after leaving school also has its problems: in many jobs, for example nursing and teaching, the veil cannot be worn at work. '"We are studying to be able to work later ... and we all know that if you wear a veil all the doors will close." Sonia Benyahia ... who wants to be a schoolteacher, fears her future could be equally blocked. "I don't know if I'll be able to take off the scarf, so I think I'll remain a housewife," she says.' (Astier 2005)

The European Court of Human Rights (ECHR) upheld the ban in 2008. There are a variety of arguments both for and against the wearing of the hijab. Muslims traditionally require women to cover their hair outside the family home, which is seen as a symbol of respectability and a central part of their identity. Some worry that girls may be kept away from school as a result of the ban and be denied an education. Those against the ban also argue that it is a sign of anti-Islamic policy and sends a message that Muslims are not welcome in French society. Those who support the ban argue that religious displays are a private, not a public, matter and that wearing the scarf is a sign of submission to men and so should not be allowed in a free society.

Muslim women who want to work in certain areas will have to make a choice between fitting in with French secular society or keeping their traditional form of dress. The difficulty of combining a career with religious affiliation was highlighted in 2010 by the reaction to a political candidate in France, who horrified people by wearing the hijab.

'Ilham Moussaid, a 21-year-old Muslim woman who describes herself as "feminist, secular and veiled", is running for the far-left New Anti-Capitalist party (NPA). . . . Despite her insistence that there is no contradiction between her clothing and her political role, Moussaid's candidacy in the regional vote due in March has angered other feminists and politicians' (Davies 2010).

The candidate's headscarf sparked deep anger in French society, with critics arguing that her appearance went against secular principles as well as women's rights. A feminist group filed an official complaint against the NPA's list of candidates in protest against what they called an 'anti-secular, anti-feminist and anti-republican stunt' (Davies 2010). The anger towards Moussaid shows that in modern France, wearing a visible religious statement in public life has now become taboo.

Summarised from Astier (2005); Davies (2010).

Activities

1   'Faith is in the heart.' Discuss the arguments for and against allowing religious displays in public places.

2   The veiled political candidate, Ilham Moussaid, stated, 'It is with great sadness that I watch . . . my life reduced to my headscarf. It is with great sadness that I hear that my personal beliefs are a danger to others while I advocate friendship, respect, tolerance, solidarity and equality for all human beings' (Davies 2010). Reflect on whether you agree or disagree with those who complained about Moussaid's wearing of the headscarf.

Project idea

FIFA recently overturned a ban on headscarves, thus allowing Islamic women to play football at an international level. Sport is a shared passion across many cultures, yet bans on religious displays may prevent some people taking part. Research the effects of previous bans and the effects of recent changes. A useful newspaper article on the topic is available at www.guardian.co.uk/sport/the-womens-blog-with-jane-martinson/2012/jul/23/sports-hijabs-muslim-women-olympics.

Revision questions

1 List some functions of religion in society.

2 Outline the origins and main beliefs of three religions.

3 What is the 'golden rule'?

4 List two death rituals and two marriage rituals from different cultures.

5 Explain the term 'fundamentalism'.

6 Explain the term 'sectarian' and describe a modern sectarian conflict.

7 List some historic examples of religious persecution.

8 Define the term 'secularism'.

9 Describe some ways in which Irish society has become more secular in recent years.

10 Outline the conflict between secular and religious views in France.

CHAPTER 4

Research Methods and Culture Shock

By the end of this chapter, students should be able to:

- Distinguish between primary and secondary data and discuss the advantages and disadvantages of each.
- Distinguish between quantitative and qualitative data.
- Understand these research terms: *survey*, *survey population*, *hypothesis*, *sample* and *representative sample*.
- Understand and use the seven types of question in designing a questionnaire.
- Design a questionnaire and identify and avoid 'problem questions'.
- Recognise two types of interview style and understand how bias may affect an interview.
- Understand the notion of 'culture shock' and the difficulties faced by those entering a strange culture.
- List several organisations that help migrants adjust to Irish society and aim to combat racism and discrimination.
- Discuss the impact of the recession on society's attitudes and on funding for organisations.

Research

'What makes the views of sociologists different from those likely to be aired in a pub, in the canteen at work . . . is that sociologists try to provide evidence to back up what they say. This evidence is collected from a variety of sources and through the use of a number of research methods' (Browne 1992:395).

As Browne states, research is essential in establishing facts. Anyone can air an opinion, but individual opinions are worthless without some form of proof. In order to make informed judgements, researchers must carefully gather and examine information.

Primary and Secondary Data

Information can be classified as either primary or secondary data.

'Primary data is that which is collected by sociologists (or researchers) themselves . . . such information is usually obtained by carrying out a social survey or by participant observation' (Browne 1992:396). The benefit of gathering primary data is that the researcher can focus on the specific information required and be assured that it is not biased. However, gathering primary data can be costly and time-consuming.

'Secondary data has already been collected by others' (Browne 1992:396). Examples include official statistics such as census results, other researchers' work, mass media such as newspapers and television, and various other sources such as diaries, letters and photographs. An advantage of using secondary data is that it is 'readily available and so is cheap and easy to use' (Browne 1992:396). Researchers do not have to find the time and money to assemble their own data. A disadvantage of this type of data is that the material can be inaccurate, biased or unrepresentative (only apply to a small group of people). Also, relying on statistics may not show the full picture. For example, Department of Social Protection statistics may not give an accurate picture of unemployment levels as they will only show those who are on the Live Register. Those who are unemployed but are not eligible for unemployment assistance because their spouse is working will not be represented in these statistics.

Summarised from Browne (1992).

Surveys

Quantitative and Qualitative Data

When gathering primary data, a survey is often conducted. The purpose of a survey is to systematically gather information from a particular group, and this can be done using a questionnaire or an interview. Organising a survey involves making considered decisions regarding what type of material to gather, who to gather it from and how to gather it. In deciding what sort of data is wanted, a choice must be made between two types of data – quantitative and qualitative.

'Quantitative data is anything that can be expressed in statistical or number form or can be "measured" in some way, such as age, qualifications or income' (Browne 1992:395). One example of quantitative data is a census return listing the number of people in each household.

'Qualitative data is concerned with people's feelings about some issue or event, and tries to get at the way they see things' (Browne 1992:395). An example of qualitative data is a survey or poll in which people are asked to deliver an opinion or judgement.

Summarised from Browne (1992).

Activities

1 If you were conducting a survey on attitudes to immigration, what would be the benefits of using either quantitative or qualitative data?

2 Discuss how bias might affect a secondary source.

Project idea

Primary data is difficult and expensive to gather. Contact the Central Statistical Office and find out the cost of running a census, how long it takes to collect and process results, and how it is organised.

Survey Population

The next decision is to define the survey population, which is the group of people to be studied. These people will be selected according to the researcher's focus of interest. The researcher will have a hypothesis: 'an idea which the sociologist guesses to be true, but which has not yet been tested against the evidence' (Browne 1992:400). For example, the researcher may have an idea that teenagers spend more time watching television than doing homework, and so the survey population will be made up of teenagers. Of course it would be impossible to survey every teenager in the country, so a sample will be used. 'A sample is simply a small group drawn from the survey population' (Browne 1992:400).

In order to give an accurate picture of an entire group, the researcher must ensure that the sample is representative. If one is surveying the television-watching habits of teenagers, there is no point in interviewing a group of boys from just one locality – a representative sample must include more than one gender, age group, social class or ethnic group.

Summarised from Browne (1992).

Questionnaires

Having decided on the survey population, the next step is to design a questionnaire. 'A questionnaire is a printed list of questions to be filled in either personally by the respondent (the person answering the questions) or by an interviewer' (Browne 1992:405).

Questionnaires are primary methods of research and are widely used for collecting information. They can be conducted in three ways: by post; face to face; and by telephone.

Questionnaires are a useful research tool but must be carefully planned so that they are relevant and easily understood by the respondent. The questions themselves must be chosen carefully. There are seven main types of question:

1 *Closed question*: The respondent is required to answer simply 'yes' or 'no'. An advantage of this type of question is the speed with which it can be completed, but a disadvantage is that there can be no expansion or explanation of answers. An example of a closed question could be:

Have you experienced racism at work?   *Yes* ◯   *No* ◯

2 *Forced question*: This is similar to a closed question because it supplies answer categories, but it obtains more information than a Yes/No answer. A common forced question is:

Are you: *Male* ◯   *Female* ◯

3 *Multiple choice question*: The respondent is given a list of possible answers and asked to choose one or more from the list. Some examples of a multiple choice question are:

What is the most difficult thing about adjusting to life in Ireland? (Please tick only one)

Adjusting to a new language	◯
Lack of community	◯
Finding accommodation	◯
Finding employment	◯

Which of the following have you found difficult since arriving in Ireland? (Please tick all that apply)

Adjusting to a new language	◯
Finding accommodation	◯
Finding employment	◯
Finding a school for children	◯

4 *Ranking question*: Respondents are asked to rank their answers in order of importance. For example:

Which of the following have you found most difficult since arriving in Ireland? Please use numbers to indicate importance, with number 1 for the most difficult and number 4 for the least difficult.

Adjusting to a new language	◯
Finding accommodation	◯
Finding employment	◯
Finding a school for children	◯

An alternative approach to this type of question is to allow respondents to give their own answers in rank order. For example:

What have you found most difficult since arriving in Ireland? Please list in order of importance with 1 being the most difficult and 3 being the least difficult.

1 _____

2 _____

3 _____

5 *Filter questions*: These direct respondents on to relevant questions depending on their answer, for example:

   1 *Are you married?*   *Yes* ◯   *No* ◯

   If No, please move to question 5

6 *Likert scale*: 'This scale was devised by Likert in order to measure the attitudes and opinions of respondents. The main characteristic of this method is that statements are provided and, on the basis of a 5-point scale, respondents are asked whether they strongly agree, agree, neither agree nor disagree, disagree or strongly disagree.' (McDonald 2009:50). An example of this type of question is:

All landlords are suspicious of foreigners.

SA	A	NA/D	D	SD
1	2	3	4	5

Important points to consider when using a Likert scale are 'Scales should consist of an equal number of positive and negative statements . . . format of scales should ensure that negative and positive statements are adequately dispersed' (McDonald 2009:50).

7 *Open questions*: Respondents are encouraged to give detailed responses in their own words. This allows for more variety and individual experience. However, one disadvantage is that respondents may feel daunted, depending on their literacy and fluency levels, and so may not want to participate. Some examples of open questions are:

Are you happy with the choice of/availability of your own foods in Ireland?

_____

_____

Have you been the target of racist abuse or a racist attack?

_____

_____

_____

Summarised from Browne (1992); McDonald (2009).

Problem Questions

In order to be successful tools for research, questionnaires must be clear and relevant. Eileen Kane (1983) points out the importance of avoiding problem questions that may be confusing to the respondent. She gives examples of some common problem questions:

1 *Double question*: The wording may make a question difficult or even impossible to answer, by containing two unrelated or contradictory parts. For example, 'Do you eat Chinese food or enjoy cooking?'

2 *Wrong choice question*: A question may not allow the respondent to answer accurately. For example, a question such as 'Do you vote for Fianna Fáil, Fine Gael or Labour?' will not allow respondents who vote for other parties/independents to answer.

3 *Kitchen sink question*: This type of question attempts to ask too many questions at once. An example is, 'Please list previous addresses for the last five years and rate them from 1 to 5, according to satisfaction with public transport, local schools, choice of shops, quality of pubs and restaurants.' This type of question confuses the respondent. Each part of a question like this would be better asked separately.

4 *Leading question*: This type of question might encourage respondents to give a particular answer and not allow them to answer truthfully. For example, 'Why is Ireland such a great place to live?' will only allow respondents to make positive statements about their experience of Ireland.

5 *Hearsay question*: For example, 'Do you think Chinese people enjoy going to pubs?' This provides inaccurate data on Chinese social habits as it does not ask Chinese people themselves. 'Do not ask one person the opinions or attitudes of another' (Kane 1983:79).

6 *'Dream' question*: 'Hypothetical questions do not necessarily produce comparable answers from different respondents' (Kane 1983:79). For example, a question such as 'How do you think your local school could be improved?' might garner too wide a range of responses from those seeking the ideal, e.g. 'The school should have brand new classrooms and its own Olympic-sized swimming pool. Students should be given their own laptops and there should be one teacher for every eight students' to others who are more realistic, e.g. 'The canteen facilities need to be more spacious.'

7 *'Fuzzy word' question*: Certain words can mean different things to different people, for example 'frequently', 'often', 'occasionally', 'rarely' and 'a lot'. A question like 'Do you go to the cinema often?' is vague because one respondent might think once a month is often, while another might think anything less than once a week is not often. Where time is involved, it is better to specify time periods such as 'weekly', 'daily', 'monthly'.

8 *'Cover-the-world' question*: This type of question is not specific enough. For example, 'What do you think of current government policy?' is too broad. The respondent will wonder whether the question relates to policy on education, employment, taxation, welfare, health or many other areas, and consequently their answers will be so varied as to not be useful to the researcher. A more tailored question would be, 'What do you think of current government policy on health?'

Summarised from Kane (1983).

Browne (1992) and McDonald (2009) give further recommendations for designing successful questionnaires.

1 Questionnaires should not be too long, so keep the number of questions to a minimum, choosing only the most relevant to your research. 'Respondents may be unwilling to spend a long time answering questions' (Browne 1992:408).

2 Instructions for completing the questionnaire should be clear and easily understood.

3 Questions should be phrased in simple, everyday language. Avoid technical jargon or slang, for example instead of asking a question on marital status, ask if the respondent is married, has never married, is divorced or widowed.

4 Provide a title for your questionnaire and an introduction describing the purpose of the questionnaire and what college or organisation it is done in conjunction with or authorised by.

5 Include clear instructions for completing the questionnaire.

Summarised from Browne (1992); McDonald (2009).

Activities

1 Discuss the drawbacks and limitations of each type of question listed above.

2 Write some sample questions that deliberately ignore the above recommendations. Swap with a classmate and establish the type of mistake in each question.

Project idea

Design and carry out a questionnaire on an issue that interests you.

Interviews

An interview, which is another primary method of research, may involve using a questionnaire, but it will not necessarily do so. Interview styles can range from very informal, even 'chatty', to a very ordered set of questions. There are two basic types: structured/formal; and unstructured.

1 *Structured/formal*: Every respondent is asked the same pre-set questions in the same order. This is exactly the same as a questionnaire except that the researcher fills in the answers themselves. It is useful when interviewing a large number of people but provides a limited amount of detail.

2 *Unstructured*: The interviewer will have less rigid pre-set questions than on a questionnaire. They may have more open-ended questions or even just a list of topics to discuss. This approach gives a more in-depth sense of a person's opinions and feelings, Browne describes it as 'a bit like a TV chat show' (Browne 1992:411). However, an unstructured interview is best managed by an experienced interviewer to avoid straying off into irrelevant areas.

Browne (1992) points out that interviewer bias can affect the interview. 'Interviewer bias is the way in which the presence or behaviour of the interviewer may influence in some way the answers given by the respondent' (Browne 1992:411). A respondent's answer might be adapted to try to suit the interviewer; for instance, the status, class, age, gender or ethnicity of the interviewer may influence the respondent to avoid giving their true opinions. For example, an immigrant being interviewed by an Irish person may be uncomfortable answering questions relating to difficulties encountered in Ireland. They may think the interviewer does not want to hear negative stories so may try to please the interviewer by only saying positive things. A good interviewer will be very neutral in their expression and tone and not show any signs of favour or disfavour at answers received.

Summarised from Browne (1992).

Challenges Faced by People Living in a Strange Culture

Culture Shock

People living in a strange culture face many problems and challenges. We are all attached to our own culture and the familiarity of our surroundings is something that we take for granted. Those entering a new culture may experience culture shock. 'Culture shock is nothing more than the inability to "read" meaning in one's surroundings. We feel lost and isolated, unsure of how to act, and sometimes frightened – a consequence of being outside the symbolic web of culture that joins individuals in meaningful social life' (Macionis & Plummer 2002:100).

Living in a strange environment can very stressful, as all the habitual routines and interactions of a familiar society are replaced by new and threatening surroundings. 'When individuals relocate to a new socio-cultural environment they have to make adjustments in how they meet their needs . . . Migrants have to manage demands not encountered in their society of origin, such as language difficulties or racist abuse' (Ryan *et al.* 2007:113).

Communities and institutions can make an effort to host intercultural days and events, so that they can learn about other people's culture and teach newcomers about their own. McCann James, de Róiste and McHugh list some inclusion policies suitable for children, but that apply also to adults: 'learning about their different cultures, special cultural days and religious events . . . Equally, helping such children understand Irish norms and ways of life can assist them to understand and feel more as if they belong in Irish society' (McCann James *et al.* 2009:10).

The norms of everyday life are understood by us all through absorption from childhood, but to a newcomer they are incomprehensible. For example, in some countries people haggle over goods anywhere, but in Ireland this is done only occasionally at market stalls. Everyday norms that we take for granted, such as being quiet when entering a library or the distance to stand from the next person in a queue may not be so obvious to someone from another culture.

It may take time for a person to adjust, but with patience and time, they can become integrated into a new culture. Where children are involved, the help of an adult to encourage acceptance may be crucial, as this interview with a Vietnamese man, who arrived in Ireland as a child, shows:

> First I got a very bad time because I couldn't communicate with the children there. I got a very strange look from the local kids . . . I feel very scared but the teachers there have helped me through a lot of it by talking to the kids . . . and I get very good treatment from the kids afterwards, they offered me sweets and at lunchtime they offered to share with me their sandwiches and all, like this. I joined, I played football in school . . . I even played some Gaelic football and I joined the school Gaelic team. And I travelled too, you know, playing against all the schools, having great fun. (Interview in Sheridan 2007:136)

Summarised from Macionis & Plummer (2002); McCann James *et al.* (2009); Ryan *et al.* (2007); Sheridan (2007).

Language Barriers

Language is of supreme importance in making us feel comfortable in our surroundings. Without it we are unable to undertake even the most basic interactions in society, for example asking for directions or buying a bus ticket. Apart from not being able to communicate our needs, we are also shut off from the outside world – an incomprehensible announcement at a train station or airport leaves a person confused and worried. The practicalities of everyday life, such as finding accommodation or schools, are impossible without understanding the language. An added difficulty is that of different alphabets, such as the Chinese or Arabic alphabet: an immigrant can be rendered illiterate by street signs and notices in an unfamiliar alphabet.

Newcomer children commonly go through a period of muteness on entering school because they are so afraid to speak (NCCA/IILT 2003:4). Adults also may be embarrassed and frightened of trying to master a new language and consequently may become shut off from society. 'Before I came here, I had a university degree and a good job. Now I am a baby. I sound like a baby, I am treated like a baby, not an adult. I shamed myself when I went out, always repeating, and no one understanding. So I stayed home all the time, not even understanding TV' (Moldovan woman, 29 years old, www.spirasi.ie).

If a person does not have language skills, their qualifications may be of no use and so they will have to set about finding a different type of work. Jobs that do not require language skills will usually be low paid. Workers may also be vulnerable to exploitation because the language gap means that they will not understand employment rights.

SPIRASI, which provides free language classes for migrants, states that lacking language skills in a new society is frustrating and isolating, and that sadly locals may not always be very helpful.

> Just getting on the bus or shopping at local stores can be a formidable undertaking which often requires more courage and confidence than many people newly arrived to this country may have. Unfortunately, in this society, people who do not speak English are often treated with distrust and condescension, making the goal of feeling at home in Ireland that much more difficult to reach. (www.spirasi.ie)

They also point out that research – including the White Paper on Adult Education (2000) and *Asylum Seekers in Adult Education: A Study of Language and Literacy Needs* (Ward 2002) – confirms that poor English skills are a major block to integration into Irish society.

Apart from needing the language to meet daily needs such as banking, shopping and finding a job, non-English-speaking immigrants will be socially isolated and unable to make friends. Fáilte Isteach, a volunteer programme that gives free English lessons, has found that immigrants are motivated to learn the language not just to deal with the practicalities of life but also 'to meet new people and make new friends within the project itself, and in the wider community' (www.thirdageireland.ie). English classes are essential for a migrant to become integrated into society. 'When I came to English class, no one laughed, and I made friends and learned. Now I am a little afraid of speaking to Irish people, but I try, I try' (Congolese male, 37 years old (www.spirasi.ie)).

Summarised from NCCA/IILT (2003); www.spirasi.ie.

Dietary Requirements

Certain religious groups have particular dietary needs: Jewish people must eat only kosher food; Muslims must eat only halal meat. Outside large cities, it may be difficult to find these specific foods. Cultures that do not have religious dietary restrictions may still want to eat food they are familiar with from home. Some supermarket chains have responded by providing a range of ethnic foods in their shops. In 2010, Tesco added 'specialist Turkish, Sri Lankan, Latin, Filipino, African, South African and Greek-Cypriot ranges to a roster that already includes Asian, Oriental, Afro-Caribbean, Kosher, Polish, and Halal foods' (Wright 2010). Their Polish range has increased from just 20 products in 2006 to 260 in 2010.

Religion

It is important for many people to worship regularly and it may be particularly important when they find themselves alone in a new culture. It might be disorienting rather than comforting to attend a service in an unknown language, but churches have been quick to respond to people's needs and provide foreign language masses. CatholicIreland.net (www.catholicireland.net) lists Spanish, Portuguese, Romanian, Polish, Korean, French, Filipino, Italian, Chinese and African masses available in Dublin. Many institutions, such as hospitals, nursing homes and colleges, have multi-denominational prayer rooms so that people of all faiths can find a quiet space to worship.

Previous Trauma

Immigrants, particularly refugees, may have had terrible experiences before coming to a new country. 'Violence, torture, rape, murder, kidnapping, traumatic bereavement and natural disasters, such as earthquakes and floods, are examples of some of the forms of trauma encountered' (McCann James et al. 2009:12). Schools, hospitals and social services need to be aware of trauma and how to deal with it effectively.

SPIRASI is an organisation that provides assistance to survivors of torture and also trains bodies such as the health service to recognise and help those affected in this way.
Summarised from McCann James et al. (2009); www.spirasi.ie.

Racism

Sadly, many immigrants will encounter racism in Ireland. This may take the form of verbal abuse or even violence. Racism in schools is a common occurrence: 'the fears of black and other immigrant parents that their children will encounter racism are well founded. A study published by the Teachers' Union of Ireland (TUI) . . . involving 332 second-level and third-level . . . teachers found that 28 per cent were aware of racist incidents that had occurred in their school or college during the last month. African children were identified as particularly vulnerable to such incidents' (Fanning 2012:210).

Schools can take many steps to deal with this and the National Council for Curriculum and Assessment (NCCA) has produced guidelines on intercultural education, which include steps to tackle racism at both primary and secondary level. It advises teachers to try to get students to engage at an emotional level with issues like racism, rather than just learning facts.

> Young people will identify that they have been treated unfairly at one time or another, whether that means having had someone else getting preference over them unfairly, or having had assumptions made about them because of the way they look or where they live, or having someone in authority refuse to listen to them. Such experiences mean that students can often readily empathise with others who are victims of discrimination. (NCCA 2006:17)

There is a high level of racist abuse in Ireland. 'I get abused in Ireland almost every day . . . for example, if I'm driving the car in Lucan or Blanchardstown, and if I stop at the lights, someone walking by will shout "black bastard"' (Fanning 2012:206). Fanning also gives an example of the ongoing harassment of Dexter, a Filipino man living in Dublin, who had stones thrown at his car, his house and his three-year-old child. He endured constant abusive language and fire crackers were thrown at his house. He called the Gardaí on many occasions, but they never came to his house. As a result he no longer allows his children to play outside and feels powerless. 'I feel useless, I'm the father of a family and I can't protect the family' (Fanning 2012:215). Many victims of abuse or harassment do not report the incidents to the Gardaí because they feel the reports are not taken seriously. 'Various case studies . . . find that some victims perceive the Gardaí as unresponsive or uninterested in their experiences of racism' (Fanning 2012:234).

Fanning notes that assaults on immigrants by groups of teenagers, including girls, are common and there have been several racist murders in Dublin. In 2002, a Chinese man, Zhao Liu Tao, was assaulted with an iron bar and later died. Racist abuse had accompanied the assault. Also in Dublin, in 2008 two Polish men, Mariusz Szwajkos and Pavel Kalite, were stabbed to death, again after racist abuse. Toyosi Shittabey, a 15-year-old black boy, was stabbed to death in 2010, and again there were allegations of a racist motivation.

Summarised from Fanning (2010); NCCA (2006).

Institutional Racism

To be on the receiving end of racism from an individual is distressing. However, when the racism or discrimination comes from an official institution, it is even more dangerous, as the power of the institution to do harm is greater. 'Foreign nationals on legitimate trips to Ireland were arrested from time to time by immigration officials. For example, in November 2000 six Pakistani businessmen travelling on valid passports

. . . were imprisoned for a weekend in Mountjoy jail' (Fanning 2012:97). The National Consultative Committee on Racism and Interculturalism (NCCRI), which is now closed, received many complaints of institutional racism: 'complaints by persons who had received racist abuse not only from immigration officials at Dublin airport but even from officials in the Department of Justice' (Bacik 2004:200).

There have been efforts to tackle institutional racism in the Garda Síochána. First, changes were made so that immigrants were not barred from joining the Gardaí. 'The removal in 2005 from the selection criteria for the Gardaí of a qualification in the Irish language was replaced with one for any second language [which] got rid of an obvious institutional barrier' (Fanning 2007:2).

Second, studies have shown that many immigrants do not report crime, both because they do not trust that the Gardaí will respond adequately and because they fear negative consequences. A 2004 report by the NCCRI found that non-reporting of racist crime was high because of 'negative perceptions of police by recent migrants to Ireland, a reluctance to report crime out of fear that it might jeopardise residency in Ireland and, crucially, inconsistencies in the way the Gardaí respond to racist crime' (Fanning 2012:234).

In response to criticisms, the Gardaí have taken many steps both to try to combat racist crime and to reach out to new communities who may be afraid or unwilling to approach them.

The Gardaí have set up a Racial, Intercultural and Diversity Office (GRIDO), which provides anti-racism and intercultural awareness training and supports community groups. All racially motivated incidents reported to the Gardaí must be recorded on the Pulse system and then individually followed up by GRIDO. Ethnic liaison officers are responsible for creating links with ethnic minority communities, informing them of Garda services and monitoring racist incidents. 'Furthermore the Gardaí have put in place procedures for victim support and family liaison to keep victims informed of progress in investigations. In some divisional areas the Gardaí hold regular clinics to reach out to immigrant communities. One example of such good practice is a regular clinic held at the mosque at Clonskeagh in Dublin after prayers on Friday (Fanning 2012:234).

Summarised from Bacik (2004); Fanning (2012).

Activities

1 Devise and discuss some guidelines on helping newcomers adjust for institutions such as schools, colleges, workplaces and public facilities.

2 Students who have lived abroad: reflect on and write about your own experience of 'culture shock' and how you coped. Students who have not lived abroad: reflect on a time when you felt 'at sea' or out of your 'comfort zone' and what steps you took to cope.

3 Reflect on your reaction to the stories of racist abuse above.

4 If children are hearing prejudiced ideas from their parents, can schools make a difference? Discuss.

Irish Organisations and Events that Aim to Promote Belonging

Immigrant Council of Ireland (ICI)

The ICI sees the integration of migrants as crucial and it works to overcome barriers to migrants becoming involved in Irish society. 'The ICI's work in the area of integration is aimed at promoting participation and leadership, political, economic, social and cultural integration in Ireland' (www.immigrantcouncil.ie).

It has a number of functions:

- It provides information for migrants on immigration matters such as residency status and citizenship.
- It offers a limited legal service in very complex cases or for people who are especially vulnerable, such as unaccompanied minors and women who have been trafficked for the sex industry.
- It has a support system for people who experience racism.
- It keeps a database of all racist incidents reported to it, and it uses this information to compile research papers and to campaign for reform.
- It gives training on immigration legislation and policy along with immigrant rights and entitlements to a range of groups and organisations.
- It campaigns for the reform of current immigration legislation, which it views as outdated and inadequate.
- It is currently involved in the 'Turn Off the Red Light' campaign, which aims to end prostitution and sex trafficking in Ireland by making it a crime to pay for sex.

Summarised from www.immigrantcouncil.ie.

Migrant Rights Centre Ireland (MRCI)

MRCI is a national organisation 'working to promote justice, empowerment and equality for migrant workers and their families' (www.mrci.ie).

It aims to promote equality for migrant workers and prevent exploitation in the workplace. It provides information and assists in legal cases involving employment rights: 'MRCI has assisted hundreds of migrant workers in lodging formal complaints, and in receiving settlements and awards for unpaid wages and other gross violations of their employment rights. Breaches typically include payment below the minimum wage, non-payment of holidays, and excessive working hours' (www.mrci.ie). It also provides training on migrants to bodies such as the Gardaí, trade unions and Citizens Information Centres. The MRCI is a member of the European Network Against Racism (ENAR) and it undertakes research on racism and racist incidents. It produces reports and leaflets, many of which are available to download from its website. It campaigns for reform in employment policy and practices and aims to help those who are trapped in a forced labour situation, which may result from being illegally trafficked into the country. Indicators of forced labour are:

1 Threats or actual physical harm to the worker.

2 Restriction of movement and confinement to the workplace or to a limited area.

3 Debt bondage: the worker works to pay off a debt or loan, and is not paid for his or her services. The employer may provide food and accommodation at such inflated prices that the worker cannot escape the debt.

4 Withholding wages or excessive wage reductions that violate previously made agreements.

5 Retention of passports and identity documents, so that the worker cannot leave, or prove his/her identity and status.

6 Threat of denunciation to the authorities, where the worker is in an irregular immigration status. (www.mrci.ie)

Summarised from www.mrci.ie.

SPIRASI

'SPIRASI enables access to specialist services to promote the well-being of the human person, and encourages self-reliance and integration into Ireland' (www.spirasi.ie).

SPIRASI is an organisation that works with refugees and migrant groups, providing free English and IT classes along with other activities such as an art and media skills programme, an integration programme and a mentoring programme. It has observed that as a student's English improves, they begin to feel more confident and in control. Another benefit of attending classes is 'a stability of routine and social aspects previously absent in their everyday lives . . . they have access to a strong peer support system and begin the process of socialisation' (www.spirasi.ie).

SPIRASI also provides specialised care for survivors of torture, with access to a team of doctors, psychologists, therapists and psychosocial workers. Torture involves deliberately inflicting severe pain for a particular purpose – to gain information, to punish or to create an atmosphere of fear among people. 'The aim of torture is not to kill the victim, but to break down the victim's personality . . . to destroy the identity of the individual, to humiliate, weaken and destroy the personality' (www.spirasi.ie). The tortured person is used to control society by serving as an example of what will happen to those who do not obey. After the body of the tortured person heals, severe psychological pain often remains and victims often need specialised care to help them cope and heal. SPIRASI is the only specialist centre in Ireland for the rehabilitation of survivors of torture. Some of the free services that SPIRASI provides to survivors of torture are medical assessments, individual and group psychotherapy, psychosocial and integration support, complementary therapies and support groups. SPIRASI also provides professional training to other healthcare professionals.

Summarised from www.spirasi.ie.

Third Age

Third Age is a national voluntary organisation for older people, which aims at demonstrating 'the value of older people remaining engaged and contributing in their own community for as long as possible' (www.thirdageireland.ie). One of its projects is Fáilte Isteach (which means 'welcome'), which involves older people volunteering to teach conversational English to migrants. Third Age hopes that as well as learning English, the students will also feel welcomed into the community and it sees the classes as also benefiting the teacher, who can feel that they are making a valuable contribution to society.

Fáilte Isteach began in 2006 in Summerhill, Co. Meath, when it was noticed that many new migrants had difficulty with English but there was a lack of free classes available. It began with six students and within a year 70 students who had begun with no English had progressed to basic, intermediate or even advanced level. The project proved a great success and spread nationwide; to date there are 53 Fáilte Isteach projects in Ireland. 'Every week over 540 volunteers teach over 1,600 students from over 63 countries, collectively offering over a thousand hours of tuition each week' (www.thirdage.ireland.ie). Fáilte Isteach has been listed on the European Commission's website on integration (ec.europa.eu/ewsi/en/) as meeting best practice requirements in its field and has been noted as a project that is adaptable to any EU country.

Summarised from www.thirdageireland.ie.

Tralee International Resource Centre (TIRC)

TIRC aims 'to support integration between local and international communities in Tralee, Co. Kerry' (www.tirc.ie). It provides support services to asylum seekers and other immigrants by providing a drop-in facility and networking with other groups and agencies. It gives advice and information on a range of issues and provides a range of classes, along with social activities, such as parent and toddler groups. The activities and classes are free, which is very important for asylum seekers who only receive €19.10 a week and are not allowed to work. It also arranges Gardaí and legal clinics, so that people can obtain information in an informal atmosphere.

Summarised from www.tirc.ie.

Show Racism the Red Card Ireland

Show Racism the Red Card is an anti-racist charity that operates in Ireland, the UK, Norway, Sweden, Denmark and Finland. Its aim is 'to challenge racism through providing education resources and intercultural activity which support integration' (www. theredcard.ie). Its educational materials are suitable for both primary and secondary school use, and its factsheets give a brief history of racism, highlight the current problem of racism in Ireland and give advice on how individuals and organisations can deal with it. The website also has a confidential facility for reporting experiences of racism – individuals can choose whether the information will be reported to another authority. Each country's campaigns involve education through sport but are also tailored to the specific country. In Ireland the organisation emphasises connections with the Gaelic Players Association and the Irish Rugby Union Players Association. Summer camps and competitions take place regularly.

Summarised from www.theredcard.ie.

ENAR Ireland and European Week against Racism

ENAR Ireland is part of the European Network Against Racism, which is based in Brussels. It co-ordinates a range of anti-racist groups and organisations on a national level and 'aims to work collectively to highlight and address the issue of racism in Ireland' (www.enarireland.org). It is involved in organising European Week against Racism, which takes place in March every year. The week centres on the International Day Against Racism, which takes place on 21 March and commemorates the 1960 Sharpeville massacre in South Africa. The 2012 theme of the week was 'Open Your Mind – Speak Out Against Racism'. Events that took place in Ireland included poster displays in schools, fashion shows, competitions, football games and children's events.

Summarised from www.enarireland.org.

The Impact of the Recession

The National Consultative Committee on Racism and Interculturalism (NCCRI) was set up in 1998 with the aim of being an expert body in Ireland on racist and intercultural matters. It was involved in research and produced a National Action Plan Against Racism, which was a blueprint for promoting an inclusive Irish society. However, as a result of government cut-backs, the NCCRI was closed in 2008, and the National Action Plan was discontinued. Other bodies suffered in the 2008 budget: the Equality Authority budget was cut by 43 per cent and the Irish Human Rights Commission (IHRC) also had its budget cut drastically.

The recession may also be a factor in increased racist incidents, as people unfairly target immigrants as scapegoats for the economic crisis.

> A number of Filipino focus group participants recalled that they had experienced considerable hostility when they first came to Ireland around the turn of the millennium but that overt expressions of racist verbal abuse had risen again since the start of the economic crisis . . . 'It's like when we [first] came, now we are going through it all over again for the past two years, since the start of the recession.' ('Anabelle', in Fanning 2012:205)

Summarised from Fanning (2012); www.nccri.ie.

Activities

1 Discuss reasons why racism might increase during a recession.

2 Many Irish people are emigrating to find work. If any friend/family member is working abroad, discuss with them how the local population responds to immigrants.

Project ideas

1 Research what services or projects for migrants are available in your town or area. If possible, visit the project and speak to both organisers and participants.

2 Design a questionnaire that aims to discover what migrants find most daunting on arrival in Ireland and how they have adjusted.

Revision questions

1 Outline the difference between primary and secondary data.

2 List some advantages and disadvantages of both types of data.

3 Outline the difference between quantitative and qualitative data.

4 Explain the following terms: hypothesis, survey population, representative sample.

5 List the seven types of question used in a questionnaire.

6 Explain, using examples, what a 'problem question' is.

7 Describe some challenges faced by those living in a strange culture.

8 List two groups that help migrants in Ireland and describe their work.

CHAPTER 5

Prejudice

By the end of this chapter, students should be able to:

- Define ethnocentrism and understand how it can be resolved with cultural relativism.
- List and explain four theories of prejudice.
- List and discuss patterns of majority–minority relationships.
- Define *genocide* and be aware of two twentieth-century cases of genocide.
- Evaluate and discuss various prejudices towards immigrants.

Ethnocentrism

Ethnocentrism can be defined as 'A suspicion of outsiders combined with a tendency to evaluate the culture of others in terms of one's own culture' (Giddens 2001:254). Another way of putting it is 'the belief that our culture is superior to all other cultures' (Curry *et al.* 2005:37).

We have all been socialised into our own culture, which results in us thinking of our own way of life as 'normal', while those who behave differently may make us feel uncomfortable. Because of our attachment to our own culture, it is unsurprising, even inevitable, that most of us 'view other cultures with a mixture of curiosity, acceptance and loathing' (Curry *et al.* 2005:37).

When we judge others by the standards of our own culture, we may find that other cultures do not conform to our expectations of the way things 'should' be, which may lead to a negative attitude toward these cultures.

If we examine different societies we can see many differences between what is considered acceptable or unacceptable. 'Some people in our society are disgusted when they learn that people from other cultures eat dog meat. The mere fact of eating a dog disgusts them, and they think anybody who would eat a dog must be degenerate. On the other hand, we, who eat baby sheep and baby cows, consider ourselves normal' (Curry *et al.* 2005:37).

Ethnocentrism involves judging, and it is a normal human reaction which we all share – 'On one level, some ethnocentrism is inevitable if people are to be emotionally attached to a cultural system. On another level, however, ethnocentrism generates misunderstanding and sometimes conflict' (Macionis & Plummer 2002:112) – but this attitude can create problems if we do not think it through.

When we perceive people as different from us, we may not treat them with the same respect as we do others; and at worst we may regard them as less than human and thus as not having the same human rights as us. 'It is easy to see how ethnocentrism combines with stereotypical thought. Outsiders are thought of as aliens, barbarians or morally and mentally inferior' (Giddens 2001:254). Lack of tolerance for differences in human behaviour and belief systems often leads to prejudice and discrimination.

Summarised from Curry *et al.* (2005); Giddens (2001); Macionis & Plummer (2002).

> ### Activity
>
> 'The easiest idea to sell anyone is that he is better than someone else' (Allport (1954), cited in Jandt 2004). Discuss this statement.

Cultural Relativism

In order to avoid ethnocentrism we need to make an effort to adopt a mindset known as cultural relativism, which is 'the practice of judging a culture by its own standards' (Macionis & Plummer 2002:113).

It is not easy to break the habit of making judgements. Because we are all socialised into a particular culture, it is challenging to mentally step into another's shoes. 'Cultural relativism is a difficult attitude to adopt because it requires that we not only understand the values and norms of another society but also suspend cultural standards we have known all our lives' (Macionis & Plummer 2002:113).

'Cultural relativism recognises that each culture is unique and valid' (Curry *et al.* 2005:37). Some of the child-rearing methods of other cultures outlined in Chapter 2 are very different from our own society's expectations and norms, yet each is appropriate to its particular society. Realising that the motivations and values of other people are as valid as our own is essential if we want to avoid ethnocentric thinking.

This can, of course, be difficult. 'Not only can it be hard to see things from a completely different point of view, but sometimes troubling questions are raised. Does cultural relativism mean that all customs and behaviours are equally legitimate? Are there any universal standards to which all humans should adhere?' (Giddens 2001:25). Sometimes a damaging or unfair practice is defended on the grounds of cultural tradition. Giddens raises the example of the Taliban in Afghanistan and their attitude to women. In Afghanistan, the Taliban established strict Islamic Sharia (religious) law. Women had to be covered from head to toe, including the face, and could neither work nor be educated. This type of repressive regime could not be defended on the grounds of cultural relativism. The Council of Europe states that cultural practices are only to be respected where they do not contradict human rights and equality. 'Cultural traditions, whether they be "majority" or "minority" traditions, could not trump principles and standards of the European Convention on Human Rights' (Council of Europe 2008:10).

In Chapter 3, it was mentioned that the practice of suttee (a widow burning herself on her husband's funeral pyre) in India was outlawed by Lord William Bentinck in 1829. Because of the penalties imposed for abetting suttee, the practice largely came to an end and many women who would have felt pressured by their society to end their lives were now saved from this fate. It could be argued that it was ethnocentric for an Englishman to impose his values on Indian society, but it could also be argued that he acted humanely and for the best.

Ethical problems can appear alongside cultural relativism because 'virtually any kind of behaviour is practiced somewhere in the world; does that mean that everything is equally right?' (Macionis & Plummer 2002:113). Trying to get the balance right is not always easy, but it is best to realise that there are no simple answers and to avoid making snap judgements. Ask yourself why other cultures do things in a particular way rather than just reacting from your own experience. In keeping an open mind, it might be helpful to imagine how an outsider might regard certain norms in our own society: 'Think about your own way of life as others might see it' (Macionis & Plummer 2002:113).

Summarised from Council of Europe (2008); Giddens (2001); Macionis & Plummer (2002).

Activities

1 Make a list of what you consider important values in the organisation of society. Consider how your list might differ from a person from another culture.

2 Depending on the values of a culture, others will be judged on how they reach that standard. Studies show that Japanese perceive Americans as very loud and aggressive because in Japan direct eye contact is seen as aggressive while raised voices signal anger instead of enthusiasm. Japanese people also disapprove of public displays of affection and the use of informal language when speaking to older people (Jandt & Taberski 1998). Make a list of aspects of your own culture that a person from another culture might disapprove of.

3 The Tour Egypt website (www.touregypt.net) gives the following advice on Egyptian social mores. 'In general, Egyptians are most accommodating and they will go out of their way to help you and respond to any questions you have. Most Egyptians require little personal space and will stand within inches of you to talk. You will find that whenever you start talking with an Egyptian, you will inevitably draw a crowd, and

often the Egyptians will start discussing among themselves over the correct answer to a question.'

Discuss the importance of such cultural information when travelling abroad.

4   Look at a travel book or website and note what tips it gives on local customs and what to avoid. Include Ireland in this search and see if you agree and what you might add. A useful website is www.culturecrossing.net.

Theories of Prejudice

Sociologists have examined prejudice in society and have formed various theories to explain it. There are four major theories concerning prejudice.

1 Scapegoat Theory

A scapegoat is 'a person or category of people, typically with little power, whom people unfairly blame for their own troubles' (Macionis & Plummer 2002:263). People who feel that their life circumstances are unfair may wish to hold a 'scapegoat' responsible. This theory proposes that disadvantaged people, instead of venting anger at those above – who are too powerful to be attacked – blame others below or in some disadvantaged position. It will not improve the person's circumstances, but it allows them to vent their anger and gives a comforting feeling of being superior.

Unemployed people may prefer to blame foreigners for 'taking their jobs' than to blame a multinational whose concern for their profits has led them to relocate in a cheaper country. 'Scapegoat theory holds that prejudice springs from frustration' (Macionis & Plummer 2002:262).

Summarised from Macionis & Plummer (2002).

2 Authoritarian Personality Theory

This theory, formulated by Theodore W. Adorno and colleagues in 1950, claims that prejudice is an individual personality trait. His research showed that people who hold strong prejudice towards one minority group are usually prejudiced toward all minorities. Studies showed that when respondents who had shown prejudice towards known ethnic groups were polled on their attitudes towards non-existent ethnic groups such as the 'Danireans', 'Piraneans' and 'Wallonians', they 'were also antagonistic towards these other three groups, sometimes even advocating that restrictive measures be taken against them' (Hartley (1946), Jahoda (1960), cited in Farley 1982:20). This study demonstrated that prejudice is an internal attitude rather than one brought about through any experience of other ethnicities.

'Such people exhibit authoritarian personalities, rigidly conforming to conventional cultural values, envisaging moral issues as clear-cut matters of right and wrong and advocating strongly ethnocentric views' (Macionis & Plummer 2002:263–4). This type of person also looks on society as 'naturally competitive and hierarchical, with "better" people (such as themselves) inevitably dominating those who are weaker' (Macionis & Plummer 2002:264).

Adorno also found that people who were tolerant of one group were generally tolerant of all groups, believed that everyone should be equal and felt uncomfortable with the exercising of excessive power. Those who displayed strong prejudice were often unwilling to see any faults in themselves and were completely uncritical of their parents, reserving their judgement for people separate from themselves, while more tolerant groups tended to have a more realistic picture of their own faults and an ability to recognise imperfections in their own parents.

Summarised from Farley (1982); Macionis & Plummer (2002).

3 Cultural Theory

This theory holds that prejudice is common because of attitudes that are deeply embedded in a culture. Socialisation is seen to be an important factor in creating prejudice, often at an unconscious level. 'Frequently, young children see their parents as all-knowing and all-powerful. Thus, the parents' prejudices are taken for truth by the children, often with very little thought or awareness of what has happened' (Allport (1954), cited in Farley 1982).

The superiority of certain groups may be a 'core value' of some cultures. Emory S. Bogardus came up with the idea of the social distance scale – the concept was based on how close people feel on a scale to those of different cultures. His research showed a similarity of views throughout the USA, which led him to believe that 'such attitudes are culturally normative' (Macionis & Plummer 2002:264). US society responded most favourably to those of English, Canadian and Scottish descent and would welcome close relationships, even marriage, with them. French, German, Swedish and Dutch backgrounds were less popular, while African and Asian people were regarded most negatively.

MacGreil's research in Ireland in the late 1980s showed similar results. 'When asked if an American person would be welcome into the family, 78.6% said that they would welcome a white American, while only 26.2% would welcome a black American; 95.6% said they would have white Americans as a next-door neighbour, but only 59% said they would similarly welcome black Americans' (MacGreil, quoted in NCCA 2006:7).

Pressure to conform to the cultural attitudes of the surrounding society is very powerful as it is always easier to 'fit in' rather than disagree. 'All agents of socialisation reward behaviour and expression of attitudes that conform to their norms and punish those who do not' (Farley 1982:29). Research has shown that college students who privately expressed ideas of racial equality were unwilling to appear publicly – on marches, in newspapers or on television – stating these beliefs, because of fears of what others might think of them (DeFleur and Westie (1958), Fendrich (1967) and Evans & Ehrlich (1969), cited in Farley 1982:30).

Summarised from Farley (1982); Macionis & Plummer (2002); NCCA (2006).

4 Oppression of Minorities

'A fourth view claims that powerful people utilise prejudice as a strategy to oppress minorities' (Macionis & Plummer 2002:264). If the general public looks down on minorities, then employers can pay people from minority groups lower wages for their hard work. The policy of 'divide and conquer' has long been a recipe for success. Workers who have to face pay cuts might blame immigrants for lowering wages, but their energies might be more productive if they were united. 'Elites benefit from prejudice that divides workers along racial and ethnic lines and discourages them from working together to advance their common interests' (Geschwender (1978) and Olzak (1989), cited in Macionis & Plummer 2002:264).

In the case of the Irish Ferries dispute, which will be discussed in more detail later, it was found that resentment was directed not only towards the company who were eager to maximise a profit, but also towards those who had been hired below the minimum wage. 'Resentments towards immigrants may increase, particularly among low-skilled workers, if they perceive migrant workers as presenting a cheaper option' (Krings 2006:33). In this case, however, the policy of 'divide and conquer' was not successful and unions forced the company to comply with employment law and pay the minimum wage.

Summarised from Farley (1982); Krings (2006); Macionis & Plummer (2002).

Activities

1 'Most people are concerned about what others think of them and will tend to conform to gain or keep the acceptance of others' (Farley 1982:30).

   Have you ever remained silent on something you disagreed with in order to fit in? Write a short reflective piece on the consequences of standing out from the crowd.

2 Scapegoat theory holds that we take our frustrations out on those less powerful than ourselves. Hold a class discussion on this, trying to find examples from your own lives.

3 How do the theories of scapegoating and oppression of minorities combine?

4 Discuss the four theories and which you consider to be most dominant in your society.

Patterns of Majority–Minority Relations

Where societies are not mono-ethnic there are several typical patterns of majority–minority relations. These are assimilation, pluralism, segregation, expulsion and annihilation/genocide.

Farley (1982) points out that the terms 'majority' and 'minority', when used sociologically, are not defined strictly on a numerical basis:

> The sociological meaning of majority group . . . is any group which is dominant in society. . . . Typically, a majority group is in a position to dominate or exercise power over other group in society. A minority group may be defined as any group that is assigned an inferior status in society – that is, any group that has less than its proportionate share of wealth, power, and/or social status.' (Farley 1982:6–7)

For example, we have seen how the white population in South Africa was a minority numerically but enjoyed majority status.

Assimilation

Assimilation was previously defined as 'The blending of the culture and structure of one racial or ethnic group with the culture and structure of society' (Curry et al. 2005:199). Curry et al. divide the outcome of assimilation into two forms:

1 The 'majority group remains the same whereas the minority changes and becomes like the majority group' (Curry et al. 2005:201) – newcomers take on the culture of the dominant majority and abandon their own culture. Over time the distinction between groups disappears. For example, in Ireland after the Norman invasion, the Normans settled into Irish life, intermarried, spoke Irish and adopted Irish customs. They are said to have become 'more Irish than the Irish themselves' (www.teachnet.ie).

2 'Melting pot – a situation in which the culture and social structure of both the minority and the majority change in such a way that a new blended grouping emerges that combines some features of both groups' (Curry et al. 2005:201). The traditions and customs of immigrants become blended with the host culture to form a new cultural pattern; for example, the modern USA is a fusion of many cultures.

Pluralism

This is defined as 'A situation in which separate racial and ethnic groups maintain their distinctiveness even though they may have approximately equal standing' (Curry et al.

2005:201). In a pluralist society numerous cultures are seen as equally valid and all have the same rights, while differences are respected and celebrated. Groups remain distinct, but this is through their own choice rather than because they are regarded as outsiders. There are two key reasons given for the stability of pluralist societies. First, distinctly different groups share a 'common cultural core' (Curry *et al.* 2005:202) in obeying the country's laws and abiding by many shared customs of the society. Second, a shared government unites all the cultures and 'provides avenues for resolving disputes' (Kallen (1924), cited in Curry *et al.* 2005:202).

Segregation

Segregation was defined in Chapter 1 as 'The physical and social separation of categories of people' (Macionis & Plummer 2002:678). Under this system, groups of people remain entirely separate and are not treated equally. Often the majority holds power, but the (numerical) minority may be dominant, as in apartheid-period South Africa. Segregation is sometimes referred to as 'group closure' and often results from an ethnocentric viewpoint: 'Ethnocentrism and group closure frequently go together. "Closure" refers to the process whereby groups maintain boundaries separating themselves from others . . . such devices include limiting or prohibiting inter-marriage between the groups, restrictions on social contact or economic relationships like trading, and the physical separation of groups' (Giddens 2001:254).

Expulsion

This is 'the forceful exclusion of a racial or ethnic group from a society' (Curry *et al.* 2005:202). Curry *et al.* give many examples of expulsion:

- In 1492 in Spain, Jews were ordered to convert to Catholicism or leave Spain. Most left.
- In 1838 the US government forced 16,000 Cherokee Indians to march from Georgia to a reservation in Oklahoma. A quarter died on the journey
- In 1972 the Asian–Indian population of Uganda were ordered to leave the country.
- During the 1990s in the former Yugoslavia, Croats, Bosnians, Serbs and Muslims attempted to drive each other out to create mono-ethnic territories.

Expulsion may be linked with genocide because being forcibly driven out can result in many deaths, as in the Cherokee example given above, and the estimated 500,000 people who died in the Bosnian conflict. A new term for expulsion, so-called 'ethnic cleansing', emerged during the violence in the former Yugoslavia. 'Ethnic cleansing involves the forced relocation of ethnic populations through targeted violence, harassment, threats and campaigns of terror' (Giddens 2001:257–8). Some commentators, such as Stephen

Poole, dislike the mainstream use of this term as it signifies acceptance that 'some ethnicities are dirtier and more corrupted than others' (Poole 2006:91). He also points out that when the Nazis spoke of the deportation and extermination of Jews, they used the term Säuberungsaktion, which means 'cleaning process'.

Genocide

Giddens describes genocide as 'the systematic elimination of one ethnic group at the hands of another' (Giddens 2001:258). The aim of genocide is not just to gain territory, power or wealth but to completely wipe out a group of people. Giddens mentions several genocides of the 20th century:

- 1 million Armenians were killed under the Ottoman Empire.
- In 1994 in Rwanda, 800,000 of the Tutsi minority were killed by the Hutu majority.
- Under the Nazi regime six million Jews were killed, along with one and a half million Roma.

Genocide can be attempted in different ways: 'by rounding up all the members of a particular group and then executing them or incarcerating them under such brutal conditions that they slowly perish . . . Another tactic is to spread disease among a group or allow its members to perish for lack of food, shelter and medicine' (Curry *et al.* 2005:203). The US Cavalry spread smallpox through the native American tribes by deliberately leaving clothes infected with the smallpox virus (Alvin Josephy, quoted in Curry *et al.* 2005:203); British settlers in Tasmania hunted the natives for sport and wiped them out. The Khmer Rouge in Cambodia killed two million people 'for supposedly representing capitalist culture . . . teachers, bureaucrats, lawyers, officials and anyone who spoke English' (Hinton (1998), cited in Curry *et al.* 2005:203).

Ideally, countries with an ethnic mix could live harmoniously in a pluralist society. However, this is sadly not the case. Most modern wars are fought internally between different ethnic groups in one country: 'between 1989 and 1992 there were 80 armed conflicts – but only three of them were between countries. The rest were within countries' (Macionis & Plummer 2002:259).

Summarised from Curry *et al.* (2005); Farley (1982); Giddens (2001); Macionis & Plummer (2002); Poole (2002).

Case study: Genocide in Rwanda

In 1994, three-quarters of the Tutsi tribe in Rwanda were killed by the Hutu majority. The slaughter took place over three months and an estimated half a million Tutsis were wiped out.

The minority Tutsis had been in power in Rwanda in the past, but a revolution in 1959 had overthrown them. Some Tutsis stayed in Rwanda at this time, but many fled to other countries. The Tutsi refugees were treated badly in Uganda, so they decided to return home. However, the Rwandan authorities refused to recognise them as having Rwandan nationality, so they were forced to return to the refugee camps.

Tutsi refugees in Uganda created a party known as the Rwandan Patriotic Front (RPF), who wished to return to Rwanda. The RPF attacked Rwanda in 1990 with the intention of removing the then President Juvénal Habyarimana and ensuring that the Tutsi refugees could return to Rwanda. Throughout the war, divisions between Hutus and Tutsis increased and were encouraged by Hutu government propaganda. The government also encouraged militias (irregular armies of civilians) to form and armed them with machetes.

A ceasefire was declared in 1992 and peace negotiations began. However, Hutu leaders continued to make plans to slaughter Tutsis and any opposing Hutus. In April 1994, the plane carrying President Habyarimana was shot down. Responsibility for this has never been established, but his death signalled the start of the slaughter.

Close associates of the president took control of the government and decided to continue with the extermination plan. Almost immediately, 'Soldiers and militia ... began systematically slaughtering Tutsi. Within hours, military officers and administrators far from the capital dispatched soldiers and militia to kill Tutsi. . . . After months of warnings, rumors and prior attacks, the violence struck panic among Rwandans and foreigners alike. The rapidity of the first killings gave the impression of large numbers of assailants, but in fact their impact resulted more from ruthlessness and organization than from great numbers' (Human Rights Watch 1999).

UN peacekeeping troops, who were present in the country to monitor the ceasefire, were ordered by their superiors to withdraw to their posts. Countries such as France, Belgium and Italy sent troops to evacuate their citizens but the UN Security Council did not order any intervention. 'The leaders of the genocide held meetings in the center and south of the country to push hesitant local administrators into collaboration. At the same time, they sent assailants from areas where slaughter was well under way into those central and southern communes where people had refused to kill and they used the radio to ridicule and threaten administrators and local political leaders who had been preaching calm' (Human Rights Watch 1999).

Orders to kill were passed from the highest level of government down to small communities, through local meetings which presented the genocide as self defence. 'Slaughter was known as "work" and machetes and firearms were described as "tools"' (Human Rights Watch 1999).

The compliance or non-compliance of villagers was then reported back to the top and any Hutus who would not obey the orders to kill were themselves endangered. In some areas where Tutsis were well integrated, Hutus had joined with them to resist attack, but unity was impossible to maintain without support and eventually this protection collapsed. Even those who were at first reluctant were increasingly drawn into the violence:

.

> Only when military and civilian authorities resorted to public criticism and
> harassment, fines, destruction of property, injury, and threat of death did these
> Hutu give up their open opposition to the genocide. In some places, authorities
> apparently deliberately drew hesitant Hutu into increasingly more violent behavior,
> first encouraging them to pillage, then to destroy homes, then to kill the occupants
> of the homes. Soldiers and police sometimes threatened to punish Hutu who
> wanted only to pillage and not to harm Tutsi. (Human Rights Watch 1999)

Throughout the country, soldiers, police, militia and civilians set about a horrific and highly organised slaughter of the Tutsis. Tutsis were easily identifiable: they had earlier been forced to carry ID cards; and even without these they were recognisable by their physical appearance. No one was spared. Tutsi children were murdered with the same ruthless efficiency as their parents. 'Authorities first incited attacks on the most obvious targets – men who had acknowledged or could be easily supposed to have ties with the

RPF – and only later insisted on the slaughter of women, children, the elderly, and others generally regarded as apolitical' (Human Rights Watch 1999).

The RPF resumed fighting and began to gain ground throughout Rwanda. In July 1994 the RPF took the capital and by July the government forces had admitted defeat. The Tutsi RPF had gained control in Rwanda and so many Hutus fled to neighbouring countries in fear of retaliation for the genocide they had committed.

A UN-appointed tribunal investigated and sentenced those most responsible for organising the genocide. The UN are presently engaged in helping to rebuild and stabilise Rwanda.

Summarised from BBC (2012b); Human Rights Watch (1999); UN (http://rw.one.un.org).

Case study: Genocide by the Nazis in World War II

Adolf Hitler, head of the Nazi party, came to power in Germany in 1933. The Germans wanted to expand into and dominate Europe, and this eventually led to World War II. The Nazi party believed that Germans were a super race and had little regard for other nationalities: 'Hitler looked upon people like the Poles and Russians as fit only to be "slaves for the Germans"' (Neill 1975:101). They were ruthlessly efficient in killing those whom they thought of as little more than animals: in 1941 the German army wanted to reduce the population in the Russian city of Kharkov and coldly executed 100,000 Russians in one day. 'A hundred thousand civilians were rounded up, handed picks and shovels, and told to dig a colossal trench on a hill outside the city. This took all day. At the end of the day an SS lorry drove slowly along this trench, and collected the picks and shovels. Then it drove back, and machine-gunned all the diggers. A bulldozer followed to push the bodies in' (Neill 1975:115).

Although the Nazis regarded other nationalities as only fit to serve the German people, there were others they thought were not even fit to serve, and a system of elimination was organised for both the Roma and the Jewish people. 'Roma were the only other population besides the Jews who were targeted for extermination on racial grounds in the Final Solution. Up to one and a half million Romani lives were lost by 1945' (www.theredcard.ie).

Hitler wanted total elimination of the Jews and his plans for this were called the Final Solution. The Final Solution involved rounding up Jews throughout Europe and transporting them to concentration camps such as Auschwitz, Buchenwald, Dachau and Treblinka. Mass shootings were seen as too slow, so it was decided to use gas to kill large numbers of people. At each camp the Nazis built enormous gas chambers and crematoriums for disposing of the dead. The gas chambers were 'huge dance-hall-sized rooms into which two thousand Jews at a time were crowded. Once filled, the doors were closed and the taps which brought poison gas into the chambers were opened' (Neill 1975:116). Apart from those who were murdered on arrival, such as children and old or sick people, the average life expectancy of a prisoner was less than three months. Those who had been selected for work and so allowed to live a little longer were not the lucky ones:

> The Sonderkommando (Special Squad) was a group of Jewish prisoners whom the Germans forced to carry out the most horrifying labour. . . . Their 'job', which they endured day after day until they themselves were killed and replaced by a new group of 'living dead', was to empty the gas chambers, pry open the mouths of the dead and pull out gold teeth, cut the dead women's hair, and then burn the bodies in the ovens or in pits. One survivor explained afterwards: 'Certainly I could have killed myself or got myself killed; but I wanted to survive, to survive to avenge myself and bear witness. You mustn't think that we are monsters; we are the same as you, only much more unhappy.' (Bruchfeld and Levine 1998:61)

By the end of the war in 1945, six million Jews had been killed by the Nazis. The Nazi genocide of the Jews is known as the Holocaust.

Summarised from Bruchfeld and Levine (1998); Holocaust Memorial Day Trust (http://hmd.org.uk/genocides/the-holocaust); Neill (1975); Show Racism the Red Card Ireland (www.theredcard.ie).

Myths and Misinformation

Prejudice towards newcomers is often fuelled by myths and misinformation. Fictions and half truths become part of popular belief and if left unchallenged and unexamined can fuel hatred. If we examine assumptions and rumours, we may find that certain facts are more complex than they first seemed. In considering our attitude towards migrants to Ireland, we might also do well to remember our own history of emigration. Here are some common myths.

All Asylum Seekers are Lazy

A big problem for asylum seekers in Ireland is that they are not allowed to work while waiting for a decision, so they are forced to rely on the state for their needs. The Refugee Act of 1996 denied the right to work to asylum seekers. The then minister for Justice, Equality and Law Reform, Nora Owen, stated, 'I do not consider it appropriate to allow people, with temporary permission to remain in the State, to work and put down roots' (Fanning 2012:99).

Because they are forced to be dependent on the state for their needs, some people have classified them as lazy. 'The perception has been fostered among some sectors of the Irish population that they are "scroungers" because they do not work' (Bacik 2004:188).

Surveys among asylum seekers show that most were employed in their home country and many are well educated. Ninety-five per cent of asylum seekers surveyed in a 2006 study in Waterford had been employed before coming to Ireland (Waterford Area Partnership *et al.* 2006:36), while a 2002 survey in Cork found that 80 per cent of the asylum seekers they surveyed had trained for a career such as teaching, banking, nursing or accountancy (Collins (2002), cited in Waterford Area Partnership *et al.* 2006:17). Most asylum seekers would rather earn their living and live independently.

When Irish people flooded to the USA during the Famine years, they at first represented a great threat and crisis. Between 1847 and 1851 848,000 Irish people arrived in New York: 'This unprecedented onslaught of destitute, ill and unskilled immigrants burdened the city with its first social service crisis . . . their arrival also stretched the limits of existing institutions like the Almshouse Department, the Lunatic Asylum, Bellevue Hospital and the House of Refugees' (Ruckenstein & O'Malley 2004:255). They were, of course, allowed to work and soon changed from being a threat to the city's resources to productive citizens.

Summarised from Bacik (2004); Fanning (2012); Ruckenstein & O'Malley (2004); Waterford Area Partnership *et al.* (2006).

Direct Provision Centres are like Holiday Camps

From 2000, the system of 'direct provision' for asylum seekers replaced social welfare payments. Direct provision means that the state pays for accommodation and meals at an approved centre or hostel, along with a cash allowance, which is currently €19.10 a week for an adult and €9.60 for a child. Asylum seekers have no choice of which centre they are placed in and many have criticised the conditions in these centres. The Waterford study mentioned above found that rooms were shared by four to six men (Waterford Area Partnership *et al.* 2006:8) and the food was often inadequate or inappropriate for religious reasons: 'Muslim respondents also expressed concerns as to whether the meat they were served was Halal. "Rice everyday. Same food everyday and the quality of the food. I am Muslim and sometimes he put pork in the food and this is not legal according to our Islam"' (Waterford Area Partnership *et al.* 2006:34). Complaints were also made about the lack of fresh fruit and vegetables in the centres.

Other rumours about asylum seekers suggest that they get all sorts of goods and services free. 'Myths about asylum-seekers have spread like wildfire through the country – myths that they get free phones, cars, prams, even hair-dressing vouchers from the state' (Bacik 2004:188).

These rumours are completely untrue. Asylum seekers receive their room and board in a designated centre, a small cash allowance, a medical card and free education for their children. They can apply for assistance towards clothing and other exceptional needs from the Department of Social Protection, but this is by no means an easy process. The same exceptional needs payments are available to anyone – pensioner, carer, unemployed person – whose only income is a social welfare payment; they are not available to asylum seekers only, as some rumours suggest.

The Department of Social Protection guidelines state that 'a single payment may be made to help meet essential, once-off, exceptional expenditure, which a person could not reasonably be expected to meet out of their weekly income. . . . The payments would be for items such as special clothing in the case of a person who has a serious illness, bedding or cooking utensils for someone setting up a home for the first time, costs in relation to funerals, visiting relatives in hospital or prison etc.' (Department of Social Protection 2012).

Free legal aid is available to asylum seekers to help with the application process and possible appeals. This is not special treatment – any Irish person who does not have the means to pay for their own legal services is entitled to apply for legal aid. Legal aid in criminal matters is completely free, while a contribution according to means is required for civil cases such as divorces.

Summarised from Bacik (2004); Citizens Information; Department of Social Protection (2012); Waterford Area Partnership *et al.* (2006).

We're being Flooded by Foreigners

Some people may resent the number of migrants coming to Ireland and see immigration as a threat. Sometimes the complaint is that foreigners are living on social welfare; at other times it is that foreigners are taking all the jobs.

In answer to those who complain that foreigners are living on social welfare, the 2011 Census shows that a higher percentage of the Irish labour force are unemployed. Of the non-Irish labour force there were 268,180 employed and 77,460 unemployed, which is an employment rate of 74.2 per cent. Of the Irish workforce there were 1,494,487 employed and 339,064 unemployed, an employment rate of 60.1 per cent (CSO 2011b:25). The top eight nationalities of non-Irish workers were Polish, British, Lithuanian, Latvian, Indian, Romanian, Filipino and Slovak (CSO 2011b:26). Twelve per cent (544,357) of the Irish population in 2011 were not of Irish nationality, the most numerous other nationalities being Polish, British, Lithuanian, Latvian, Nigerian, Romanian, Indian, Filipino, German, American, Chinese and Slovak (CSO 2011b:33).

Those who complain that foreign people are taking all the jobs might consider the number of jobs taken by Irish people all over the world. There are currently 34.7 million US residents of Irish descent and approximately 144,588 current US residents of Irish birth (www.history.com). 'By 1900, there were more Irish people to be found living outside Ireland than inside' (O'Brien 1995:5).

The total number of Irish people now resident in Ireland who have lived and worked abroad (during the period 1971 to 2011) and have now returned to Ireland is 892,370 (CSO 2011a:32).

CSO figures also show that between 35,000 and 40,000 people a year emigrate (RTÉ News 2012). So when we take into account the number of Irish people who have used and do use the right to live and work abroad, it seems a fair exchange.

Some people worry that there are too many asylum seekers settling in Ireland, but statistics show that the numbers of those granted residency are quite low: 'Of the 3,910 first-stage applications considered in 2009 just 97 (2.4 per cent) were granted. By 2010 Irish acceptance of asylum claims was the lowest in the EU at 1.3 per cent' (Fanning 2012:99).

Summarised from CSO (2011a,b); Fanning (2012); O'Brien (1995); RTÉ News (2012); www.history.com.

They are Undercutting our Wages

This claim will remind many people of the Irish Ferries dispute of 2005 when 500 Irish staff were made redundant and replaced with cheaper Eastern European workers. The response by Irish workers – strikes and pickets – forced Irish Ferries to cancel most of their operations for two weeks, while unions lobbied for a resolution. Anti-immigrant feelings also increased at this time.

> There already has been some evidence that resentments towards migrant workers increased during the Irish Ferries dispute . . . there is little doubt that conflicts such as the Irish Ferries dispute reinforce the perception, in particular among less skilled Irish workers, that migrants are a threat to their job prospects. (Krings 2006:38)

If foreign workers seem to offer cheaper labour, resentment from the Irish workforce will obviously follow. However, Krings offers a solution to this problem – which is to ensure that migrant workers are entitled to the same rights as Irish workers so that wages cannot be undercut. 'If migrant workers appear as a potentially cheaper alternative to Irish workers, resentment towards the former may grow. To prevent the emergence of a two tier labour market, stratified along ethnic lines, migrant workers should be entitled to the same rights as Irish workers' (2006:31). This was the eventual solution found in the Irish Ferries case. The flag of Cyprus had been flown on some of the Irish Ferries vessels so that they could not be held accountable under Irish labour law – a necessary step as they were paying less than half of the minimum wage.

The dispute escalated and both government bodies and unions sought to resolve the issue. Eventually the company was forced to pay the Eastern European contract workers the minimum wage – therefore no saving was made, so there was no reason not to hire Irish workers. The new social partnership agreement – Towards 2016 – contains a section on 'Employment Rights and Compliance' which involves 'increased penalties for non-compliance with employment law' (Kring 2006:33). Legislation such as this is essential in order to protect workers of all nationalities and ensure a decent wage. 'If properly implemented, these measures should offer better protection to both indigenous and migrant workers alike and ensure that established labour standards are not undermined' (Krings 2006:37).

They All Stick Together and Don't Mingle

Many immigrants will indeed form their own communities on arrival in a new country, but this does not mean that they are unfriendly or unwilling to integrate. Language is an enormous barrier to integration and racism may also lead to newcomers forming friendships mainly among people of their own nationality. 'A 2009 study undertaken on behalf of the Fundamental Rights Agency (FRA) placed Ireland among the worst five of the EU's twenty-seven member states where people of African origin had experienced racist crime or victimisation such as theft, assault or harassment' (Fanning 2012:205). The old saying, 'there's safety in numbers' rings true: many migrants stay together as they find it difficult to gain acceptance except among their own. Irish emigrants in the past have concentrated themselves in certain areas – Queens in New York and Cricklewood in London, for example – but eventually become part of their new country.

Immigrants are Taking Houses and Jobs from Irish People

Fanning cites a 2007 estate management study by Fingal County Council that noted that hostility was targeted towards immigrant families on a housing estate in Dublin. There was much ill-feeling towards these families on the basis that their houses had been denied to Irish people. However, on investigation, it was found that no Irish people had applied for the new housing there. 'The claim that immigrants were taking houses from local people was a species of urban myth, invoked to promote and justify hostility towards immigrants' (Fanning 2012:212).

Certainly, jobs are taken by non-Irish workers, but in return Irish people have access to a range of jobs in other countries. EU workers are free to work here and in return we enjoy the same privileges abroad. Restrictions on non-EU workers mean that they find work permits hard to come by. A work permit is only available for a non-EU worker if the position has been advertised and it is found that no other worker is available for the job.

Irish People are Born Here – Foreigners Never Fit In

When migrants arrive in a new place, they will not adapt overnight. Because of our island status and our own history as emigrants, Irish people are unused to others setting up home here. Some studies suggest that Irish people are particularly fixated on having to be born here to be Irish and do not accept foreigners even when they have lived here for many years.

An interview with a Bosnian man who had lived in Ireland for 15 years demonstrated this lack of acceptance. 'Irish people always ask you, "when will you go home?" I am not a refugee any more, I have a passport, I have the citizenship . . . yet they always ask, "When are you going to go home to your own country?" . . . it's like I am sitting in their own living room all the time' (Halilovic-Pastuovic 2007:160).

Irish people were not always welcome abroad because of similar assumptions that they would not fit in. Irish people who emigrated centuries ago have passed an Irish identity down to their descendants who combine their heritage with the national identity of the country in which they live. St Patrick's Day parades are huge events in America, organised and attended by Irish Americans, yet no one considers that this dual identity shows disloyalty to the USA.

Activities

1   In 2011 there were 78,600 children under 14 of non-Irish nationality living in Ireland (CSO 2011a:34). As these children attend school and grow up in Ireland, will they ever be seen as Irish or will they remain foreign? Discuss what factors may prevent them from being seen as 'Irish'.

2   Discuss any negative stories you have heard about immigrants and examine them with regard to whether they are based in fact or myth. If possible, contact relevant authorities or services to establish the facts.

3   Try to apply some of the theories of prejudice to negative perceptions of immigrants.

4   Discuss whether you agree or disagree with the law forbidding asylum seekers to work.

Project idea

Research and present the experiences of asylum seekers in the direct provision system. A useful link to start off is www.thejournal.ie/readme/interviews. Search for the article entitled '"I love the food" – First-hand stories from asylum seekers in Ireland' dated 26 June 2012.

Revision questions

1 Define and describe ethnocentrism.

2 Explain the term 'cultural relativism' and the difficulties associated with it.

3 List and explain the four theories of prejudice.

4 Explain how majority and minority groups are not always determined on a numerical basis.

5 List two examples of patterns of majority–minority relations.

6 Explain the background to the genocides in Rwanda and Germany.

7 Discuss some common arguments used by people who promote prejudice against immigrants.

CHAPTER 6

Colonialism and Racism

By the end of this chapter, students should:

- Understand the terms *colonisation* and *colonialism* and describe their links with racism and ethnocentrism.
- Be aware of the treatment of Native Americans by European settlers.
- Be aware of the development and extent of the British Empire.
- Be able to describe racist attitudes toward black and Irish people.
- Be able to discuss how colonisation economically benefited the British.
- Be aware of post-colonial problems for new states.
- Be aware of aid programmes in the developing world.
- Be aware of the history of slavery and civil rights in the USA.

Colonialism

Colonisation involves taking land from its native population 'when one group migrates into an area where another group is present and conquers and subordinates that indigenous group' (Farley 1982:95–6). Colonialism is the policy, mindset and justification of colonisation.

Colonisation was often linked to ethnocentrism and racism, as native culture was continuously viewed as inferior to European culture. Racist views also meant that native people could be regarded as sub-human and so not deserving of human rights. 'The spread of the colonizing powers, or of their emigrants . . . took one of two forms or some combination of the two: (1) the removal of the indigenous peoples by killing them off or forcing them into specially reserved areas . . . or (2) the conquest of the indigenous peoples and the transformation of their existing societies to suit the changing needs of the more powerful militarily and technically advanced nations' (C. E. No., *Encyclopaedia Britannica*, Macropaedia Vol. 4 1982:890).

The British Empire is an example of an aggressive pursuit of wealth and glory to the exclusion of the rights of native people. An attitude that the subdued population benefited from colonisation often masked the economic rewards the British acquired from their territory. The Viceroy (the British queen's representative) of India, George Curzon, declared, 'In the Empire we have found not merely the key to glory and wealth, but the call to duty, and the means of service to mankind' (quoted by Morris 1968:122) A poem by Rudyard Kipling written in 1899, 'Take Up the White Man's Burden', is often quoted as summarising the belief that the Europeans were carrying out the well-intentioned task of bringing 'civilisation' to other lands. Racist attitudes in modern Britain have been linked to the colonial ethos of superiority: 'Four hundred years of conquest and looting, four centuries of being told that you are superior to the Fuzzy-wuzzies and the wogs, leave their stain. This stain has seeped into every part of the culture, the language and daily life; and nothing much has been done to wash it out' (Salman Rushdie, quoted in Thompson 2008:55).

Summarised from *Encyclopaedia Britannica*, Macropaedia Vol. 4 (1982); Farley (1982); Morris (1968); Thompson (2008).

Early Colonialism

From the 1500s, European powers pursued a strategy of colonising overseas territories. This began with the discovery of America and new sea routes around Africa and involved countries such as England, Portugal, Spain, France and the Netherlands. Colonisation brought great wealth to the European powers, for as well as acquiring territory, they also had access to materials that were in high demand, such as tea, coffee, sugar, spices, textiles, precious metals and furs. Trade in slaves was also highly lucrative and the English were a major part of this trade. In the mid-18th century, about 150 ships a year sailed from British ports to Africa, each with a capacity of 40,000 slaves, and by the end of the century 'the British were the leading slave traders, controlling at least half of the transatlantic slave trade' (Ha. Ma., *Encyclopaedia Britannica*, Macropaedia Vol. 4 1982:892).

Summarised from *Encyclopaedia Britannica*, Macropaedia Vol. 4 (1982).

America

The English established themselves in North America in 1607. The settlers were first located in Virginia and Massachusetts, but soon expanded to 13 colonies. Initially the relationship with the Native Americans (commonly called Indians) was one of trade, but it soon changed to conquest. The English view of the natives was that they were 'ungodly heathens not subject to conversion or worthy of human association' (Farley 1982:110) and so their rights in regard to land were not considered.

The American War of Independence (1775–1783) dislodged the British, but the new United States continued the policy of expansion. America became a popular destination for European settlers in the late 18th and 19th centuries and the frontier continuously advanced. Land was taken from the Native Americans, whose population declined rapidly, due to 'massacres during wars, susceptibility to infectious European diseases and hardships endured during forced migrations' (Ha. Ma., *Encyclopaedia Britannica*, Macropaedia Vol. 4 1982:894). The Native Americans were at a disadvantage: internal tribal warfare prevented a united resistance and the Europeans had superior weapons. Disease was critical in weakening the native population – they had no immunity to European diseases. Their cultural beliefs also put them at a disadvantage: their notions of communal ownership of land made them willing to share, while their belief in the sacredness of treaties left them easily deceived. The settlers did not regard these treaties as binding and repeatedly broke them

when more land was wanted for the increasing number of Europeans.

The Native Americans were pushed further and further west, and forced long-distance marches to reservations resulted in many deaths. These reservations were usually on the worst land that was considered unsuitable for farming by settlers, and attempts were made to destroy the native culture. 'Practice of native religions and other displays of Indian culture were forbidden. The Sun Dance, an annual religious ritual practiced by many plains tribes was banned . . . Indian children in reservations were frequently taken from their homes and forced to attend boarding schools run by whites. At these schools, they were required to speak only English' (Farley 1982:114). Natives were not regarded as citizens and so had no vote.

The settlers regarded their own culture as superior and convinced themselves that they were 'doing the native people a favour' by bringing British civilisation to them. Racism was a convenient justification for their actions. 'The English settlers were aware that they were taking land away from an established people. To justify this, they developed an image of the Native American as a helpless savage who could only benefit from being Christianized, civilized, and brought into a modern agricultural system. As pressures for land increased, so did racist stereotyping of Indian people and the image of the Indian as a lawless barbarian replaced the earlier image of the "noble savage"' (Nash (1970), cited in Farley 1982:115–16).

The original population of Native Americans is estimated at 40 million, but by the mid-19th century they had been reduced to a population of 250,000. They remain a disadvantaged group today with a suicide rate of twice the national average and an alcoholism rate eight times the national average (Curry *et al.* 2005:206).

Summarised from Curry *et al.* (2005), *Encyclopaedia Britannica*, Macropaedia Vol. 4 (1982); Farley (1982).

Activities

1　'As pressures for land increased, so did racist stereotyping of Indian people.' Discuss how and why the settlers justified their mistreatment of the natives.

2　Have you ever 'badmouthed' someone when you were in the wrong? Reflect on what attraction this attitude has.

Case study: The British Empire

The Act of Union of 1707 formally united England (and Wales) and Scotland into one nation of Great Britain. Britain had lost America by 1783, but it kept Canada, soon expanded into India, and of course still had many other territories, including Ireland. The Industrial Revolution fuelled demand for raw materials and new markets, and expanding the Empire met both these needs. 'By 1815, despite the loss of the 13 colonies, Britain had a second empire, one that straddled the globe from Canada and the Caribbean in the Western Hemisphere around the Cape of Good Hope to India and Australia' (Ha. Ma., *Encyclopaedia Britannica,* Macropaedia Vol. 4 1982:892).

Maritime power was the key to dominance and British expansion was aided by the supremacy of the British navy. During the late 19th and early 20th centuries other European powers such as Germany, Belgium and Italy also became eager to acquire empires, resulting in the 'Scramble for Africa', which led to the continent being divided up between European powers. Before this period, European traders had remained in trading posts along the coast, but by the late 19th century, they had advanced into the interior of Africa. In 1800 European powers had controlled 55 per cent of the world, but by 1914 this had extended to 85 per cent. By 1914 Britain was the overseer of 80 separate territories including Canada, Australia, New Zealand, South Africa, Newfoundland, India and, of course, Ireland. By the early 20th century, the British Empire covered a quarter of the world; it was boasted about as the empire 'where the sun never sets'. There was, however, not enough land to satisfy the European powers, and competition and rivalry led eventually to the outbreak of World War I in 1914. After the war, much of the energy was gone from the drive for empire, but most territories did not gain independence until after World War II.

Summarised from *Encyclopaedia Britannica*, Macropaedia Vol. 4 (1982).

Activity

After the British Empire had disintegrated, many former colonies joined the Commonwealth, with Queen Elizabeth as their shared head of state. Research what advantages this gave to these states.

Colonial Ethnocentrism and Racism

Racism was common in the British Empire, and those who had been conquered were consistently ridiculed. The attitude was that the natives needed to be ruled by their 'betters' for they were incapable of managing themselves. An American traveller, listening to racist outpourings by the English, 'concluded that it was a law of nature to hate those we oppress' (quoted in Brendon 2008:124).

Native religions were often condemned – 'the "filth and obscenity" of heathen idolatry' (Brendon 2008:125) – and efforts were made to convert the colonised nation. The British colonists had enormous self-pride and assumed their accomplishments would dazzle the natives. They saw their technological achievements as evidence of their utter superiority. 'Our steamboats and our miraculous railways are the advertisements and vouchers for our enlightened institutions' (Cobden, quoted in Darwin 2008:14). The humbler and more basic society of Africa served to heighten their sense of being an entirely different and better type of human being. 'When Mary Kingsley returned home from exploring West Africa she felt like embracing "the first magnificent bit of machinery" she saw, since it was a "manifestation of the superiority of my race". The corollary was that peoples with few mechanical achievements to their credit were inferior' (Brendon 2008:150).

Advanced weaponry, such as machine guns, allowed the easy conquest of Africa during the late 19th and early 20th centuries and is said to have 'turned colonial fighting into hunting' (Brendon 2008:145), with the native Africans even being referred to as 'game'. Despite the fact that the British had abolished slavery in 1807, they still held Africans in contempt. They believed in freedom, but only a freedom that involved Africans acknowledging the British as their superiors. Some have argued that the abolition of slavery was simply achieved because it was not as economically necessary to Britain as it was to the USA. They had justified slavery on the basis that 'They did not "have souls" and were "much on a level with beasts". They were a "brutish, ignorant, idle, crafty, treacherous, bloody, thievish, mistrustful, and superstitious people"' (Brendon 2008:19) and later justified colonisation on the basis that Africans were 'mentally dormant and morally undeveloped' (Brendon 2008:151). A West African doctor of the time attempted to remind the British that in Roman times, the Britons had been sneered at as stupid and ugly barbarians incapable of being taught the finer arts, but his point fell on deaf ears.

PUNCH, OR THE LONDON CHARIVARI.—May 20, 1882.

THE IRISH FRANKENSTEIN.

"The baneful and blood-stained Monster * * * yet was it not my Master to the very extent that it was my Creature? * * * Had I not breathed into it my own spirit!" * * * (*Extract from the Works of* C. S. P-RN-LL, M.P.)

The Irish were white, Christian and European, so it would seem likely that they would not be held in quite the same low regard as Africans and other non-white natives, yet the Irish were also seen as an entirely different type of human being. The prejudice ranged from mild, such as regarding the Irish as 'wayward children ... one had only to look around to realise that they needed strong leadership' (Morris 1968:463), to more extreme views: 'Englishmen of refined sensibilities likened Irish peasants to "white negroes", "apes" and "human chimpanzees" ... and a company of low, vulgar, lazy wretches, who prefer beggary to work and filth to cleanliness' (Brendon 2008:121, 124).

The Irish Famine of the mid-nineteenth century saw the British send troops to Ireland to ensure the continued export of corn while people starved. Many argued against giving any help to the Irish, preferring to blame the Famine on Irish fecklessness. Sir Charles Trevelyan was in charge of administering some small relief to Ireland, but his own attitude that famine was God's way of reducing surplus population meant that his main goal was to spend as little as possible. Only £8 million was given to Irish relief while £20 million had been paid to compensate British slave owners in the West Indies when slavery was abolished.

Summarised from Brendon (2008); Darwin (2008); Morris (1968).

Activity

The English novelist Thackeray visited Ireland in 1842. He was horrified by the poverty he saw, but instead of feeling any sympathy or shame, 'He was more inclined to blame the Irish themselves, their indolence and partiality for dirt, for the problems they faced' (Hall 2008:214). Discuss reasons for this attitude.

The Purposes of Empire

Economic

Financial gain was an important incentive to colonise, though this was often masked by a pretence that the colonisers were acting for the good of civilisation. Foreign trade was a massive boost to the British economy, 'where the prize was not territory or rule over peoples but access to markets, suppliers and customers' (Darwin 2008:7). A policy of colonialism provided goods such as spices, tobacco, rubber, sugar, coffee, cotton, tea and wool as well as land for settlers. Surplus population could also be offloaded and have access to opportunities not available at home – 100,000 migrants left Britain in 1830 alone (Darwin 2008:9). The Industrial Revolution increased production, so new markets were wanted as well as raw materials. A British parliamentary speaker stated in 1839, 'The great object of the Government in every quarter of the world was to extend the commerce of the country' (quoted by Darwin 2008:8). Colonies were 'essential outlets for surplus capital, goods and population' (Wakefield, quoted in Dilley 2008:104) and a desire to protect trade routes often influenced Britain's colonial policy: during the 'scramble for Africa', 'Britain's main goal was to defend the routes to India via the Cape and Suez, both threatened by escalating crises in Southern Africa and Egypt' (Robinson & Gallagher, quoted in Dilley 2008:105).

The needs of other peoples were always less important than British financial gain. The Opium War in China demonstrates this. In Britain there was a strong demand for tea, which was imported from China and was largely financed by exports from India. 'The tea Britain bought in China was paid for by India's exports of opium and cotton to China' (Ha. Ma., *Encyclopaedia Britannica,* Macropaedia Vol. 4 1982:898). Britain controlled India, so this trade triangle was very convenient. However, many Chinese people became addicted to opium, so in the 1830s the Chinese authorities banned its import. In 1840, a British fleet arrived in China and the Opium War began. The Chinese surrendered in 1842. The opium trade resumed and Hong Kong was taken by Britain along with five other treaty ports. Hong Kong was not returned to the Chinese until 1997.

Summarised from Darwin (2008); Dilley (2008); *Encyclopaedia Britannica,*
Macropaedia Vol. 4 (1982).

Surplus Population: Deportation

Colonies could also be used for ridding Britain of anyone considered a social problem. Initially Australia was a penal colony. From the late 1700s to the early 1800s it was a destination for criminals only. Most of these were first time offenders convicted of stealing. They were mostly young British and Irish people – over 70 per cent were aged between 15 and 29, and 34 per cent of convicts were Irish. By 1853, convict transportation to eastern Australia had stopped, but it continued to western Australia until 1868. The total of transported convicts is estimated at between 157,000 and 163,000. Sentences ranged from seven years to life. Transportation was a way of dealing with overcrowded jails; most convicts came from large cities, where overcrowding was a problem.

The first 'free settlers' arrived in 1793 but numbers remained small. During the Irish Famine, Australia became a favoured destination for Irish people who were escaping death at home. The Irish orphan scheme during the Famine also sent many young girls to Australia, exporting a social problem as well as providing women for this largely male country: '4,000 girls between the ages of 14 and 18 were despatched to Australia from Irish workhouses in 1848 and 1849' (Fedorowich 2008:82). One can only assume that the girls were glad to escape starvation, but they were given no choice about leaving their home.

The British also sent many children in orphanages or care homes to the colonies. Many still had parents alive, but they were told that they were dead and shipped off as 'home children' to Australia and Canada. The policy of sending children abroad has been called 'philanthropic abduction' (Parr, quoted in Fedorowich 2008:87). The aim was to prevent slum children falling into juvenile delinquency and also to boost the white population in Australia and Canada. The exact number sent is unknown, but 87,699 were sent to Canada alone between 1868 and 1916.

These 'home children' were supposedly going abroad for a better life, but many reported being beaten, abused and treated as slaves. This policy of exporting children continued up to the 1960s.

Summarised from Fedorowich (2008), Thorne (2011).

The Post-colonial World

Problems Following Independence

'The world's post colonial areas often are scenes of protracted and violent conflicts: ethnic, as in Nigeria's Biafran war, national–religious, as in the Arab–Israeli conflicts, the civil wars in Cyprus and the continual clashes between India and Pakistan' (R. A. We., *Encyclopaedia Britannica*, Macropaedia Vol. 4 1982:905).

A consequence of colonisation is often a period of unrest following independence. For example, in Nigeria, a former British territory, civil war broke out on independence. The two main tribes were the Ibo, who lived in the East, and the Yoruba, who were given central government by the British. 'The Ibos and Yorubas were as different as any two nationalities, yet the European cook – Great Britain – had thrown them into the same pot' (Neill 1975:168). In 1967 the Ibos tried to break away and form their own country, Biafra. A cruel civil war followed, which lasted until 1979, when the Ibos had to give in. Biafra was cut off by Nigeria from the outside world, and a million civilians died: 'For several years the area was literally starved to death, as Ibo leaders were too proud to give in' (Neill 1975:169).

Israel and Palestine

War in the Middle East has also been a consequence of colonial powers dividing power unfairly. On the collapse of the Turkish empire after World War I, Britain and France took many lands in the Middle East that had previously been under Turkish rule. They called these occupancies 'mandates', not colonies, as the plan was a system of temporary rule 'until such time as they (European powers) thought the people there were "fit" to govern themselves' (Neill 1975:200).

The Arabs waited for their independence, but the British decided to designate one of their mandates – Palestine – as a homeland for Jewish people, to be called Israel. The Jews had suffered persecution even before World War II and had long lobbied for their own homeland. In 1917, the British declared support for a Jewish state to be established in Palestine, displaying ethnocentric disregard for the Arab population: 'Unfortunately, Israel was not an empty land; the new Jewish house already had tenants' (Neill 1975:202). The Arab desire for their own independent state in Palestine was quashed. An Arab delegate to the Versailles peace conference in 1919 protested: 'This cannot be. The country is ours and has been so of old. We have lived in it longer than they did . . . The number of Jews in Palestine does not exceed one tenth of the number of the natives. Does justice then allow the violation of the rights of the majority?' (quoted by Neill 1975:203).

The British had a purpose in backing Israel. Many Jews were European, and the Americans and British had an interest in trade routes, so it was beneficial to have a state that favoured the West. Arab needs were ignored, leading to an Arab revolt against the British in 1936, which was crushed. Jewish immigration continued, and by 1939 the Jewish population had increased from the 1914 level of eight per cent to 30 per cent.

The extermination of six million Jews in Nazi Germany increased European support for a Jewish state and the USA now favoured it along with the British. The British declared that their mandate would end in 1948 and the Jewish state of Israel was established in that year. Originally Palestinians were left with 40 per cent of their original land. However, in 1948 Israel was invaded by the combined forces of Egypt, Jordan, Iraq and Syria – Arab states that were determined to aid other Arabs. They were defeated and the result was to lose more land, so the Palestinians were now left with 20 per cent of their original territory. The Palestinians were pushed out, often to refugee camps in Jordan, Syria and the Lebanon. The area remains in conflict to this day.

Summarised from Neill (1975); *Encyclopaedia Britannica*, Macropaedia Vol. 4 (1982).

Britain and Immigration after World War II

After the break-up of the Empire, the British Nationality Act of 1948 affirmed the right of people from former countries of the Empire to settle in the 'mother country'. This conveniently helped to fill the labour shortage of the time. By the mid 1970s one and a half million new residents had arrived, comprising three per cent of the population and mainly concentrated in cities and urban districts. From 1962 on, this 'open door' policy changed and a series of laws were passed that controlled residence. The 1981 Nationality Act has been seen as an example of institutional racism: under the Act citizenship is allowed on the basis of having had a parent or grandparent born in the UK, so the law favours the white descendants of settlers to America, New Zealand, South Africa and Australia. During the 1960s, immigration began to be seen as a problem; immigrants became unwelcome and were often viewed as outsiders. In 1978 the British Prime Minister Margaret Thatcher spoke of British culture being swamped by aliens (Dominell 2008:27). Britain today faces ongoing issues of inequality and lack of full integration.

Summarised from Dominell (2008); Thompson (2008).

Aid and Trade

Many countries that gained their independence continued to suffer from the effects of colonisation. They had suffered badly under colonial rule and it was not so easy to start afresh. Being under another's rule had left them no chance to develop their own systems and so they inherited not a new world, but an old system. 'Despite seeking to assert their political and cultural autonomy, anti-colonialists demanding independence found they had little choice but to operate within this system, since it was the only one that was also imaginable to their rulers' (Cooper (2003), cited in Chiriyankandath 2007:45). They had been forced into the conditions of a modern state instead of going through a gradual change in society, so many new states were unprepared. Africa had traditionally been divided into tribes rather than countries, which meant that the notions of state, central government and borders were not part of their culture. The handovers were often hurried and suddenly new people, who had no experience of being in charge, were in control. Not surprisingly, instability often followed.

The western world and the developing world remain unequal socially and developmentally, so there is a policy in the West of giving foreign aid in order to try to change this imbalance. Programmes focus not just on supplying immediate basic needs but also on building societies.

Irish Aid is Ireland's official programme of assistance abroad. It focuses on ending poverty and inequality, and does this in a way that builds towards the future rather than focusing purely on short-term needs. Poverty is tackled, not simply by providing food and clothes, but by breaking the vicious circle of poverty by supporting local development of businesses and industry. Other aims include universal primary education, environmental sustainability and reducing child mortality. The old proverb, 'Give a man a fish and feed him for a day; teach a man to fish and feed him for life' sums up the long-term goals of programmes such as Irish Aid.

Apart from government programmes bringing aid to developing countries, there are popular movements, such as the fair trade movement, that also aim to improve life in the poorest countries. Global trade often favours western countries, with people in the developing world working for low wages to supply goods often exported to the West. Multinational companies that export goods such as cocoa beans and coffee often pay low prices, keeping those in the developing world in poverty. Movements such as fair trade aim to help tackle poverty in the developing world by allowing people to earn a decent wage for their work. The Fairtrade label guarantees that the workers who made or grew the product have decent working conditions and are paid a fair wage. The scheme also ensures that the environment is also protected. The cost of each product covers not only wages but an amount of money that is used by the community to invest in essential local needs such as education, water supplies, health and transport. Fairtrade products are now stocked by many supermarket chains and restaurants. Consumer spending on Fairtrade products in Ireland is increasing, growing from €118 million in 2009 to €138 million in 2010.

Summarised from Chiriyankandath (2007), Fairtrade Ireland (www.fairtrade.ie); Irish Aid (www.irishaid.ie).

Activity

Discuss whether you believe that the developed world has a responsibility to help developing countries to improve their standard of living.

Project idea

Research in detail a development programme supported by either Irish Aid or Fairtrade.

Case study: African-Americans – from slavery to the present day

Slavery in the USA

The first slaves were brought to North America in 1619 and many more were to follow. The average life expectancy was only ten years after arrival, so a constant supply was needed. Traders from Britain, France, Holland, Spain and Portugal exchanged goods for slaves along the African coast.

Williamson gives a vivid description of visiting a former Dutch slave house in Senegal, where captives waited for transportation. 'Guides explain how slaves were stuffed into pens measuring ten by six metres, and inspected and priced like animals; how they were chained to the walls, and seawater was piped into the rooms to keep them subdued and in partial submersion; how they were forced to fight for food, to ensure that only the stronger specimens survived' (Williamson 2007:2).

Fifteen million slaves arrived in America over three centuries, but so many died on the journey that the actual number who were transported is estimated at 35 to 40 million. The voyages could last up to ten months and conditions on board were dreadful; slaves were chained and squeezed so tightly below deck that many died from disease, dehydration and suffocation. Sharks often followed slave ships, drawn by the huge number of corpses thrown overboard. 'The air on the slave decks was so fetid that candles would not burn, and a traveller on one ship reported that the floor was "so covered with blood and mucus . . . that it resembles a slaughterhouse. It is not in the power of the human imagination to picture to itself a situation more dreadful or disgusting'" (Williamson 2007:4).

In the Deep South of the USA there was a high demand for labour as the industry there involved back-breaking work on tobacco, rice, sugar and cotton plantations. By the late 17th century, 23,000 of the 28,000 slaves in the USA were located in the southern states. African slaves – unfortunately for them – were extremely useful in the South, due to their knowledge of hot weather farming techniques and ability to cope with the climate. They were profitable for their owners even when the seasonal field work was slow, as owners often leased their slaves out to construction companies: 'they were cheaper to employ than poor whites, and there was less trouble if they were whipped and beaten and died on the job' (Williamson 2007:4). By the early 19th century there were one million slaves in America, concentrated largely in the South.

On arrival, slaves were sold and families were often split up – father, mother and children could all be sold to different plantations. The slaves were also isolated from each other, and since they came from many different parts and tribes of Africa, they had no common language. The work was hard and it made no difference to the owner how long a slave survived, for they could always buy another. 'Field slaves were expected to work from "can to can't"' (Williamson 2007:5), that is from dawn to dusk. Whippings were common and any escapees were hunted down by dogs and savagely whipped, sometimes to death, as a deterrent. The effect of the 1808 ban on the import of slaves at least made conditions a little better, because it made slaves a more valuable resource. "'The time has been", wrote a planter in 1849, "that the farmer could kill up and wear out one Negro to buy another. Negroes are too high in proportion to the price of cotton, and it behoves those who own them to make them last as long as possible"' (Stampp (1956), cited in Farley 1982:104).

Much was written on how to manage slaves, for they had not been slaves before they arrived in the USA. Advice was given on breaking their will and training them into a submissive attitude. Absolute obedience was demanded; slaves had to 'know their place' and know that their master's word was law. The intention was for them to be in awe and fear of their masters and to make them feel helpless and dependent. They were not encouraged to become too skilled – any training was for menial work only. For slaves who were slow to submit, whips and chains were used to correct any supposed insolence.

The longer slavery continued, the more racism increased, 'so that by the mid-nineteenth century there was a pervasive racist ideology in the South unlike anything that existed when slavery was first established' (Wilson (1973) and Jordan (1968), cited in Farley 1982:100). The belief that black people were inferior and simple-minded was used to justify slavery, reflecting the need for traders and owners to absolve themselves. For if they believed 'that slaves were less than human, that they were heathens and savages incapable of being civilised, they might be able to convince themselves and others that slavery was not so bad. Indeed they could even claim it was morally good' (Farley 1982:101).

The system was easy to maintain because there was so little possibility of revolt. Slaves had no access to weapons, they were scattered, forbidden to travel alone and so were unable to assemble. Most important, they were surrounded by an entire land that supported slavery, so they had nowhere to escape to.

Summarised from Curry *et al.* (2005); *Encyclopaedia Britannica*, Macropaedia Vol. 18 (1982); Farley (1982); Williamson (2007).

Activity

'The plantation system in the Deep South was dependent on cheap labour to maintain their wealth. Three per cent of the white southern population owned over half the slaves' (Stampp (1956), cited in Farley 1982:99). Link this statement with a theory of prejudice from Chapter 5.

Independence and Abolition

The War of Independence from Britain began in 1775 and by 1783 an independent USA was in existence. The 1776 Declaration of Independence stated that all men are created equal, but this was taken in the South as 'not applying to slaves, who were regarded as property not persons' (Williamson 2007:5).

In 1807, Britain banned the slave trade and in 1808 the USA followed suit by banning the importation of slaves. However, it was only importation that was banned; slavery itself was still legal. There were already one million slaves in the country and smuggling of slaves continued. The descendants of slaves could still be sold, and a 'breeding' slave was highly valuable.

Campaigns to end slavery had grown in the north of the USA, leading to a deepening rift between North and South. Many Northern states began to abolish slavery, but the South wanted to keep their slaves, both for economic reasons and because they feared retribution from freed slaves. Many believed that Africans were uncivilised and needed to be disciplined by having masters. 'Most Southern whites resolutely refused to

believe that the slaves, if freed, could ever co-exist peacefully with their former masters'
(D. H. D., *Encyclopaedia Britannica*, Macropaedia Vol. 18 1982:968).

Lincoln became president in 1860, and his opposition to slavery prompted the South
to secede from the Union in 1860 and form the Confederate States of America. Carolina
was the first state to secede and was soon followed by other Southern states. Civil
war began in 1861 and in 1863 Lincoln issued the Proclamation of Emancipation, which
encouraged half a million slaves to flee north, many of whom served as soldiers on the
Northern side. The Confederates surrendered in 1865.

Summarised from *Encyclopaedia Britannica*, Macropaedia Vol. 18 (1982); Farley (1982);
Williamson (2007).

Activity

Southerners defended slavery 'on Biblical, economic and sociological grounds'
(*Encyclopaedia Britannica* 1982:968). Research and discuss the reasons why the
South continued to defend slavery.

After the Civil War

After the Civil War, the North began a policy of reconstruction in the South, which was
designed to establish a new and equal society. Among the measures brought in was the
introduction of the vote for the newly freed slaves and the removal from office of those
who had long held power. However, efforts to alter the society failed. There was much
opposition in the South and radical white supremacist groups such as the Ku Klux Klan
grew in power. Also, Lincoln had been assassinated in 1865, after which Vice President
Andrew Johnson became president. Johnson's attitude was crucial. He was Southern-born
and had owned slaves himself, and he 'shared the white Southerners' attitude toward the
Negro, considering black men innately inferior and unready for equal civil or political
rights' (D. H. D., *Encyclopaedia Britannica*, Macropaedia Vol. 18 1982:971).

Northern intervention was not a success and the South was gradually left to its
own devices. Power returned to the same old hands. The Fifteenth Amendment to the
Constitution allowed black people to vote, but organisations such as the Klan were
successful in keeping them from the polls. Southern state governments began to adopt
new laws, which segregated and restricted the rights of black people. These laws were
known informally as the 'Jim Crow' laws and were to shape Southern life for decades.
Limits on black people being allowed to vote, serve on juries and own property were
introduced. By the 1890s most Southern states had removed the right to vote from black
people.

Segregation laws were passed in the South that justified white supremacy. Supposedly
whites and blacks were 'separate but equal', but the actual result was that black people

became second-class citizens. 'Formal sanctions blocked access to decent housing, jobs, schools, hospitals and public transportation, and ensured that African Americans were kept unskilled, uneducated and living in poverty' (Williamson 2007:8). Some rights were retained. Black people could now set up their own churches and could marry – under slavery they had no right to spouse or family as they were property, not people.

Although improved, the life of the newly freed black population was still extremely harsh. The sharecropping system was the most common way of making a living. Under this system the black worker leased the land of the plantation owner in return for splitting the crop 50:50. However, the owner would deduct what had been given on credit: housing (a basic shack), food, clothing, seed and tools. The illiterate sharecropper had no way to check the fairness of the calculation and often found himself in a cycle of permanent debt with no possibility of saving to buy his own farm.

The elite of the South needed poor and powerless people to exploit for cheap labour and the sharecropping system was perfect for this. Poor whites who also worked as sharecroppers were now in competition for land and jobs, giving the elite more power to set the terms. The ruling class 'was happy to sit back and benefit from racism. As long as working-class whites and blacks saw each other as the enemy, there was little chance of a united, class-based movement against those who controlled the real wealth of the South.'

Apart from physical inequalities, the social distance system was important. Whites wanted to maintain a system where white had value and superiority, 'where whiteness conferred status; a system of social distance' (Farley 1982:133). These ideas of superiority were essential to maintaining Southern white pride after their defeat in the Civil War. Attempts to unite black and white under a common cause were unsuccessful. The Populist Party attempted to promote unity among the poor : 'You are made to hate each other because upon that hatred is rested the keystone of the arch of financial despotism which enslaves you both. You are deceived and blinded that you may not see how this race antagonism perpetuates a monetary system which beggars you both' (speech by Tom Watson, quoted in Woodward (1966) and cited in Farley 1982:134). These efforts were in vain and racial hatred persisted.

Patterson describes how the Southerners longed for the 'old Negro', 'mentally retarded but uncomplaining, faithful, humble, childlike, religious and endearing' (Patterson 1998:214).

The Southerners dreaded any signs of independence or advancement in black people, which was known as being 'uppity',and ensured that the black population was continuously kept in place. This is demonstrated in the writings of the African-American Richard Wright, who described his experiences as a boy in the Deep South. His first job was in a factory, where he worked with white men. All went smoothly enough at first, as he took care to be docile and respectful. However, one day he made the mistake of trying to learn more about the work.

I asked Morrie one day to tell me about the work.
He grew red.
'Whut yuh tryin' t' do, nigger, get smart?' he asked.
'Naw, I ain' tryin' t' get smart' I said.
'Well, don't, if yuh know what's good for yuh!' (Wright 1938)

Thinking that there had been a misunderstanding, he questioned another man, Mr Pease. The response was the same.

'Nigger, you think you're white, don't you?'
'Naw, Sir!'
'Well, you're acting mighty like it!'
'But Mr. Pease, the boss said...'
Pease shook his fist in my face.
'This is a white man's work around here, and you better watch yourself!'

(Wright 1937)

Soon after this incident, Wright was attacked by Morrie and Pease and told to leave. Reaction at home confirmed his place: 'When I told the folks at home what had happened, they called me a fool. They told me that I must never again attempt to exceed my boundaries. When you are working for white folks, they said, you got to "stay in your place" if you want to keep working' (Wright 1938).

In another incident he was beaten up by a group of young white men for forgetting to say 'sir' when answering a question. After beating him they told him he was lucky to have got off lightly. 'When they left they comforted me with: "Nigger, yuh sho better be damn glad it wuz us yuh talked t' tha' way. Yuh're a lucky bastard, 'cause if yuh'd said tha' t' somebody else, yuh might've been a dead nigger now"' (Wright 1938).

Where intimidation did not work, violence was the next step in keeping African-Americans in line. 'Organisations such as Ku Klux Klan ... sought to punish so called uppity negroes and to drive their white collaborators from the South' (*Encyclopaedia Britannica* 1982:972). Lynch mobs kept down any who drew attention to themselves, and black-owned businesses risked vandalism or arson. There were an estimated 5,000 lynchings between the end of the Civil War and 1968. Victims were usually alleged to have committed crimes, but the main motivation was very often to stop African-Americans getting 'uppity'. Lynchings were gruesome public affairs, with children often present. Patterson recounts the experience of one man who met some children near where a lynching had happened. A girl of about ten was eager to tell him of 'the fun we had burning the niggers' (Patterson 1998:196). There are horrific accounts of how the victim would often be tortured and mutilated – castrated, his fingers, toes and ears cut off –

before being strung up and burned slowly. People often took body parts for souvenirs and there was a brisk trade in photos. The body was often displayed in the black part of town as a warning to behave. 'In the presence of nearly 2000 people, who sent aloft yells of defiance and shouts of joy Sam Holt was burned at the stake in the public road. Before the torch was applied to the pyre, the Negro was deprived of his ears, fingers and other portions of his body' (Patterson1998:194).

Lynching was socially accepted as a method of control and police collusion was rampant. Victims were seen as violent and deserving of their fate until a black journalist named Ida Wells Barnett began to investigate the circumstances around lynchings. She had herself believed that those lynched were guilty of crime and that law-abiding people would be safe. But she discovered that those lynched had often just been seen as troublemakers, had committed no crime or even been accused of one. Ida campaigned and raised much awareness around the issue.

Racial issues in the North were also troubled. After slavery was abolished in the North, blacks and whites – particularly low-skilled immigrants – often had to compete for jobs. From 1890 on, race relations had worsened due to this increased competition between white and black workers. Blacks who were desperate for work would often work for lower wages, which stirred up hatred against them. Unions were being started, but they excluded blacks from membership, stupidly playing into the hands of employers. Black workers had no union to support them in demanding fair treatment, so they were often hired for lower wages or to break strikes. The unions, by excluding them, weakened their own power. 'Northern race relations took an abrupt turn for the worse, with a great upsurge in both prejudice and discrimination ... there seem to be a number of reasons for this change, and it is striking that most of them in some way arose from the economics of the era, from some kind of competition for scarce resources' (Farley 1982:141).

This continued well into the 1920s. 'Black and white workers, because of their mutual fear and mistrust of one another – and their inherently weak bargaining position in an era of low wages and surplus labour – were easily played off against one another' (Farley 1982:142–3). Hatred often resulted in violent outbursts and riots from 1917 to 1919. Police moved in only when blacks struck back but took no preventive measures. At this time, Catholics, Jews, Asians and Mexicans were also seen as a threat to society.

Summarised from Curry *et al.* (2005); *Encyclopaedia Britannica*, Macropaedia Vol. 18 (1982); Farley (1982); Williamson (2007).

Project idea

Research the story of either Emmett Till or Ida Wells Barnett.

The Civil Rights Movement

After World War II, the system began to be challenged more strongly. The 1950s and 1960s were more economically prosperous, so it was a favourable time for change. Also many black people had served in the army during the war, which helped to break down barriers.

A series of protests resulted in increasing civil rights legislation. In 1946 segregation on government transport was ruled illegal and in 1954, segregated schools were ruled illegal. Further civil rights laws passed during the 1960s protected African-Americans' voting rights and outlawed discrimination in employment, providing goods and services and selling or renting houses.

One part of the battle was legal change, but getting compliance with the law was a different matter. In 1955, a black woman called Rosa Parks was arrested for refusing to give up her seat to a white man on a bus in Montgomery, Alabama. This incident led to a campaign against segregation. Dr Martin Luther King, a minister, was involved in that campaign. Other campaigns mushroomed after victory in Montgomery and King soon became a national leader. He advocated non-violent resistance, although protesters were often attacked, even by police. Many businesses still refused to serve African-Americans, and mass sit-ins were organised in these places. Schools continued to be segregated and resistance to this was enormous. In Little Rock, Arkansas, an order was issued to the governor in 1957 to desegregate a high school. He failed to do so, and President Eisenhower had to send in troops to carry out the order.

An enormous demonstration in Washington in 1963 (the 'March for Jobs and Freedom') was attended by a quarter of a million of King's supporters, both black and white. He gave his famous 'I have a dream' speech, which urged supporters to remain peaceful and meet 'physical force with soul force'.

Civil rights laws were enacted piecemeal and peaceful protesters became impatient. Marches and demonstrations were often attacked by white mobs or even by the police, for example in 1963 in Birmingham, Alabama. Those impatient with the slow progress of the civil rights movement turned to other leaders and movements such as Bobby Seale of the Black Panthers and Malcolm X of the Nation of Islam, who urged 'Black Power' – economic equality and political power, not just civil rights. Malcolm X also favoured self-defence rather than passive resistance, and – not having any belief in the possibility of real integration – the separation of black and white. Feelings of frustration began to spill over into rioting. In 1968 King was assassinated, which led to violent outbursts. The 1970s saw mass protest, especially among young black people.

The government commissioned a special advisory board and instigated the policy of affirmative action. This meant that a certain number of black people had to be hired by the public services, such as the police force.

The USA today still has major racial issues. Affirmative action has proved problematic: many white people oppose this system, saying that it discriminates against whites. In 1996 California voters passed Proposition 29, which banned state affirmative action programmes. Some African-American groups say that the US government should pay reparations for past slavery, which would be used to improve black education and housing.

Race issues are of major importance in American society. One in four African-American male youths are in jail, on probation or on parole, but only one in five are in college; the majority still live in segregated neighbourhoods and attend all-black schools. (Collins and David (1990), Johnson (1990), Krivo and Peterson (2000), all cited in Curry *et al.* 2005). But with the election, and re-election, of Barack Obama as President of the USA, hope for an improvement in race relations has grown.

Summarised from Curry *et al.* (2005); *Encyclopaedia Britannica*, Macropaedia Vol. 18 (1982); Farley (1982).

Activities

1 Read or listen to Martin Luther King's 'I have a dream' speech. Discuss your response to it and why you think it is so lastingly famous.

2 Discuss why some civil rights campaigners became impatient with peaceful protest. Reflect on which movement you would be attracted to if you were a black student of the time.

3 Look up Norman Rockwell's painting 'The Problem We All Live With'. Write down your instant reactions to the picture. Why did Rockwell choose this title?

4 Read about Ruby Bridges and the incidents around her enrolment at school. Discuss why her parents put her in that position.

5 The famous American writer John Steinbeck observed the protests against Ruby Bridges. He wrote that he knew many kind, decent people in New Orleans and wondered where they were while this was taking place, 'the ones whose arms would ache to gather up a small, scared, black mite?' Discuss why people who disagree with certain actions stay silent.

Revision questions

1 Explain what colonisation is.

2 Outline briefly the history of the colonisation and settlement of the USA.

3 Describe how the Native Americans were treated and why their numbers and culture declined.

4 Describe the British opinion of Africans and Irish people in the 19th century.

5 Outline the economic benefits of the Empire to the British.

6 Describe how countries have been affected by colonialism after independence.

7 Describe how developing countries are helped by one government and one non-government agency.

8 Outline briefly the history of slavery in the USA.

9 Explain the term 'Jim Crow laws'.

10 Describe the civil rights movement in the USA.

CHAPTER 7

The Print Media, Attitudes and Objectivity

By the end of this chapter, students should:

- Understand the importance of the media in determining cultural attitudes.
- Understand the terms *agenda setting*, *gate keeping* and *norm setting*.
- Be aware of bias in the media.
- Be aware of legislation that limits media content.
- Understand the role of the Press Council and Press Ombudsman.
- Understand the terms *moral panic* and *folk devil*.
- Be aware of issues around ethnicity in the magazine industry.

Introduction

As we saw in Chapter 2, the mass media is an agent of socialisation, helping form our values, beliefs and identity. 'The media are central in the provision of ideas and images which people use to interpret and understand a great deal of their everyday existence' (Golding (1974:78), cited in Marsh & Keating 2000:708).

Apart from direct contact with other people, most of our knowledge of the world comes from media sources, which may or may not be accurate. 'If most of our opinions are based on knowledge obtained "second hand" through the mass media, then this raises the important issue of the power of the mass media to influence our lives' (Browne 1992:146). With so much of our information coming from the media, it is vital that the information is accurate and fairly presented. We might take it for granted that what is reported by the media is true, but this assumption needs to be examined.

Important questions to ask are:

- How is the information selected?
- Are some issues presented favourably and others harshly?
- Do the media exaggerate issues and give distorted perceptions?
- How do profit motives and the control of ownership influence the media?
- Is there bias in the media?

Summarised from Browne (1992); Marsh & Keating (2000).

Newspapers

Browne (1992) mentions three types of newspaper: 'quality'; 'middlebrow'; and 'popular'. 'Quality' or broadsheet newspapers such as the *Irish Times* tend to be the largest, have the fewest pictures and are 'serious in tone and content' (Browne 1992:150); they give in-depth coverage of politics, economics and world events. They aim for a neutral tone, except in specific opinion pieces.

'Popular' or tabloid newspapers such as *The Mirror* cover a lot of 'human interest' stories to do with scandals and celebrities and contain a large amount of pictures. Sensational stories, such as crime, are the main focus of news reporting, and entertainment and sport are given a large amount of coverage. They use bold headlines and the writing style uses simple, colloquial language.

'Middlebrow' newspapers fall somewhere between 'quality' and 'popular' – they are more serious than a tabloid but have a lighter tone than a broadsheet.

The tabloid press is the section of the press most often accused of inaccurate or insensitive reporting, but other newspapers, although more subtle, will still be involved in gate keeping, agenda setting and norm setting (see below).

Summarised from Browne (1992).

Activity

Choose a story that is reported in both the tabloid and the broadsheet press. Compare the two styles of reporting. If possible, follow the same story for a week.

Commercial Interest and Control

One aim of a newspaper is to inform the public, but we must not forget that it is also a business and must make a profit to survive. 'The popular press is financed by its readers; two thirds of its income derives from sales, only one third from advertising' (Marsh & Keating 2000). The media are market-driven, so they are designed to satisfy the majority, while minority groups are often ignored. Advertising targets those who have disposable income to spend, not powerless groups such as the old and poor.

The question of ownership of the media also raises questions of how information can be controlled by powerful individuals. 'Owners have always sought to intervene in media production to further their own commercial and political interests or those of others whom they support' (Marsh & Keating 2000:732).

In Ireland, there is a concentration of media ownership in few hands. The Independent News and Media Group (INM) is extremely powerful, owning many national daily and Sunday newspapers – the *Irish Independent*, *The Star*, the *Evening Herald*, the *Sunday Independent*, the *Sunday World* – along with 13 regional newspapers and many newspapers abroad (INM). The Communicorp group is another very powerful media organisation, owning 40 radio stations in eight countries, including six in Ireland.

Some commentators have stated that the concentration of media ownership in too few hands is unhealthy for democracy. 'A new concentration of ownership suggests we need to consider how that influence is applied and how that unaccountable power might be used to deflect attention from uncomfortable truths, how it might be used to silence valid criticism or even objective commentary' (*Irish Examiner* 2012).

Fintan O'Toole points out that ownership of the media gives a person or group extreme power. As well as the news being about what is said, 'news is also about what is not said, and . . . the ability to control what can and cannot be said about you is an indispensable form of power' (O'Toole 1997:40).

Summarised from INM (www.inmplc.com); *Irish Examiner* (2012); Marsh & Keating (2000), O'Toole (1997); www.communicorp.ie.

Freedom of Speech

The Irish Constitution guarantees us the right to express opinion freely, but there are restrictions on saying anything that might undermine public order, morality or state authority. Freedom of expression is also restricted in the interests of national security, public safety and the protection of an individual's reputation and rights. It is also a criminal offence to publish blasphemous material. (Blasphemy refers to 'grossly abusive or insulting' statements about the sacred beliefs of a religion.) The Official Secrets Act 1963 and the Prohibition of Incitement to Hatred Act 1989 also limit what can and cannot be said by the media.

The Defamation Act 2009 provides protection against any untrue statement 'which tends to injure a person's reputation in the eyes of a reasonable member of society'. In order for court proceedings to take place, the statement must be published, must be false and must clearly refer to the complainant. Statements made on television and radio are regarded as being 'published' as these media forms can be preserved in the same way as a newspaper cutting. Eighty per cent of all defamation actions are brought against the media, and if such an action is successful it will cost dearly, as the defendant will have to pay damages along with all costs. The highest damages payment ever awarded in an Irish defamation case was €10 million. However, it is also risky to take a case, as if the case goes against the complainant, they will have to bear the cost.

Summarised from Irishbarrister.com; Irish Statute Book (1963, 1989).

At times the media may publish material that, although it is not outlawed by any legislation, is insulting or causes offence to the reader. In this case the reader has an option to complain to the Press Ombudsman.

The Press Ombudsman

The Office of the Press Ombudsman responds to complaints about the press. It aims to regulate the press in the best interests of the public but also to ensure the continuing freedom of the press. The public can make a complaint to the Press Ombudsman and it will then be decided if there are grounds for the complaint and what action to take. The complaint must be made within three months of publication of the offending piece and can only relate to publications that have signed up to the Code of Practice (see below). Member publications include all daily and Sunday newspapers, the Irish editions of UK newspapers, the majority of regional newspapers, and most Irish-published magazines.

A formal complaint must first be made by writing to the editor of the publication. If the outcome is not satisfactory, an attempt at conciliation will be made. Conciliation involves a case worker attempting to negotiate between the complainant and the editor. If this is not successful a decision will be made by the Ombudsman, based on the Code of Practice, or will be referred directly to the Press Council. If the complaint is upheld, the newspaper will be asked to print an apology or clarification.

The Press Council of Ireland

The function of the Press Council is to ensure appropriate ethical standards in the Irish print media (newspapers and magazines). The Press Council is an independent body that deals with complaints and oversees the principles set out in the Code of Practice for Newspapers and Magazines. It aims to establish a co-operative and supportive relationship with editors and journalists, rather than one of censorship. The Press Council is responsible for appointing the Press Ombudsman and also decides on any appeals arising from decisions of the Ombudsman.

Code of Practice for Newspapers and Magazines

The Code of Practice outlines certain principles for professional journalism, which editors and journalists voluntarily agree to. It is based on ten principles:

1 *Truth and accuracy*: All print media must aim to be accurate and in the event of a mistake must publish an apology or clarification (33 per cent of the complaints made in 2011 were based on this principle).

2 *Distinguishing fact and comment*: Opinion is perfectly acceptable, but it must not be presented as fact. Rumours and unconfirmed reports must not be presented as fact (10.2 per cent of complaints in 2011 were based on this principle).

3 *Fairness and honesty*: Journalists must not gain information through harassment or deception and must attempt to present a balanced and truthful report (9.2 per cent of complaints in 2011 were based on this principle).

4 *Respect for rights*: Journalists must respect a person's good name and must not publish accusations without thoroughly checking facts (8.4 per cent of complaints in 2011 were based on this principle).

5 *Privacy*: Privacy is a human right which must be respected but must not prevent the investigation of matters of public interest. Publishing details of the private lives of those in the public eye is justified only when it relates to the person's credibility in public affairs (10.8 per cent of complaints in 2011 were based on this principle).

6 *Protection of sources*: Journalists must respect confidentiality of sources (there were no complaints based on this principle in 2011).

7 *Court reporting*: The presumption of 'innocent until proven guilty' must be respected and information must be recorded accurately so as not to deny a fair trial (1.9 per cent of complaints in 2011 were based on this principle).

8 *Prejudice*: Material likely to deeply offend or stir up hatred against a person on the grounds of race, religion, nationality, colour, ethnic origin, membership of the Travelling community, gender, sexual orientation, marital status, disability, illness or age should be avoided (23.5 per cent of complaints in 2011 were based on this principle).

9 *Children*: Publications must be particularly careful and sensitive in regard to publishing information involving children (2.7 per cent of complaints in 2011 were based on this principle).

10 *Publication of the decision of the Press Council/Press Ombudsman*: If requested, any decision on a complaint should be published (0.3 per cent of complaints in 2011 were based on this principle).

Summarised from Press Council of Ireland (website).

National Union of Journalists (NUJ) Guidelines on Race Reporting

In addition to the Code of Practice, the NUJ also has its own guidelines on race and reporting. They advise journalists:

• not to mention race or ethnicity unless it is relevant (the guidelines ask, 'Would you mention race if the person was white?')

- to think carefully about the words used and avoid stereotypes
- not to make assumptions about a person's cultural background
- not to sensationalise race issues
- not to promote prejudice and fear over asylum and immigration issues
- not to repeat statements without cross-checking with another source.

Summarised from NUJ (2007).

It should be noted that the guidelines and code of practice discussed above are only examples of best practice and are not legally binding.

Agenda Setting, Gatekeeping and Norm Setting

Of the many events that happen in the world each day, a certain few are selected to become 'news'. This gives an enormous amount of power and responsibility to those who decide what to report. 'Journalists and editors are not only gatekeepers of news events but also actively involved in the creation of news through the criteria by which they select "newsworthy" stories' (Marsh & Keating 2000:729).

The media have the power to highlight or ignore events, and only a small number of issues make it to the public's attention. 'There is no limit to what might be reported. The number of observable events is infinite . . . we often fail to realise what a very, very limited selection of events it is that appears on our table at breakfast time' (Whitaker (1981:23), cited in Marsh & Keating 2000:729). Being aware of the limited number of events that are reported may help us realise that we are offered a selective picture of the world. It can be argued that the media may present only one point of view, while neglecting others. We rely heavily on the media to tell us what to think and what to believe.

> The processes of agenda-setting, gate keeping and norm setting mean some events are simply not reported . . . some that are reported may be singled out for particularly unfavourable treatment . . . the mass media can decide what the important issues are, what 'news' is, what the public should and should not be concerned about, and what should or should not be regarded as 'normal' behaviour in society. (Browne 1992:168)

Agenda setting refers to the method by which the media select the agenda (subjects) for public discussion. They choose what to inform people about, and can choose to include or not include certain items. This in turn will influence public interest and public opinion. 'What they choose to include in or leave out . . . will influence the main topics of public discussion and public concern' (Browne 1992:155). Obviously not every issue can be covered, and local newspapers will often cover issues that are of interest to a smaller group of people, yet there are major world events that receive little or limited coverage.

Gate keeping is concerned with the exclusion of coverage of certain issues. Browne argues that issues that are damaging to the powerful and don't square with the business interests of the elite are often not reported:

> For example, strikes are widely reported (nearly always unfavourably), while industrial injuries and diseases . . . hardly ever get reported. This means there is more public concern with tightening up trade union laws to stop strikes than there is with improving health and safety laws. Similarly, black crime gets widely covered in the media, but little attention is paid to attacks on black people by white racists . . . A final example is the way welfare benefit 'fiddles' are widely reported but not tax evasion. (Browne 1992:156)

Norm setting is the process by which the media promote socially desirable behaviour and present certain groups as threatening. 'Norm-setting means the mass media emphasise and reinforce conformity to social norms, and seek to isolate those who do not conform by making them the victims of unfavourable public opinion' (Browne 1992:156).

According to Browne the media are active in both encouraging conformist behaviour and discouraging nonconformist behaviour. Nonconformist behaviour is presented in sensational stories of violence, riots and hooliganism. This coverage of the worst aspects of society convinces people that it is best to 'stay in line' and behave themselves, reinforces what is acceptable and respectable and emphasises the consequences of straying from core values. 'Politically, the ruling ideas set the agenda, excluding some possibilities and normalizing others so that they become "just common sense" . . . consequently, there is a striking lack of diversity within media messages' (Haralambos & Holborn 2004:835).

Browne argues that young people and people from ethnic minorities are 'frequently used as scapegoats for many of society's problems. Scapegoats are simply groups or individuals blamed for something which is not their fault' (Browne 1992:161). Stan Cohen argued that 'Young people have been used as scapegoats to create a sense of unity in society, by uniting the public against a common "enemy". Young people are relatively powerless, and an easily identifiable group to blame for all of society's ills' (cited in Browne 1992:163). Cohen's description of a scapegoat group as powerless and easily identifiable can easily be applied to ethnicity.

Activity

Read through a selection of newspapers, taking in not just the news, but any messages that are contained in each article. For example, who or what is it critical of or favourable towards? Who does it target as a reader? What sort of language does it use?

Moral Panics and Folk Devils

Exciting and sensational stories help to sell newspapers. Certain groups are pinpointed as being a threat to society and the media focus often leads to exaggeration and the creation of 'folk devils'. Folk devils are groups that are popularly seen as posing a major threat to society, and media labelling often causes an over-reaction, known as a moral panic. 'The folk devils become visible reminders of what we should not be' (Browne 1992:163), and are easy targets for outrage and hatred.

Examples given by Browne (1992) of folk devils and moral panics in the UK media are acid house parties and Aids in the 1980s; and joyriding and dangerous dogs in the 1990s. Irish examples would include divorce and family breakdown in the 1990s; and contemporary moral panics around gang violence, immigration and gay marriage.

Alia and Bull also mention the latest moral panic about new folk devils – asylum seekers. 'In recent years, representations of asylum seekers have merged with criminal imagery. In this scenario, refugees are portrayed as "bogus" and destined to "milk" the State of resources, or dangerous and motivated by criminal intent' (Weber (2002), cited in Alia & Bull 2005:26)

Kenyon points out that journalists' focus on asylum seekers is overwhelmingly negative, even when confronted with extreme examples. When the frozen body of an eight-year-old boy was found attached to the wheel arch of a plane that had arrived in England from Kenya, the media aim was to 'reassure' the public that if there had been any surviving stowaways, they would have been unable to escape from the airport undetected. There was 'not a mention of what drove him to cling on to a plane at 10,000 metres with barely a wisp of oxygen in temperatures of 60 degrees below' (Kenyon 2010).

Five recurring myths about asylum seekers presented by the media have been identified by Mollard (2001) and Baird (2002), cited in Alia and Bull (2005:27):

1 *The numbers myth*: The media exaggerate the number of people seeking asylum with phrases such as 'swamping' and 'flooding', which lead people into false beliefs about actual numbers. 'A 2005 survey found that the average person thinks asylum seekers and refugees make up about 23 per cent of the UK population, yet research shows the actual figure is 1.98 per cent' (*The Independent* (2005), cited in Alia & Bull 2005:27).

2 *The ineligibility myth*: The media claim that asylum seekers' claims are mostly bogus, but research shows that asylum seekers are motivated by push factors (fear in their own country) rather than pull factors (desire for a better lifestyle).

3 *The cost myth*: The media give an inaccurate picture of asylum seekers receiving better treatment and more benefits than the local population and ignores the contribution they could make in tax if they were allowed to work. Kenyon points

out that asylum seekers he spoke to were far from the 'dole-scroungers' portrayed by the press. 'They wanted to find work. Building, welding, cooking; to do nothing would be culturally unacceptable to them and an insult to the families waiting at home to share their earnings' (Kenyon 2010).

4 *The social cost myth*: The media present immigration as a threat to a country's way of life and stir up fears that newcomers will destroy the host country's culture and identity.

5 *The criminality myth*: Allegations are made linking asylum seekers to crime waves, while no proof or statistics are given to support this claim. One study in Kent showed a fall in the crime rate in a period when the number of asylum seekers in the area increased, but the media ignored this type of evidence. Kenyon points out that asylum seekers are often portrayed as criminals because they must pay organised gangs to bring them to another country, and questions are often asked about how they fund this. 'Firstly, people fleeing conflict or persecution have to use unorthodox methods to travel to countries of safety . . . they rely on professionals to get them out' (Kenyon 2010) .

Activity

Before reading the figures below, write down how many asylum applications you think are made each year in Ireland and how many are successful. Compare your estimate with the actual figures.

(There were 1,290 applications in 2011. Of 2,785 decisions made in 2010, 2,655 were rejected.)

Bias

Bias involves presenting a one-sided version of events, rather than being fair and balanced. In Britain, there are very few editors and journalists from ethnic minorities; proportionally far fewer than the ethnic mix who buy newspapers. White reporters dominate, 'with little understanding of the cultures and religions of the communities they were reporting' (Cole (2004), cited in Alia & Bull 2005:10). Most reporters and editors are white and male, so they may be biased, either deliberately or through ignorance.

Bias in the media can influence both the selection and the presentation of material. Apart from the content of each article, attention must also be paid to captions, headlines, photos and how far from the cover the article is placed. 'Years ago in the segregated South it was not uncommon for local newspapers to run all sex-crime accusations against blacks on page one, even if the incident took place on the other side of the country' (Steinhorn and Diggs-Brown 1999:594).

Headlines and captions are often not written by the reporter who researched and wrote the story, so may not accurately capture the full story. Headlines may also sensationalise and distort in order to grab the reader's attention. Research shows that many readers only glance through the headlines and do not read the full article (Thompson (1953, 1954, 1955), cited in Alia & Bull 2005). Alia and Bull found that headlines often feature ethnic labels, particularly in regard to violent and sexual offending, but 'white' is never used as a label. They quote examples from New Zealand newspapers: 'Maori's attack on white girl'; 'Maori guilty of murder'.

The language used is also of major importance. Often descriptions of events and people are not neutral but are designed to influence the reader's outlook. In 1991, *The Guardian* newspaper compiled a selection of words and phrases from various British media describing the British and Iraqi armies during the first week of the Gulf War in 1991. The comparison of the words used is an excellent example of how bias can influence perception.

BRITISH	IRAQIS
Army, navy and air force	War machine
Reporting guidelines	Censorship
Press briefings	Propaganda
Eliminate	Kill
Neutralise	Kill
Boys	Troops
Lads	Hordes
Professional	Brainwashed
Cautious	Cowardly
Confident	Desperate
Heroes	Cornered
Young Knights of the skies	Bastards of Baghdad
Loyal	Blindly obedient
Resolute	Ruthless
Brave	Fanatical
Collateral damage	Civilian casualties
Precision bomb	Fire wildly at anything in the sky

(Compiled by *The Guardian*, January 1991, quoted in Browne 1992:170).

The media can minimise public outrage by reporting events in a muted way. Naomi Wolf, writing on the media coverage of banking scandals, notes how 'bank fraud is portrayed as a case, when it surfaces, of a few "bad apples" gone astray' (Wolf 2012). She states that the evidence is of massive global banking fraud, yet instances are played down by the media and presented as mistakes and oversights rather than deliberate decisions. 'The mainstream media need to drop their narratives of "Gosh, another oversight". The financial sector's corruption must be recognised as systemic' (Wolf 2012).

While choosing to play down some events, the media can also choose to inflame public opinion by using language that is deliberately sensational and designed to cause outrage. The Parekh Report in Britain highlighted "'a series of increasingly vitriolic press campaigns. Targeted groups have included Tamils, Turkish Kurds and Somalis." The report quotes a Dover newspaper which lumps asylum seekers together with other undesirables. The paper said "illegal immigrants, asylum seekers, bootleggers and scum-of-the-earth drug smugglers . . . have targeted our beloved coastline. We are left with the backdraft of a nation's human sewage."' (Parekh *et al.*, quoted in Haralambos & Holborn 2004:162).

Activity

Try to make a list of words that are neutral and similar words that are more sensational and that might influence the reader towards a certain viewpoint. For example stated/revealed, asked/pleaded, criticised/slammed, angry/crazed . . .

The Media and Crime Reporting

'For many people, the news media are the principal source of information about 'law-and-order' issues (McGregor (1993), cited in Alia & Bull 2005:18). Sensational stories about crime often raise people's fears and can lead to distorted perceptions about the crime rate.

While actual events are reported, certain details may be omitted, giving an inaccurate picture. Black and Asian people are often invisible in the media, except in news reports on crime. This may give a misleading picture that every member of an ethnic group is involved in crime, instead of acknowledging that the majority spend their lives as peaceful citizens. 'These ethnic minorities often only appear in the media in the context of crime, drugs and inner city riots, as scapegoats on which to blame these problems' (Browne 1992:163).

'Bad news is more newsworthy than good news' (Haralambos & Holborn 2004:842), so we will see negative images of groups and if we do not know any of these groups in real life, we may assume that this is the entire picture. The stories may be true, but they are not representative of the whole group. Tabloids are seen as the worst offenders: 'Tabloid newspapers often stereotype the cultural values and norms of behaviour of some minority groups. Stories are frequently cast in terms of the threat posed by minority ethnic groups: by their increasing numbers or criminality' (Haralambos & Holborn 2004:853).

> **Activity**
>
> Read through a newspaper and note what crimes have been committed and by whom.
> Does crime reporting give an accurate picture of the society you live in?

Media Coverage of Refugees in Ireland

Print media is extremely influential in Ireland: Ireland has the highest per capita newspaper readership in Europe. In 2003 the National Consultative Committee on Racism and Interculturalism (NCCRI) and the Equality Authority produced a study that investigated media coverage of refugees and asylum seekers in Ireland. Their report claims that irresponsible newspaper coverage often fuels racism: 'Some tabloid newspapers continue to persist in presenting a misleading picture of asylum seekers' entitlements through totally unfounded claims of social welfare support for cars, mobile phones and entertainment allowances' (NCCRI & Equality Authority 2003:3).

Refugees are often perceived as liars, criminals and terrorists, and the media have at times been responsible for this perception. International conferences against racism highlight the importance of fair and accurate reporting, avoiding stereotyping, depicting diversity in society, avoiding labelling and not linking a person's origin to individual behaviour. Often the actions of an individual are used to stigmatise an entire group.

The report found that the use of the words 'flood' and 'tide' was common, with the implication that Ireland would be overwhelmed by an unstoppable force. Another common theme was the linking of asylum seekers with criminal activity. A particularly strong example was the headline from *The Star* on 13 June 1997: 'Refugee Rapists on the Rampage'. The article went on to state, 'Gardaí have warned women to stay away from refugees after a spree of sex assaults. Prostitutes and minors are the main targets of rapacious Romanians and Somalians, according to top Garda sources' (NCCRI & Equality Authority 2003:15). When questioned, the Gardaí stated that there was no such crime wave.

Many newspapers also reported that refugees were not genuine and were targeting the state for money rather than fleeing persecution. Some newspapers stated that asylum seekers were dressed in designer clothes. Another example, from the *Daily Mirror* (16 December 2002), stated: 'Free Cars for Refugees: Cash Grants buy BMWs' (NCCRI & Equality Authority 2003:17). Efforts were made to clear up this issue, with press statements issued by health boards, the Department of Social Protection and the Department of Justice, but such claims continue to be made.

Despite the NUJ guidelines on race reporting and the press Code of Practice, misleading reports continue to be written because headlines like those quoted above grab a reader's attention and so help sell papers. The journalist Nuala Haughey has argued, 'When it comes to racism, the ethical issue is pretty clear-cut. Journalists have a duty to not be racist, just as we have a duty to not be sexist. . . . New guidelines and codes are great things to have, but they are pretty useless if they are not implemented. Unfortunately, sections of the Irish media have been consistently flouting best practice in their coverage of the asylum/refugee/race issue in the past few years' (Haughey 2001, quoted in NCCRI & Equality Authority 2003:27).

There is a low risk of legal action being taken both because of the costs involved and the importance of a free press. Some attempts have been made to prosecute journalists under the Prohibition of Incitement to Hatred Act, but the cases did not go to court.

Summarised from NCCRI & Equality Authority (2003).

Activity

The old sayings 'Mud sticks' and 'There's no smoke without fire' suggest that once an image has been formed, it is very difficult to erase. Discuss whether and how it is possible to correct misleading information and negative images once they have been established.

Ethnic Minority Press

There are a number of publications in Ireland specifically aimed at migrant communities. *Metro Éireann* is a weekly newspaper, both printed and online, which was set up by two Nigerian journalists, Chinedu Onyejelem and Abel Ugba, in April 2000. Both men came to Ireland as asylum seekers and were granted refugee status. The newspaper focuses on immigrant and ethnic communities.

Polski Express is an online magazine in Polish and English aimed at the Polish community in Ireland. It is particularly aimed at Polish people who have already settled here and 'for whom Ireland has become their second home' (www.polskiexpress.ie) rather than meeting the needs of new arrivals.

Other publications include *Nasha Gazeta*, a Russian language fortnightly newsletter, and the *Sun Emerald*, a weekly Chinese newspaper.

Ethic Minority Representation in Magazines

The fashion industry – including fashion magazines – has been criticised for its representation of ethnicity, for the scarcity of ethnic models featured and the presentation of these models. White models are most often used and where non-white models are used they are often presented in a particular stereotypical way. For example, South American models are often 'portrayed as being sultry and seductive . . . growling or purring or doing something else that's totally fierce' (Alvarez 2008). Black models used are often lighter-skinned with straightened hair, while Asian models very often have pale complexions. White models are chosen for a specific standard of beauty: 'The gold standard of white beauty is a woman who is thought of as being the least "ethnic" and most "neutral" as possible. Fair skin, fair hair and thin, often lacking in curves' (Alvarez 2008).

Despite the success of some high-profile black models such as Naomi Campbell and Tyra Banks, model agents have stated that it is difficult to find work on photo shoots and fashion runways for black models. An English agent stated, 'We have had casting briefs which say "no ethnics". But we are better in London than Paris and Milan; there if you offer a black girl they will drop the book like it's hot' (Sharp 2008).

However, Solomos and Back state that there have been major changes in ethnic representation in the media. 'A particularly important change is the increased use of multicultural images. As world markets have become more global, some advertisers have used multicultural images to associate their products with an anti-racist stance, as well as trying to make them appeal to a wide variety of people' (quoted in Haralambos & Holborn 2004:193). Adverts with multicultural images are a good indicator of a more diverse society, yet they can cause controversy. Haralambos and Holborn describe how a series of Benetton ads produced very different and even extreme reactions. In one advert, 'The hands of a black man and a white man are shown handcuffed together. In the USA people complained because it conjured up images of slavery, and in the USA and Britain some people associated the image with black criminality. In France a racist group threw a tear-gas cylinder into a Benetton shop after Benetton released a poster of a black woman breastfeeding a white baby' (Haralambos & Holborn 2004:193).

In 2007, the American magazine *Glamour* was involved in a controversy around race. An associate editor of the magazine, Ashley Baker, was giving a presentation on corporate fashion when she dismissed wearing black hair naturally with the comment, 'Just say no to the "fro". . . . No offense, but those political hairstyles really have to go.' There were many complaints made to the magazine, which led to Baker resigning and a front page apology from the editor.

The issue of beauty for black women is complex, as lighter skin and smooth hair have often been seen as preferable to a more natural look. 'African-American women who

chose to wear their natural hair have been stigmatized over the years' (Reese, quoted in Dorning 2007). Many black women straighten their hair, chemically and electrically, but it has been argued that this is not a straightforward choice, that it is to do with what is considered an 'acceptable' look. 'Over the years corporations ranging from MCI Communications to American Airlines have been sued because black women said that they were fired for wearing their hair in braids or dreadlocks' (Dorning 2007). Black women are seen as more acceptable, in everyday life as well as in the workforce, if their look conforms to society's standards. 'More corporate environments are accepting ethnic hairdos, but others quietly regard them as "unprofessional"' (Padgett 2007).

However, others have argued that conservative hairstyles, for any ethnicity, are most appropriate in a workplace. Padgett quotes a black businessman who disagrees that it is a racial issue: 'White guys can't wear mohawks, women can't wear dreadlocks like Whoopi Goldberg' (Padgett 2007).

Summarised from Alvarez (2008); Dorning (2007); Haralambos & Holborn (2004); Padgett (2007); Sharp (2008).

Activities

1 In 2008, Rob Sharp reported that 'The March issue of *Vogue* – with more than 400 pages of editorial and advertising – has 14 shots with black or Asian women – two of them featuring Naomi Campbell. This month's 362-page *Marie Claire* has eight photographs featuring black women and four examples are in the current 312-page *Glamour* magazine.'

   Look through some current issues of fashion magazines and see how many ethnic models are used. Also note how they are presented – do they conform to a European ideal of beauty?

2 Discuss whether you agree or disagree that 'ethnic' hair is not suitable for the workplace.

Revision questions

1 Why are the media so important in forming our outlook?

2 List three types of newspaper.

3 What does the Defamation Act protect against?

4 Outline the role of the Press Ombudsman.

5 Describe three principles of the Code of Practice for Newspapers and Magazines.

6 Explain the terms 'agenda setting' and 'gatekeeping'.

7 Explain the term 'folk devil' and give three examples of folk devils through the decades.

8 Describe the representation in magazines of people from minority ethnic groups.

CHAPTER 8

Ethnicity and Culture in Television, Cinema and Music

By the end of this chapter, students should:

- Be aware of the difference between primary and secondary sources.
- Be aware of the responsibilities of state broadcaster RTÉ concerning minorities.
- Be aware of the importance of properly representing ethnicity, both in children's television and in news programming.
- Be able to discuss representations of race in current cinema.

Primary and Secondary Sources

Studying culture and cultural change often involves examining primary and secondary sources. Primary and secondary sources are not to be confused with primary and secondary data (outlined in Chapter 4).

- A *primary source* is any record, document or object that was made during a particular time. For example, if we were researching society during World War II, primary sources would include any photos, newspapers, diaries, films, books and documents from that time.

- A *secondary source* is removed from the time it relates to, makes use of primary sources and often examines and interprets the era from a distance. For example, films such as *Schindler's List* and *The Wind that Shakes the Barley* revisit incidents from the past but do not immediately reflect the values and attitudes of that time.

Examining primary sources such as television, film and music can help us understand how culture has changed and what are the dominant images of our time. Cultural attitudes are often reflected in television, cinema and music. As well as reflecting a culture, they may also help to shape people's ideas and attitudes.

Summarised from Princeton University (website).

Television and Culture

Television is an enormous part of people's lives and the images they see help form and reinforce attitudes and beliefs. Gatekeeping, agenda setting and norm setting (see Chapter 7) operate within visual media, such as film and television.

RTÉ

RTÉ is the Irish state public service broadcaster and is funded both by advertising and by the public through the television licence fee. Among the guiding principles in its Public Service Broadcasting Charter (published by the Department of Communications, Marine and Natural Resources (DCMNR)) are: to avoid bias; to be fully representative of its viewers; 'to reflect fairly and equally the regional, cultural and political diversity of Ireland and its peoples'; and that 'no editorial or programming bias shall be shown in terms of gender, age, disability, race, sexual orientation, religion or membership of a minority community' (DCMNR 2004:2).

The terms of its charter require RTÉ to cater for minority interests as well as those of the majority. The charter states the aim to provide programmes that are 'socially inclusive and shall reflect the lives and concerns of all social strata in Ireland' (DCMNR 2004:3) and acknowledges 'a responsibility to reflect the full range and diversity of cultures within Ireland' (DCMNR 2004:4).

However, RTÉ has recently been criticised by Justice Minister Alan Shatter for not recognising or representing the change in Irish society. 'If we hear anything about integration or issues relating to new communities it's usually in the context of conflict or difficulty as opposed to the positive contributions that are being made. It's time we saw faces on RTÉ which represent the Ireland of 2012 rather than the Ireland of 1980' (Shatter, quoted by Reilly 2012).

Others, such as the editor of *Metro Éireann*, have also criticised the lack of coverage of cultural diversity on RTÉ programmes: 'I don't think it is right for RTÉ to be giving us travel programmes in the name of intercultural programmes, I believe they need to do more' (Onyejelem, quoted by Reilly 2012). In response to these criticisms, RTÉ has stated that its staff profile did need to better reflect a diverse population.

RTÉ has had one intercultural programme, *Mono*, which was hosted by ethnic minority presenters, but the programme was scrapped in 2006. Shalini Sinha, one of the hosts of *Mono*, expressed her disappointment with RTÉ. 'It's incorrect to pretend that Ireland has moved forward so much that a dedicated intercultural programme is no longer needed. We certainly have not. I fear that this shows in RTÉ either the result of a lack of awareness of the real situation or a lack of commitment to the type of intercultural programming that is really needed' (Sinha, quoted in *Metro Éireann* 2007). She went on to say that 'courage and leadership' are needed to have ethnic minority presenters on Irish television, and that it is up to the state broadcaster to show such leadership.

In 2007, Rotimi Adebari, who became the first black mayor in Ireland, stated his belief in the importance of representing ethnic minorities on television. 'RTÉ could start by reflecting the diversity this country now enjoys . . . I expect RTÉ to take the leading role – the acceptance is not going to happen overnight, but it is achievable' (Adebari, quoted in *Metro Éireann* 2007).

Summarised from DCMNR (2004); *Metro Éireann* (2007); Reilly (2012).

Activity

Compare the representations of ethnic minorities in British and Irish television soaps. Keep a notebook near the television and note which ethnic groups are represented and how they are represented. Compare and discuss how each programme represents a diverse society.

Children's Television

Studies have shown that children learn from an early age who is favoured or not favoured in society. 'We know from research evidence that by the time they enter primary school, white children may well be on the road to believing that they are superior' (CRE (1989), cited in Webb & Tossell 1999:91). They form these attitudes not just from their parents, but also from the programmes and movies they watch.

The success of *Dora the Explorer* has been seen by some commentators as a positive step in representing ethnicity on children's television. The creation of Dora was in direct response to a noticeable lack of bilingual and ethnic minority characters. 'Nickelodeon paid more attention to the growing diversity of their audiences and a study reported on the lack of bilingual characters on children's television, the network suggested that creators consider making the title character a Latina' (Tapia 2010). This was particularly important in the USA, where the portrayal of Latino/Hispanic American people by the media is often negatively associated with crime. The show's producers also hired advisers to ensure that the show accurately reflects Hispanic culture and they hope that the success of a bilingual character with a dark skin tone will influence children to be more open. One of the consultants expressed his hope that this will be the case: 'The Latino kids take pride having Dora as a lead character and non-Latino kids can embrace someone different. . . You can't be certain, but our hope is that young people of all backgrounds will be more open. If Dora can do that, her impact is unimaginable' (Cortes, quoted in Tapia 2010).

Summarised from Tapia (2010); Webb & Tossell (1999).

> **Activity**
>
> Think of the television programmes you watched as a child. Did they present a diverse or mono-ethnic world? Discuss what cultural messages were contained in the programmes and how the content of American/British/Irish programmes differed.

Ethnicity and News

In 1961, Langston Hughes stated, 'The only time coloured folks is front-page news is when there's been a race riot or a lynching or a whole lot of us have been butchered up or arrested' (Hughes 1961, quoted in Jandt 2004). Some would say that little has changed and that the only time minorities are mentioned is in connection with crime.

When a group is only highlighted in relation to negative events, the result is to give a distorted image in the minds of those who have no direct experience of the group. There are so many images of whiteness associated with power, respectability and wealth that when we hear of a white person committing a crime, we limit the crime to the individual rather than associating it with an entire group. But other groups whose positive achievements are ignored are likely to become labeled as villains.

> The entertainment media have displayed a fascination with Latino gangs, while the news media nationwide have given them extensive coverage. In contrast, the entertainment media have offered a comparatively narrow range of other Latino characters, while the news media have provided relatively sparse coverage of other Hispanic topics, except for such problem issues as immigration and language. The result has been a Latino public image – better yet, a stereotype – in which gangs figure prominently. (Cortes 1987)

Where the majority is in regular contact with the minority, this is not a problem because personal knowledge of the group will cancel out any impact of media images. However, if people get all their information regarding a particular group from the media, this can be problematic: 'First, whether intentionally or unintentionally, both the news and the entertainment media "teach" the public about minorities. . . . Second, this mass media curriculum has a particularly powerful educational impact on people who have little or no direct contact with members of the groups being treated' (Cortes 1987).

The news media deal with such a large amount of constantly changing material that there is a lack of space and time for complex issues or representing groups that are outside the mainstream:

> Day-to-day coverage, which doesn't produce the same attention grabbing headlines but provides on-going information that enables the broader picture

to emerge, is ignored in favor of 'violence and melodrama, the circus of the moment. . . . The result is only the affluent get covered regularly and the poor, which generally means minorities, disappear from the news except in dramatic moments' (Bagdikian, quoted in Rifkin 1988).

Also, the desire to present a dramatic, attention-grabbing news item means that that the most extreme section of a crowd or the most outspoken member of a group will be the one represented on the news. If a thousand people are protesting, and a scuffle breaks out among twenty of them, the camera will focus on the scuffle and relay that image to the world.

American NBC reporter Paula Walker believes that reporting the colour of a suspect on a news report only increases racial fear. She says: 'Typically, a reporter describing a crime will dutifully draw on the police report, which might list the suspect as a black male, five-eight, 160 pounds' (Walker, quoted in Steinhorn & Diggs-Brown 1999:593). However, there might be thousands of people walking about who fit that description and so the result is only to increase fear of the black population, while not giving enough information to help identify the suspect. 'To her, there would be nothing wrong with including race if the description also mentioned specific clothing, hair style, identifying characteristics such as a scar or a limp, and the neighborhood in which the suspect was last seen. Skin color then becomes relevant and serves a purpose' (Steinhorn & Diggs-Brown 1999:593).

Steinhorn and Diggs-Brown (1999) note that research findings clearly show that there is a distorted picture on American news programmes. Studies showed that the percentage of African-Americans shown as suspects in Los Angeles was well above the percentage of crimes committed by African-Americans and that although most victims of violent crime are of the same race as the attacker, the majority of perpetrators shown on the news were non-white and the majority of victims shown were white. This is related to the fact that more interest was shown in stories about white victims – these stories lasted 74 per cent longer than those on non-white victims. The message that is broadcast is that 'whites are vulnerable to crime, blacks are responsible for it' (Steinhorn and Diggs-Brown 1999:595).

Also, even when accused of similar crimes, there was a different portrayal of blacks than of whites. 'Whites arrested for crimes might be shown next to their attorneys, if they are shown at all, whereas blacks tend to be shown in handcuffs, on police walks, or being physically restrained by the police' (Steinhorn & Diggs-Brown 1999:594). Steinhorn and Diggs-Brown also note that names of white suspects are more often mentioned than black suspects, 'leading one scholar to conclude that the individual identity of black suspects is less important than their race' (Steinhorn & Diggs-Brown 1999:594).

News as entertainment tends to sensationalise and dramatise events. The need to provide viewer interest does not encourage an accurate picture of daily life. Steinhorn and Diggs-Brown argue that despite the increased visibility of people from minorities on television as actors and presenters, which may be a helpful step in integration, the emphasis on ethnic crime prevents any real integration because many people's perceptions are shaped by unbalanced reporting. This is not to say that crimes should not be reported, but care needs to be taken to be accurate: 'It is true that blacks commit a disproportionate share of violent crimes, especially in urban areas, but it is also true that blacks are identified with criminal acts on television all out of proportion to the number they commit . . . the relentless association between blacks and crime on the news has colored white perceptions of blacks and has seriously undermined any hope for racial integration in America' (Steinhorn & Diggs-Brown 1999:593).

Summarised from Cortes (1987); Jandt (2004); Rifkin (1988); Steinhorn & Diggs-Brown (1999).

Activity

Watch a selection of Irish, British and American news reports. Describe and discuss how their approach and style differs, and which style of reporting appeals to you most.

Cinema and Race

Mainstream film often represents a very limited view of society. In the past, unflattering stereotypical images were extremely common and some say they still are. 'Hollywood represents all ethnic identities according to semiotic codes, the most obvious of which are ethnic stereotypes such as the Latin lover, the lazy or lovable Irish' (Davies & Smith 1997).

Even if today's images are far from perfect, there has been considerable improvement in representing ethnicity. D. W. Griffith's 1915 silent film *Birth of a Nation*, set during the Civil War, is commonly cited as one of the most offensive films ever made, for its portrayal of black people as inferior, stupid, violent and lazy. The film depicts a Southern plantation where the slaves are extremely happy, dancing and singing in perfect contentment. The Southern family, the Camerons, are good friends with a Northern abolitionist family, the Stonemans. A son from each family falls in love with a daughter of the other. The Civil War intervenes but soon the families have re-established their friendships and romances.

The white characters are presented as noble, loyal and thoughtful, while the newly freed slaves are portrayed as running riot without the restraining hands of their masters. The film's main black character, the former slave Gus, attacks and attempts to rape a white woman, who jumps off a cliff in order to escape him. A black mob then attacks the Camerons, who are saved by the Ku Klux Klan. The finale of the film sees the two families united in marriage, the Klan triumphant over the black 'baddies' and the figure of Jesus standing approvingly over the scene. 'The film represents the granting of civil rights to blacks as catastrophic' (Davies & Smith 1997).

Films of this era were also extremely offensive to other ethnic groups. 'Hispanics, known as "greasers" in such silent films as *Tony the Greaser* (1911), experienced similar treatment in early silents' (Woll 1988).

Treatment of minorities in film improved during World War II, when the emphasis lay on presenting a united image to improve wartime morale. Progress in the civil rights movement also meant less negative portrayal on the big screen; but this does not mean that it is no longer an issue today. Cultural attitudes may have changed hugely, but critics say that diversity is still limited in Hollywood. Below we discuss a selection of recent films that deal with issues of race and have received both praise and criticism for their attempts to portray diversity.

Summarised from Davies & Smith (1997); Sparknotes (www.sparknotes.com); Woll (1988).

Dances with Wolves

'Cowboys and Indians' films of the 1930s to the 1950s often showed a very inaccurate and biased picture of life in frontier America. The cruelty and unfairness with which Native Americans were treated was completely overlooked and they were portrayed as aggressors while the white settlers and US Cavalry were presented as heroic. 'Many of these films distorted the truth; they showed the cowboys as always good and the Indians as always bad, when the opposite was often the case. But the popularity of Westerns was unrivalled by any other film type' (Neill 1975:91). Most audiences would have watched such films with an uncritical eye, and taken in the message that the colonisation of America by white settlers was completely justified. Films such as *The Searchers* and *Stagecoach* present stereotypical scenarios of Native Americans as aggressors.

Modern films such as *Dances with Wolves* are more sympathetic and realistic in their portrayal of the American frontier. The writer of *Dances with Wolves*, Michael Blake, states that he had strong memories of watching stereotypical Westerns as a child and wanted to tell a different story. 'Indians were widely portrayed as devils, whose destruction was purely a matter of necessity in the process of taming the West. Every publication or film I saw as a child was slanted in this way' (Blake (1990), cited in Summerfield & Lee 2001:19).

Native Americans had been continuously pushed west by settlers. By the 1860s,there were around 300,000 Native Americans living in the West and they may have finally been left in peace there as the land was undesirable. However, when gold was discovered in California there was a sudden rush to the West by Europeans and a number of military forts were established there. The Sioux tribe tried to resist this last expansion and the Sioux wars were fought for nearly 15 years. European representations of Native Americans showed only the ferocity of the Sioux tribe, ignoring the reasons for their desperate fight. The stereotypical image of them as savage and bloodthirsty ignored their individuality and culture: 'They are rarely given names or personalities, do not speak English or any other language (but do emit fierce sounds or grunts), and relish killing and scalping whites' (Summerfield & Lee 2001:27).

Most films portrayed all Native Americans as identical, ignoring the differences between different tribes. *Dances with Wolves* was one of the first movies to attempt to show the variety and differences between various tribes. It focused on the Pawnee and Lakota tribes. The film broke the mould by portraying Native Americans in a more rounded way, using the Sioux language in parts of the film, using Native American actors for the roles and paying attention to historical and cultural detail.

The film-makers sought specialist advice and undertook research to attempt to make the film as authentic as possible, even using traditional techniques to make the costumes and sets. Knowledge of cultural practices was used: for example, Native American widows would often make small cuts on themselves as part of their custom of grieving and this was reflected by a character in the film. The Native Americans were represented sympathetically, with attention paid to the values of their society and the unfairness of their treatment.

However, the film received strong criticism from some reviewers. Some pointed out that being historically accurate and presenting positive images is not very relevant or helpful to modern-day Native Americans, a third of whom live in poverty, with alcoholism, suicide and infant mortality rates three times the national average. Critics also noted that while the Lakota were shown positively as the 'good Indians', the Pawnee were represented as the stereotypical 'baddies', and that Dunbar, the white man, is always shown as the hero, saving the tribe at many points. One reviewer, Michael Dorris, wondered if the popularity of the film would result in anything positive, such as health clinics on reservations; or 'will it turn out once again, that the only good Indians – the only Indians whose causes and needs we can embrace – are lodged safely in the past, wrapped neatly in the blanket of history, magnets for our sympathy because they require nothing of us but tears in a dark theatre?' (Dorris (1991), cited in Summerfield & Lee 2001:32.

Summarised from Neill (1975); Summerfield & Lee (2001).

Slumdog Millionaire

India has its own Bollywood film industry and stars, but most of these stars and films remain unknown in the West. Most western-made big box office hits set in India have a white hero or heroine, with ethnic characters acting only as sidekicks or extras. Danny Boyle's *Slumdog Millionaire* was unusual because it featured an all-Indian cast. Audiences responded hugely to the love story, proving that ethnic stars can carry a mainstream film. It also highlighted extreme poverty and desperation, again unusual in a mainstream film. Despite being an eye-opener to many in its revelation of the inequalities in Indian society and the desperation of the very poor, it has also been criticised for ignoring the enormous issue of caste.

Under the caste system in India people's social position is set at birth. There can be no change in this social position: marriage between castes is forbidden; there is no social contact; even a person's occupation is determined by caste. Because the caste system is based on religious belief, it has proved difficult to make any changes in this system. There are five major castes: Brahmins, who are the highest caste of priests and other religious figures; Kshatriya, who are the rulers and administrators; Vaisya, who are merchants and farmers; Sudras, who do manual work; and the Dalits (Untouchables), who are social outcasts and do the lowest type of work (Browne 1992:12).

It has been pointed out that 90 per cent of the poorest people in Indian society are Dalits and that if the main character in the film, Jamal, had been a Dalit, it would have been impossible for him to overcome his situation. Varma (2009) points out that the difficulties faced by the hero and heroine, such as forced prostitution, scavenging on rubbish tips and being kept and mutilated by 'beggar masters', are most likely to happen to those of the Dalit caste. Varma states that the decision to portray Jamal as a Muslim, rather than a Dalit, was a missed opportunity for highlighting this issue.

Summarised from Browne (1992); Varma (2009).

The Help

The Help tells the story of black maids in the segregated Deep South of the USA during the civil rights era. A young white woman, Skeeter Phelan, who has recently returned home from college, encourages the maids to tell her their stories, revealing the unfairness with which they are treated by their white employers. It is an important film, because it serves to inform and remind people of issues and events that should be remembered, and also reminds us that although race relations are still difficult there has been huge improvement. 'Race relations have changed so radically in America over the last half-century that it's difficult for today's young to grasp how contentious and hate-filled things were, especially in the Deep South, during the later years of Jim Crow' (Berardinelli 2012).

Compared with earlier films that featured black characters, it also shows how much attitudes have changed. The maids Aibileen and Minny are presented as warm, funny, thoughtful and well-rounded, in contrast to earlier, mostly comic, representations of black women, such as 'Mammy' in *Gone with the Wind*.

The film has been criticised, for despite being about the experiences of the black maids, the central character is Skeeter. As with *Dances with Wolves*, which features a white hero, *The Help* is largely focused on the story of the white heroine. The maids' own stories are 'structured largely around their white female benefactor. That this is the story we keep telling ourselves is all the more puzzling – if not galling – when viewers consider that, precisely at the time that *The Help* transpires, African Americans across

Mississippi were registering to vote and agitating for political change. In other words, they were helping themselves' (Hornaday 2011).

It has also been accused of ignoring complex issues, such as how children raised by loving black nannies grow up to become racist themselves. 'The psychology of this query is too complicated for a film so hell-bent on jerking easy tears and capturing a wide audience' (Longworth 2011).

Summarised from Berardinelli (2012); Hornaday (2011); Longworth (2011).

Crash

Crash is a multi-ethnic film, featuring white, black, Hispanic, Korean and Iranian characters, all intertwined through being both victims and perpetrators of racism. It highlights how prejudice prevents people not only from empathising with each other but actually from seeing each other's personality at all and portrays how racism invades people's everyday lives on subtle and not so subtle levels. 'It shows the way we all leap to conclusions based on race – yes, all of us, of all races, and however fair-minded we may try to be – and we pay a price for that' (Ebert 2005).

The film tackles issues of modern-day prejudice that are often not discussed, and presents both sides of the argument – both the discriminators and the discriminated against are presented as fully rounded and complex characters, rather than just 'hero' or 'villain'. 'Apart from a few brave scenes in Spike Lee's work, Crash is the first movie I know of to acknowledge not only that the intolerant are also human but, further, that something like white fear of black street crime, or black fear of white cops, isn't always irrational' (Denby, quoted in Hoggard 2005). Hoggard states that Crash is a daring film because Hollywood generally steers clear of race issues, unless they are safely confined to history, so that the problem is presented as already solved.

However, Crash has also been criticised for being too simplistic: the notion in the film that everybody is prejudiced in their own way presents individuals' beliefs but ignores real issues of ongoing institutional racism. 'The film seems designed, at a deeper level, to make white people feel better. . . . In Crash, emotion trumps analysis, and psychology is more important than politics. The result: White people are off the hook' (Jensen & Wosnitzer 2007). Critics also note that in one scene the white policeman, Officer Ryan, sexually assaults a black woman, Christine, but is later redeemed and presented as a hero for saving Christine's life after a car accident. 'Ryan somehow magically overcomes his racism' (Jensen & Wosnitzer 2007).

Summarised from Ebert (2005); Hoggard (2005); Jensen & Wosnitzer (2007).

Activities

1   *Dances with Wolves* and *The Help* have been criticised for having a 'white saviour' as the central character. Many films about ethnic and racial issues contain a central white character to increase box office appeal. Think of any films you have seen that contain 'white saviours' and discuss reasons why such characters are common.

2   Watch the films listed above and discuss whether you agree or disagree with the reviewers' criticisms.

Casting Ethnic Minority Actors

Many ethnic minority actors have complained about the lack of roles, especially central roles, in Hollywood movies. Dev Patel, star of the hugely popular *Slumdog Millionaire* complained that even after the enormous success of the film 'he struggled to find work . . . because he did not want to play the usual "Asian" roles in Hollywood: terrorists, taxi drivers and geeks' (quoted in Child 2010). He said that before *Slumdog*, the last movie about India that was a mainstream success was *Gandhi* in 1982, so his choice of roles remained limited. He was not content with playing 'the goofy Indian sidekick' but was hopeful that this would not be his only option: 'I have to be realistic. Being an Asian actor, it's never going to be easy . . . Hopefully the industry is changing and the casting directors will be less focused on colour so people like myself can get through the door' (Child 2010).

Meanwhile, even when there are ethnic minority roles, they are often played by white actors in a process known as 'whitewashing' or 'racelifting'. Many recently released films have been criticised for this type of casting, for example *The Last Airbender*, in which many Asian characters are played by white actors; *Essential Killing*, which features the Italian American actor Vincent Gallo as a Taliban soldier; and *The Prince of Persia* starring Jake Gyllenhaal. Others have been annoyed that Angelina Jolie has been cast in a forthcoming film about Cleopatra, arguing that a black role should go to a black woman: 'Honestly, I don't care how full Angelina Jolie's lips are, how many African children she adopts, or how bronzed her skin will become for the film, I firmly believe this role should have gone to a Black woman' (comment quoted in Goldberg 2012). The recent film *Extraordinary Measures* was based on the true story of a couple seeking a cure for their children's rare genetic disease. The father persuades a gifted specialist doctor to work on the disease, which results in the development of effective medical treatment. The doctor is played by Harrison Ford, but the real-life doctor is Yuan-Tsong Chen, who is from Taiwan.

The reasons for this 'whitewashing' are commercial: 'The way Hollywood sees it, the more people who identify with a character, the more tickets a movie might sell' (Benshoff, quoted in Goldberg 2012). It is assumed that a white audience has a limited interest in looking at ethnic minority faces, so using white actors to play ethnic minority characters continues in mainstream Hollywood. When the plot revolves around non-white people, the use of a 'white saviour' guarantees that the central focus will be on a white character. Even in the 1982 film *Cry Freedom*, based on the life of black activist Steve Biko in apartheid-era South Africa, the story revolves largely around white journalist Donald Woods. 'Hollywood, and the film industry at large, seem to think that brown faces aren't sellable' (Peterson, quoted in Rose 2011).

Where a character's ethnicity is not explicitly stated, many directors and producers assume that a character is white and cast them as such. The limited roles for which ethnic minority actors are seen as suitable are often stereotypical: 'Time after time, black actors are cast as welfare recipients, criminals and domestic help; Asian actors as launderers and exotics; Latino actors as gang members and drug dealers; Native American actors are seldom seen at all' (Mitchell 1987).

Rodney Mitchell outlines how the casting process ensures that most actors seen are white. Agents receive a cast breakdown sheet that briefly describes the characters; then the agents submit photographs; and the directors and producers audition those who interest them. If the character description does not specifically state the character's ethnicity, agents assume that the character is white and so submit only photos of white actors. 'Longstanding industry axioms encourage many talent agents to avoid submitting minority actors unless they are specifically requested. So minority actors are denied access to even the initial interviews and auditions, which prevents them, of course, from being considered at all' (Mitchell 1987).

Summarised from Child (2010); Goldberg (2012); Leigh (2010), Mitchell (1987), Rose (2011).

Wuthering Heights and *The Hunger Games*

Even where the text indicates that a character is other than white, many film adaptations of books cast white actors in the roles. This is often not commented on, yet if a character who is generally perceived to be white is played by a non-white actor, it sparks much controversy and comment.

Emily Brontë's novel *Wuthering Heights* has been filmed many times, but a recent version directed by Andrea Arnold caused controversy by casting a black actor as Heathcliff. The decision seemed mystifying as most people have never thought of Heathcliff as anything other than white, but close examination of the text suggests that Arnold's casting decision might be more appropriate than previous versions. Heathcliff is referred to as 'a dark-skinned gypsy' and 'a little Lascar' (an Indian/Asian sailor) throughout the book; when he first arrives he does not speak English; and in one section, Nelly tells him, 'Who knows, but your father was Emperor of China, and your mother an Indian queen' (quoted in Pols 2012). Quotes such as these lead us to believe that Heathcliff is certainly not white, is most likely of mixed race parentage, yet this content in the text had been ignored in previous film adaptations. The director states: 'I think the only reason people are surprised is that they've just seen white Heathcliffs all the time and I don't think anyone's really concentrated on the text' (Arnold, quoted in Rose 2011).

What is interesting is that while Arnold's casting looked strange at first, it is stranger that nobody had ever considered it odd to repeatedly cast white actors without paying attention to what was written. 'Even though Brontë passed away in 1848, one can easily imagine the writer turning in her grave at the prospect of so many white actors portraying her "little Lascar" throughout history. . . . It suggests a certain amount of arrogance, and even cowardice on behalf of directors who were not prepared, or too fearful of audience reception, to

give the role to an actor whose ethnicity came anywhere close to matching that of the character' (Onanuga 2011).

The film *The Hunger Games* has also drawn attention recently for its choice of actors. The characters Thresh and Rue are played by black actors and many fans of the book tweeted their disappointment at seeing black actors play characters they had imagined as white. Yet Thresh and Rue were specifically described in the book as having dark skin. 'Despite certain character descriptions being spelled out in the book . . . people typically project themselves onto a character in order to empathize with that person' (Goldberg 2012). Therefore white readers had ignored indications of dark skin and imagined the characters in their own image. 'Readers of *The Hunger Games* are so blind as to skip over the author's specific details and themes of appearance, race, and class . . . the heroes in our imaginations are white until proven otherwise' (Holmes 2012).

Others have expressed disappointment at the casting of Katniss, whose character was described as having dark hair and olive skin but was played by a blonde actress who had to dye her hair and darken her skin for the part. 'A lot of things are wrong with making Katniss white. Most importantly, this decision says, loud and clear, that unless explicitly stated to be a person of color, a character is white. Unless a character says to the readers "I'm Native American", or "I'm black", that character is white' (Schueler 2012). Summarised from Goldberg (2012); Pols (2012); Schueler (2012); www.wuthering-heights.co.uk.

Music and Culture

An important aspect of culture is shared history and experience. The music of a people often reflects and shapes their culture, especially in societies where the population is largely illiterate and music becomes a way of communicating and preserving stories.

Irish Ballads: Emigration and Oppression

Many traditional Irish songs illustrate the shared experience of colonisation, poverty and emigration. Traditional Irish songs contain much sadness:

> . . . laments, long threnodies of grief and exile, banishments, hunger, disease and death and hopeless rebellions, the sad ways of our Irish life, elegies for those who emigrated and dirges for those who stayed behind. There is, though, an element of celebration in the songs, acknowledgement of endurance and survival. . . . Through these songs we learn our history. (Devlin, quoted in Dunne 2001)

Many songs recall the Famine and remind people of the horror of the situation:

> *The Great Hunger*
> In 1848
> The sky was blacker than was ever seen
> Hanging low above the country
> Dealing out her blackest queen
> Food was plenty for the gentry
> Fever raging through the fold
> Hoping that the coming winter
> Burn the demon from the ground. (Lyrics quoted in Dunne 2001)

'The Fields of Athenry' recalls Lord Trevelyan (see Chapter 6), who was in charge of distributing aid to Ireland during the Famine and also ensured that the export of corn continued. His attitude toward the Irish was that they deserved their fate, having brought it on themselves by their bad character. 'The judgement of God sent the calamity to teach the Irish a lesson, that calamity must not be too much mitigated. . . . The real evil with which we have to contend is not the physical evil of the Famine, but the moral evil of the selfish, perverse and turbulent character of the people' (quoted in O'Riordan).

The song concerns a Galway man sentenced to transportation for stealing corn for his starving family, and it contains the lines:

> By the lonely prison wall I heard a young girl calling,
> 'Michael, they are taking you away,
> For you stole Trevelyan's corn,
> So the young might see the morn,
> Now a prison ship lies waiting in the bay' (St John 1979)

The popularity of the song ensures that the name of Trevelyan is still remembered. His great great-great-granddaughter was a reporter in Ireland in the 1990s and recalled how the name was still remembered with anathema: '. . . she asked if I was related to Charles Trevelyan . . . I said I was and she asked me how I could live in Ireland when I had the blood of the Irish on my hands. She wasn't joking . . . I was constantly surprised by the amount of people who knew about Charles Trevelyan and the impact that the famine has in Ireland, more than 150 years later' (Laura Trevelyan, quoted in Meagher 2006).

Songs of emigration show the loneliness of those who have gone abroad and the regret for what they have left behind. Ireland has a long history of emigration, especially during the time of the Famine, and there are a multitude of songs expressing the despair of the exile. '"It was a characteristic much noted by officials and previous settlers of wherever the Irish fled to, that they, above all other nations, clung to their memories of their lost land", wrote an historian; and listening to these songs, we know with certitude that these emigrants felt Ireland as a living part of them which had been wrenched away' (Devlin, quoted in Dunne 2001).

The Irish Emigrant
I'm bidding you a long farewell, my Mary kind and true
But I'll not forget you, darling, in the land I'm going to
They say there's bread and work for all, and the sun shines always there
But I'll ne'er forget old Ireland, were it fifty times as fair.

Spancil Hill
I dreamt I held and kissed her as in the days of yore
She said, 'Johnny you're only joking like many's the time before'
The cock he crew in the morning he crew both loud and shrill
And I awoke in California, many miles from Spancil Hill.

An Emigrant's Daughter
They spoke of a new land far away 'cross the sea
And of peace and good fortune for my brothers and me
So we parted from townland with much weeping and pain
Kissed the loved ones and the friends we would ne'er see again.
The vessel was crowded with disquieted folk
The escape from past hardship sustaining their hope
But as the last glimpse of Ireland faded into the mist
Each one fought back tears and felt strangely alone.
(Lyrics from Ireland-information.com)

Many songs celebrate the rebellions and uprisings that took place repeatedly through Ireland's history. These rebellions were crushed but were remembered in song to inspire a new generation towards a fresh rebellion.

The 1867 rebellion is commemorated in the song 'O'Donovan Rossa's Farewell to Dublin'. The planned rising came to nothing as informers had leaked the plans to the British. O'Donovan Rossa was sentenced to life imprisonment; he served six years and then was released on condition that he never returned to Ireland.

My curse attend the traitors false
Who did our cause betray,
I would tie a millstone round their necks
And drown them in the sea.
There is Nagle, Noone, O'Brien
And Power to make four
Like demons for their conduct
In hell they loudly roar. (Lyrics from Dunne 2001)

The Easter Rising was in some senses a failure, as all the rebels were captured, the leaders executed and many others imprisoned. Yet the harshness with which the British dealt with the rebels changed the mood of Ireland and the War of Independence soon followed, which finally resulted in the founding of the Republic. The Easter Rising is celebrated in 'Erin go Bragh':

Now here's to old Dublin, and here's to her renown,
In the long generation her fame will go down,
And our children will tell how their forefathers saw,
The red blaze of freedom in Erin Go Bragh. (Lyrics from Dunne 2001)

Summarised from www.athenry.net; Dunne (2001); www.ireland-information.com, Meagher (2006); O'Riordan.

The Blues

As African culture was oral, not written, African music contained information and stories passed down through generations. There were 'songs for every aspect of day-to-day life or social occasion including hunting, pounding maize, going to war and religious ceremonies' (Williamson 2007:3). The Europeans who first heard African music were far from impressed. One observer, a man called George Pikenard, wrote in 1816: 'In dancing they scarcely moved their feet but threw about their arms and twisted and writhed their bodies into a multitude of disgusting and indecent attitudes. Their singing was a wild yell devoid of all softness and harmony' (Williamson 2007:10).

On arrival as slaves in America, Africans were stripped of their tribe's traditional ways and had to build a new culture based on their shared experience. Music was hugely important in this and songs were often used as a rhythm to work to. These work songs were often used by the plantation owners as evidence for the misconception that the slaves were happy with their status as slaves. With little else to cheer them, music was of central importance in their lives, both in the field and in their little free time on a Saturday night: 'Music was at the centre of their limited social activities' (Williamson 2007:6).

Singing was a way of releasing emotion, a rhythm to work to, a way of keeping spirits up and a way to convey information in a form that the overseer would not pick up on. Some songs conveyed information in code that could be used for planning an escape. These could be sung without any suspicion attached. 'Follow the Drinking Gourd' contained a musical map, giving instructions as to how to reach a safe place.

> When the Sun comes back
> And the first quail calls
> Follow the Drinking Gourd,
> For the old man is a-waiting for to carry you to freedom
> If you follow the Drinking Gourd
> The riverbank makes a very good road.
> The dead trees will show you the way.
> Left foot, peg foot, travelling on,
> Follow the Drinking Gourd.
> The river ends between two hills
> Follow the Drinking Gourd.
> There's another river on the other side
> Follow the Drinking Gourd.
> When the great big river meets the little river
> Follow the Drinking Gourd.
> For the old man is a-waiting for to carry you to freedom
> If you follow the Drinking Gourd.
> (Lyrics from Owen Sound 2004)

When slavery was abolished, many stayed on the plantations under the sharecropping system, but many more went to the cities. In the early 19th century, the population of New Orleans was one-third African-American. Music and dancing thrived in the city and various forms of new music emerged. Ragtime led on to jazz and the blues. Blues music was characterised by slow and mournful tunes; its themes often concerned loss and being down on one's luck. 'Blind' Lemon Jefferson wrote songs such as 'Bad Luck Blues' and 'Broke and Hungry', which described hard times.

Bad Luck Blues
I bet my money and I lost it, Lord, it's so
Doggone my bad luck soul
Mmm, lost it, ain't it so?
I mean lost it, speakin' about so, now
I'll never bet on the deuce-trey-queen no more.

Broke and Hungry
I'm broke and hungry, ragged and dirty too
I said I'm broke and hungry, ragged and dirty too
Mama, if I clean up, can I go home with you?
I'm motherless, fatherless, sister and brotherless too
I said I'm motherless, fatherless, sister and brotherless too
Reason I've tried so hard to make this trip with you. (Lyrics from lyricsmode.com)

Because of limits to where black people could gather, they often socialised in rough drinking dens known as barrelhouses, fish fries or juke joints. 'Moonshine' whiskey was served and gambling and prostitution went on alongside the music and dancing. In the 1920s, prohibition drove these places underground, but business continued. Rent parties were popular in cities – a small entrance fee was charged to see a musician and help pay the rent.

The Depression that followed the Wall Street Crash of 1929 hugely affected the lives of African-Americans and consequently their music. They had been poor before, but the Depression turned poverty into absolute poverty. Life, always hard, became even harder. Record sales shrank and so the careers of many rising blues stars were curtailed. Live music became less popular as people could not pay for it. Blues musicians eked out a bare living busking on street corners.

Billie Holiday's life was like the subject of a blues song. She was born Eleanora Harris in Baltimore and raised in extreme poverty by her teenaged mother. She moved to Harlem at the age of 12, where she was arrested for prostitution and sent to a reform school. She ran away from the reform school and was homeless for a while but eventually found work singing in a nightclub. One of her most famous songs, 'Strange Fruit', written as a poem by Abel Meeropol and recorded in 1939, tells the story of a lynching.

Southern trees bear strange fruit
Blood on the leaves and blood at the root
Black bodies swinging in the southern breeze
Strange fruit hanging from the poplar trees

Pastoral scene of the gallant south
The bulging eyes and the twisted mouth
Scent of magnolias, sweet and fresh
Then the sudden smell of burning flesh

Here is fruit for the crows to pluck
For the rain to gather, for the wind to suck
For the sun to rot, for the trees to drop
Here is a strange and bitter crop
(Lyrics from elyrics.net)

In the 1950s rock and roll eclipsed the blues in popularity but it was kept alive and rejuvenated in the folk revival. The sixties saw huge social change and an increase in the popularity of soul music. The mood was optimistic and the mournful sound of the blues receded with the new positivity of Nina Simone's 'Feeling Good' and 'Young, Gifted and Black'.

Summarised from Owen Sound (2004); Williamson (2007).

Activity

Think of some songs you know and reflect on what culture they portray.

Revision questions

1 Explain the difference between a primary and a secondary source.
2 Outline RTÉ's obligations under the Public Service Broadcasting Charter.
3 Explain why it is important to present multi-ethnic characters on children's television programmes.
4 Explain some of the ways in which news programming might increase prejudice.
5 Outline how ethnicity is treated in two films.
6 Explain the terms 'whitewashing' and 'racelifting'.
7 Outline how music reflects the history and culture of a group.

CHAPTER 9

Legislation, the United Nations and Human Rights

By the end of this chapter, students should:

- Be aware of legislation and bodies that aim to ensure equality in Ireland.

- Be aware of immigration rules relating to both EEA and non-EEA citizens and understand the conditions regarding work permits and which groups of people need work permits.

- Be aware of different categories of refugee and the legal UN definition of refugee status.

- Be aware of the steps in the asylum process in Ireland.

- Understand the terms of the Dublin Convention.

- Be aware of the direct provision system and the restrictions on and entitlements of asylum seekers waiting on a decision.

- Be aware of the various backgrounds of asylum seekers and their reasons for coming to Ireland.

- Understand the term *unaccompanied minor* and be aware of recent changes to the status of those with Irish-born children.

- Understand the roles and aims of the United Nations (UN), the European Court of Human Rights and Amnesty International.

- Be aware of the Universal Declaration of Human Rights.

Equality Legislation

There are various pieces of legislation in Ireland that aim to prevent discrimination and punish those found guilty of it. The Employment Equality Act 1998 and the Equal Status Act 2000 make discrimination illegal in employment, vocational training, advertising, collective agreements and the provision of goods and services. Goods and services include banking, transport, health, accommodation, education and other services.

Discrimination is defined as the treatment of a person in a less favourable way than another person, in a comparable situation, based on any of the following grounds:

- age
- belonging to the Traveller community
- civil status
- disability
- family status
- gender
- race
- religious belief
- sexual orientation.

To prove a case of direct discrimination, a direct comparison must be made: 'for example, in the case of disability discrimination the comparison must be between a person who has a disability and another who has not, or between persons with different disabilities' (Citizens Information).

Indirect discrimination occurs when a practice that does not immediately seem to discriminate actually has a discriminatory effect. For example, advertising a cleaning job for fluent English speakers is discriminatory, because the job does not specifically require it.

Summarised from Citizens Information (www.citizensinformation.ie); Equality Tribunal (www.equalitytribunal.ie).

The Equality Authority

The Equality Authority was set up under the Employment Equality Act. It is an independent body whose purpose is to promote equal opportunity and to ensure that everyone is treated equally. The Equality Authority assists the public with information on equality legislation and it may also provide legal assistance to people who wish to bring cases of discrimination. While it can advise and support in bringing cases, it has no power to decide a case.

Summarised from Citizens Information (www.citizensinformation.ie).

The Equality Tribunal

The Equality Tribunal investigates and mediates claims of discrimination. Complaints must be made within six months of the last act of discrimination. A mediator will help those involved in a case to reach a mediated agreement, which is legally binding. If there is any objection to mediation, the case will then be heard by a tribunal equality officer, who will hear evidence from both sides before giving a legally binding decision. The power of the Equality Tribunal to decide and enforce claims comes from the equality legislation previously mentioned.

Summarised from Citizens Information (www.citizensinformation.ie).

Activity

A database of decisions made by the Equality Tribunal is available at www.equalitytribunal. ie. Working in pairs, choose a case and write a short summary, outlining the background and outcome of the case. Discuss whether you agree or disagree with the decision made.

Immigration: Entering, Living and Working in Ireland

The right to enter Ireland is not automatic but depends on nationality and situation. Swiss and European Economic Area (EEA) nationals and their spouses or civil partners have a right of residence in Ireland for three months with no restrictions. (The EEA includes member states of the EU along with Iceland, Liechtenstein and Norway.) If a person wishes to stay longer than three months, they must be employed or self-employed. The above-mentioned nationals (apart from EEA citizens from Bulgaria and Romania) do not need an employment permit and can apply for any jobs in the public or private sector. They may enter the Irish army or the Garda Síochána. Qualifications are transferrable between EEA countries. A retired EEA or Swiss national wishing to stay in Ireland must prove that they have enough resources to provide for their needs.

Citizens of certain non-EEA countries need an entry visa before they travel to Ireland. Visas are issued by Irish embassies abroad, are for entry purposes only, and do not confer any right to live or work in Ireland. Those wishing to stay longer than three months must obtain permission to remain. A non-EEA citizen hoping to retire to Ireland must prove they can support themselves and obtain permission to remain from an immigration officer in Ireland.

Summarised from Citizens Information (www.citizensinformation.ie).

Work Permits

People from outside the EEA and EEA citizens from Romania and Bulgaria who intend to work in Ireland must obtain a work permit. Citizens of Romania and Bulgaria do need work permits, but work permit applications for this group are given preference over those for non-EEA nationals. People who have been granted either refugee status or leave to remain in Ireland, postgraduate students whose work experience is essential to their course and non-EEA nationals carrying out scientific research for an approved organisation do not need a work permit. Non-EEA students can also work without a permit, as long as they work only 20 hours a week during term time.

Work permits are not easy to obtain and carry a number of restrictions:

- Work permits are only available for jobs with a minimum annual salary of €30,000. This condition, which has existed since 2009, marks a change from migrant workers being typically engaged 'in low paid and unskilled agricultural jobs, such as fruit picking and mushroom harvesting' (Bacik 2004:189).
- Work permits are not given for certain occupations such as work riders (horse racing), domestic workers and HGV drivers.
- Work permits are granted for an initial two years and then for a further three years. A work permit may not be needed after five years.
- A labour market needs test is required with all work permit applications. This requires that the job be advertised with FÁS/EURES for eight weeks and in the national media for six days before a non-EEA citizen is allowed to take the job.
- Fees and the labour market needs test also apply to spouses, civil partners and dependents of employment permit holders.

Once an employment permit has been issued, the worker shares the same employment rights of Irish or EEA citizens for the duration of the employment.

Summarised from Citizens Information (www.citizensinformation.ie).

Activities

1   Discuss whether you think the rules relating to immigration and work permits are fair.

2   Were you aware that EEA citizens and non-EEA citizens have different rights? Discuss what advantages and disadvantages Ireland's membership of the EEA gives us.

Refugees and Asylum Seekers

'The term "refugee" is used in everyday language in Ireland to describe a number of categories of people. These categories of people may have different legal statuses' (www.citizensinformation.ie).

Because they have different legal statuses, different categories of refugee may have different rights and obligations. What they have in common is their link to the refugee process, which is based on both international conventions and Irish legislation. Categories of refugee include: asylum seekers; convention refugees; programme refugees; and those with leave to remain.

- An *asylum seeker* is a person who seeks legal recognition as a refugee.
- A *convention refugee* is a person who has received legal recognition as a refugee and has been granted refugee status.
- At times the UN will request either temporary protection or resettlement for a group of people and the government can then decide to invite these pre-selected groups, known as *programme refugees*, to Ireland. Programme refugees will not have to go through the asylum process. 'The Irish government has, at various times, welcomed groups of people who were fleeing persecution, such as those from former Yugoslav states such as Bosnia-Herzegovina during the period of genocide in that country, or at a later date, those fleeing persecution in Kosovo' (NCCA 2006:3).
- A person who does not completely satisfy the requirements to be legally recognised as a refugee may be granted *leave to remain* in Ireland for humanitarian or other reasons. People who marry or enter into a civil partnership with an Irish citizen may be granted leave to remain. A person with leave to remain has fewer rights than a refugee but is allowed to live and work in the state. They must wait a longer time before applying for citizenship and do not have the right to apply for family reunification.

Julian Assange, the Wikileaks founder, became probably the world's most famous asylum seeker when he sought political asylum at the Ecuadorean embassy in June 2012 (BBC 2012a).

In order to gain legal recognition as a refugee, a person must satisfy the definition in the UN Refugee Convention:

> Any person who owing to a well-founded fear of being persecuted for reasons of race, religion, nationality, membership of a particular social group or political opinion, is outside the country of his/her nationality and is unable, or owing to such fear, is unwilling to avail her/himself of the protection of that country; or (any person) who, not having a nationality and being outside the country of her/his former habitual residence, is unable, or owing to such fear is unwilling to return to it. (www.nccri.ie)

In Ireland, the Refugee Act 1996 is the basis for seeking refugee status. It is based on the definition of refugee contained in the UN Refugee Convention (see above). The Refugee Act 1996 states that the term 'social group' in the UN definition can include membership of a trade union, sexual orientation or gender. Refugee status is only granted if a person can prove that they meet the definition.

Once granted refugee status, the person is now entitled to work, operate a business and 'access medical, social welfare and education services on the same footing as Irish citizens." (ORAC website). They are then issued with a residence permit and may travel abroad using a Convention Travel Document.

Summarised from Citizens Information (www.citizensinformation.ie);
NCCA (www.ncca.ie); ORAC (www.orac.ie).

Applying for Refugee Status

A person may apply for asylum wherever they first enter the country and the initial paperwork and interviews will be carried out there. Photographs and fingerprints are also taken at this point. The applicant may also need to attend at the Office of the Refugee Applications Commissioner (ORAC) in Dublin. Applicants need to submit original travel documents and originals of all identity documents, birth and marriage certificates. This can prove difficult as a person fleeing their country may not have been able to take these documents with them. If an immigration officer or a member of the Garda Síochána suspects that an applicant has not made reasonable efforts to prove his or her identity, the person concerned may be detained.

The person's fingerprints will be sent by an electronic system – Eurodac – to other countries; this is aimed at preventing multiple asylum claims. Under the Dublin Convention (2003), another country may have responsibility for the asylum application. The relevant terms of the Dublin Convention are: 'Where the applicants arrive in Ireland having travelled through another EU country they may then be returned to that first EU country to have their application processed there' (Bacik 2004:186). Ireland may request another state to take charge of the application if an asylum claim had been previously made there, if another state had issued a visa or work permit or if the applicant had regularly crossed the border of another state before applying for asylum in Ireland.

At the end of the interview, asylum seekers are advised of their rights with regard to legal assistance. They first stay in a Dublin-based reception centre for a period of assessment and interviews with ORAC before being given accommodation at a regional centre. The applicant is given a Temporary Residence Certificate containing their photo and personal details, and they must live at the accommodation centre while waiting for a decision.

The Refugee Applications Commissioner will review applications and then make a recommendation either to refuse or grant refugee status. Negative outcomes may be appealed to the Refugee Appeals Tribunal. Following the recommendation of the Refugee Applications Commissioner or the Refugee Appeals Tribunal, a final decision will be made by the Minister for Justice and Equality.

Summarised from Citizens Information (www.citizensinformation.ie) and ORAC (www.orac.ie).

Direct Provision System

Asylum seekers cannot apply for social welfare but instead live under the direct provision system. They stay at a regional centre, where they receive all meals and a weekly personal allowance of €19.10 for an adult and €9.60 for each child. Extra assistance towards new clothing on arrival may be available from the Department of Social Protection. Asylum seekers are entitled to a medical card which provides them with free medical care. Legal aid is available to help with applications and appeals. Young asylum seekers are entitled to free primary and post-primary education but not to third-level education. Adults may have free access to adult literacy and English language classes through the Vocational Education Committee (VEC) or local support groups, but this is not available in every area. Asylum seekers are not allowed to work or attend vocational training, although they may become involved in voluntary community activities.

They must stay at the regional centre and they have no right to a transfer if they are unhappy in the centre, or wish to be near relatives or friends. 'You have no right to be moved to another centre of your choice. Transfer is possible, but only when we decide to allow it based on its merits and in rare and exceptional circumstances' (RIA 2011:7). They may not be absent from the centre for more than three consecutive nights, or they will be disqualified from any further assistance. Residents must obey the house rules in their centre, such as not having food or electrical items in their rooms. There is no guarantee of being served food that is suitable for particular religious groups, such as halal food for Muslims or kosher food for Jewish people. 'Where possible and practical, the centre will cater for ethnic food preferences' (RIA 2011:10). There is no obligation on the centre to provide any leisure activities. Rooms can be inspected without warning.

There have been criticisms of the direct provision system. Bryan Fanning has called it 'state-fostered segregation' (Fanning 2012:101). He states that a study carried out in 2001 found that respondents in the direct provision system often felt that food was inadequate and would have liked to buy more. He also criticises the small cash allowance as inadequate to allow a person access to wider society: 'In such centres asylum seekers were kept in place not by barred windows or barbed wire but by an inability to afford bus fares, newspapers, cups of coffee, subscriptions for clubs and leisure activities' (Fanning 2012:106).

Some local people in areas where these centres are located have protested – some on behalf of the asylum seekers, others against them. Some locals 'included demands that they [the asylum seekers] be screened for AIDS and statements that linked asylum seekers to the threat of crime', while others 'expressed concern that asylum seekers would be isolated and marginalised' (Fanning 2012:101).

Ryan, Benson and Dooley state that many asylum seekers suffer psychological distress because of worry about the outcome of their case; overcrowding and lack of privacy in the centres; and forced dependence on social welfare due to restrictions on working. They also suffer from being separated from family and friends and the traumatic experiences they had before escaping their home countries.

Summarised from Citizens Information (www.citizensinformation.ie); Fanning (2012), RIA (2011); Ryan *et al.* (2007).

Activities

1 Hold a class debate on whether asylum seekers should be able to work while waiting for a decision.

2 Discuss whether you think the direct provision system is fair or not.

Number of Asylum Applications

Statistics from Fanning show that the number of asylum applications in Ireland is falling.

Asylum Applications, Ireland 2000–2010

YEAR	NUMBER OF APPLICATIONS
2000	10,938
2001	10,325
2002	11,634
2003	7,483
2004	4,265
2005	4,323
2006	4,323
2007	3,985
2008	3,866
2009	n/a
2010	2,689

Source: Fanning 2012:98

ORAC stated in its annual report that there were 1,290 applications in 2011. The top five applicant countries in 2011 were:

- Nigeria – 14.1 per cent
- Pakistan – 13.6 per cent

- China – 11 per cent
- Democratic Republic of Congo – 5.4 per cent
- Afghanistan – 5.2 per cent.

Acceptance of asylum claims in Ireland is extremely low. Of 2,785 decisions made in 2010, 2,655 applications were rejected.

Summarised from Eurostat (2011); Fanning (2012); ORAC (2011).

Case study: Asylum seekers' experiences

Anna lived in the former Soviet Union. Because she had one Jewish parent, she became the target of ongoing harassment. Her business received threatening phone calls, as did her employees, who were told not to work for her. The threats to kill her came from men belonging to a nationalist political organisation. One day, these men broke into her home, attacked and beat her.

Her elderly mother, who witnessed the attack, died the next day. Within a week of her mother's death, Anna decided to flee, leaving her house and business behind. She paid a human trafficker who hid her in the back of a jeep. After four days' travelling she arrived in Ireland. She had not even realised she was on a ferry because she had not moved from under the blanket in the jeep. In Dublin, penniless and in poor health, she was sent to a reception centre. Anna was refused refugee status.

Alex is from Eastern Europe. He was a schoolteacher, married with two children, living in a house near his parents. War came, and Alex was unlucky enough to be a member of a persecuted ethnic minority. One day, he went to the village for food and returned to find his house and his parents' house burned to the ground. His, wife, parents and children were dead. He hid out in the mountains for two years until he was found by international peacekeeping soldiers, who arranged for him to come to Ireland. He made friends at his local church while waiting for the outcome of his case. He was granted refugee status. He now works part time, but still suffers from his past experiences.

Salam is from Africa. His country was devastated by civil war, and he and his family had to abandon their home and go and hide with relatives in the country. The family was constantly on the move, but they managed to save enough money to get one person out of the country. Salam was chosen as he was the eldest son and spoke some English. He arrived in Ireland alone and after a time there was a positive outcome to his case. Family reunification allowed his wife, father and siblings to join him.

Magda is an African woman. She was married with two daughters when conflict broke out. First her extended family were killed, then gunmen broke into her house, killed her husband in front of her and raped her. Her daughters managed to escape through a window and took shelter at a relation's house. Magda did not know where her daughters were. She managed to get enough money to bring her to Dublin but did not know if her daughters were alive or dead. She has since discovered that her daughters are safe and is missing them terribly. She is still waiting for a decision.

Summarised from Ryan *et al.* (2007).

Activities

1   The film star Angelina Jolie is a UN Special Envoy for Refugee Issues. Discuss whether celebrity involvement in politics is worthwhile or just a publicity stunt. Information on her work is available at: www.unrefugees.org (click on 'About Refugees' and then 'Angelie Jolie').

2   Refugees' stories are available to read or watch on the UN website (www.unrefugees. org): click on 'About Refugees' and then on 'Refugee Stories'. Watch and/or read a selection of these stories and then discuss what you have learned.

Unaccompanied Minors

A child under the age of 18 who is not accompanied by an adult on arrival in the state or at ORAC will be referred to the local health office. The Health Service Executive (HSE) becomes responsible for the care of the minor, will provide immediate assistance and may then apply for a declaration as a refugee on behalf of the minor. There are specific arrangements between the HSE and ORAC for processing these applications.

Children arriving alone are in a uniquely difficult situation: 'They are vulnerable to violence, have little if any voice and have great difficulty accessing services' (McCann James *et al.* 2009:3). There are also worries that some children may not receive any support from the state on arrival because they do not know who to turn to: 'Fewer than 5 per cent (of minors) are identified at port of entry' (McCann James *et al.* 2009:3).

ORAC reports that in 2011, 26 asylum applications were received from unaccompanied minors, accounting for two per cent of the total number of asylum applications.

Summarised from Citizens Information (www.citizensinformation.ie); McCann James *et al.* (2009); ORAC (2012).

Citizenship of Irish-born Children

Before the 2004 Irish Nationality and Citizenship Act, every child born in Ireland was entitled to Irish citizenship. The parents of these children did not have an automatic right of residence in Ireland and could be deported. In 1989 the Supreme Court ruled that 'it would be unconstitutional to deport the non-national parents of children born in Ireland' (Bacik 2004:194). In 2003 this decision was overturned: parents again had no right of residence, but the child could stay if the family agreed to leave without him or her.

The Irish Nationality and Citizenship Act 2004 changed the law so that children of non-Irish parents born in Ireland on or after 1 January 2005 no longer have automatic entitlement to Irish citizenship. Children born of an Irish citizen, either in or outside Ireland, are automatically Irish citizens. An Irish-born child of a British parent is also entitled to Irish citizenship. Any other non-Irish-citizen parents of Irish-born children must prove that they have a genuine link to Ireland by having been resident for three out of the four years before the child's birth. This Act entitled certain children to Irish citizenship but did not guarantee residence rights to foreign-born parents.

In 2011 the European Court of Justice (ECJ) ruled that EU member states must not refuse residence to parents of a citizen child. Parents may now apply for residence rights, including any parents who were deported from or left Ireland before this ruling. The parents may then be given permission to live and work in Ireland without an employment permit. Any parent who has been convicted of serious and/or persistent criminal offences will be unable to apply.

Summarised from Bacik (2004), Citizens Information (www.citizensinformation.ie); Irish Statute Book (2004).

> ### Activity
> Discuss whether you agree or disagree with the 2011 judgement allowing parents of Irish citizen children to remain in Ireland.

The United Nations

The UN was founded at the end of World War II in 1945. Initially it had 51 member states but now has 193, including Ireland. Its main aims are 'maintaining international peace and security, developing friendly relations among nations and promoting social progress, better living standards and human rights' (www.un.org). The UN is well known for its peacekeeping activities and humanitarian assistance, but it also works in areas such as human rights, disaster relief, sustainable development, environment and health initiatives, clearing landmines and expanding food production.

The main bodies of the UN are the General Assembly, the Security Council, the Economic and Social Council (ECOSOC), the Trusteeship Council, the Secretariat and the International Court of Justice (ICJ).

- *General Assembly*: Involved in policymaking and discussing international issues.
- *Security Council*: Responsible for maintaining international peace and security. When a dispute arises, the Security Council first tries to help countries to reach agreement by peaceful means. However, if fighting breaks out the Security Council attempts to end it quickly, for example by issuing ceasefire directives or sending peacekeeping forces to the area. Peacekeeping forces 'help reduce tensions in troubled areas, keep

opposing forces apart and create conditions of calm in which peaceful settlements may be sought' (www.un.org). Other measures include suspension or expulsion from the UN, economic sanctions or collective military action.

- *ECOSOC*: Involved with economic, social and environmental challenges facing the world. Policymakers from various governments meet to discuss challenges to a nation's development, such as education and health.

- *ICJ*: Based in The Hague (Netherlands); its role is to settle any legal disputes submitted to it by member states.

Peacekeeping

There are three principles involved in peacekeeping. First, those invol- ved in the conflict must agree to UN involvement; second, the peace- keeping forces must remain impartial; and finally, they must use force only in self defence, to protect civilians or to maintain law and order. As of

October 2012 there are 15 peacekeeping missions in operation; and there have been 67 peacekeeping operations since 1948. There are a total of 98,695 uniformed personnel (troops, police and military observers) serving, with 117 countries (including Ireland) contributing these personnel. As of 2012 Irish Army personnel are serving in Kosovo, Bosnia, Western Sahara, Congo, Afghanistan, Chad, Côte d'Ivoire, Lebanon, Haiti and the Middle East. Total fatalities since operations began amount to 3,025.

Summarised from United Nations (www.un.org).

Project ideas

1 Research in more detail the day-to-day work of UN peacekeepers.
2 A number of short videos on worldwide ECOSOC projects are available. Watch some of them and describe how useful you think each project is. Videos can be found on YouTube (www.youtube.com) – search for 'UN Economic and Social Council'.

Universal Declaration of Human Rights

After the atrocities of World War II, the UN was determined never to allow such things to happen again. It drafted the Universal Declaration of Human Rights, a document containing a list of human rights that every person in every country should enjoy. The General Assembly adopted the Declaration in 1948. It contains 30 Articles, some of the most important of which are the right to: life and liberty; equality before the law; a fair hearing in court; be presumed innocent until proved guilty; and to seek asylum from persecution. The Declaration forbids slavery, torture and unlawful detention. The Declaration is not legally binding itself, but various conventions, charters and covenants based on the Declaration do have legal force.

The European Court of Human Rights

The European Court of Human Rights is an international court based in Strasbourg, which was set up in 1959. It rules on cases involving abuses of civil and political rights as outlined in the European Convention on Human Rights. The Convention ensures the right to life; the right to a fair hearing; the right to respect for private and family life; freedom of expression; freedom of thought, conscience and religion; and the protection of property. It outlaws torture and inhuman or degrading treatment; slavery and forced labour; the death penalty; unlawful detention; and discrimination. Both states and individuals can apply for a judgement. The judgements are legally binding and have led governments to alter their laws. Forty-seven Council of Europe member states, including Ireland, have ratified the Convention and so are bound to abide by its judgements.

Summarised from European Court of Human Rights (www.echr.coe.int).

Activity

Read the Universal Declaration of Human Rights and the European Convention on Human Rights. Imagine that you have no choice but to lose three of the named human rights. As a class, discuss which are the most important and which three you are willing to let go.

Amnesty International

Amnesty International is a global organisation with over three million supporters in 150 countries. It is independent of any government or religion, is funded mainly through membership and donations and its aim is to ensure that all people enjoy full human rights as outlined in the Universal Declaration of Human Rights. It is involved in many activities, such as observing trials, interviewing victims and officials, publishing reports, publicising details of abuses, public demonstrations and letter-writing campaigns. It highlights cases of injustice and encourages people to write letters and sign online petitions in order to put pressure on governments.

Amnesty's campaigns are necessary because the media often drop a serious human rights story in favour of fresher news. Amnesty continues to campaign, sometimes over many years, reminding the victim that they have not been forgotten. For example, Amnesty campaigned for 15 years for the release of Aung San Suu Kyi, who had been under house arrest in Burma since 1989. She was released in 2010 and recently spoke about how important the support of Amnesty International had been: 'You have shown me that I shall never be alone as I go about my discharge of these duties . . . Amnesty International . . . has helped us to keep our small wick of self-respect alive, you have helped us to keep the light and we hope that you will be with us in the years to come' (www.amnesty.ie).

Summarised from Amnesty International (www.amnesty.ie).

Project idea

Find a case that interests you on the Amnesty website. Contact them for more information and present your information to the class.

Revision questions

1 Name and describe two bodies that aim to prevent discrimination.
2 Outline restrictions on living and working in Ireland.
3 Outline the conditions under which work permits are issued.
4 Explain the four categories of refugee.
5 Describe the process of applying for refugee status.
6 Explain the term 'direct provision'.
7 Explain the term 'unaccompanied minor'.
8 Outline how a child becomes entitled to Irish citizenship.
9 List three main bodies of the UN and explain the function of each.
10 Explain the role of the European Court of Human Rights.

Bibliography

Alia, V. and Bull, S. (2005) *Media and Ethnic Minorities*. Edinburgh: Edinburgh University Press.

Alvarez, A. (2008) 'Model minority: how women's magazines whitewash different ethnicities', *Guanabee*, 20 March <http://guanabee.com/2008/03/model-minority-how-womens-magazines-whitewash-different-ethnicities> accessed 4 October 2012.

Amnesty International [website] <www.amnesty.ie/about-us>; Aung San Suu Kyi: <www.amnesty.ie/welcomeaungsansuukyi> accessed 3 October 2012.

Astier, H. (2005) 'Headscarf defeat riles French Muslims' <http://news.bbc.co.uk/2/hi/europe/4395934.stm> accessed 20 September 2012.

Bacik, I. (2004) *Kicking and Screaming: Dragging Ireland into the 21st Century*. Dublin: O'Brien Press.

BBC (2004) 'French girls expelled over veils' <http://news.bbc.co.uk/2/hi/europe/3761490.stm> accessed 15 September 2012.

— (2011) 'Profile: Syria's Bashar al-Assad' <www.bbc.co.uk/news/10338256> accessed 22nd September 2012.

— (2012a) 'Q&A: Julian Assange and asylum' <www.bbc.co.uk/news/uk-18521881> accessed 15 September 2012.

— (2012b) 'Rwanda profile' <www.bbc.co.uk/news/world-africa-14093238> accessed 2 October 2012.

Berardinelli, James (2012) Review of *The Help, The Reel View* 3 February 2012 <www.reelviews.net/php_review_template.php?identifier=2416> accessed 9 October 2012.

Bilton, T., Bonnett, K., Jones, P., Lawson,T., Skinner, D., Stanworth, M. and Webster, A. (2002) *Introductory Sociology* (4th edn). Hampshire and New York: Palgrave Macmillan.

Boyle, A. and Boyle, N. (2001) *All about Faith 2: Foundations of Religion*. Dublin: Gill & Macmillan.

Brah, A. (1999) 'Asian Girls and Schooling' in P. Braham, A. Rattans and R. Skellington (eds), *Racism and Antiracism: Inequalities, Opportunities and Policies*. London: Sage.

Brendon, P. (2008) *The Decline and Fall of the British Empire 1781–1997*. New York: Alfred A. Knopf.

Browne, K. (1992) *An Introduction to Sociology*. UK: Polity Press.

Bruchfeld, Stéphane and Levine, Paul A. (1998) *Tell Ye Your Children: A Book about the Holocaust in Europe 1933–1945*. Living History Unit, Swedish Government Offices. Available at <www.levandehistoria.se/files/engelska.pdf> accessed 18 September 2012.

CatholicIreland.net [website] <www.catholicireland.net/pages/index.php?nd=336> accessed 10 September 2012.

Central Statistics Office (CSO) (2011a) *This is Ireland Part 1*: 2011 Census results <www.cso.ie/en/media/csoie/census/documents/census2011pdr/Census%20 2011%20Highlights%20Part%201%20web%2072dpi.pdf> accessed 18 September 2012.

— (2011b) *This is Ireland Part 2*: 2011 Census results <www.cso.ie/en/media/csoie/ census/documents/thisisirelandpart2census2011/This%20is%20Ireland%20 Highlights,%20P2%20Full%20doc.pdf>.

— (2011c) 'This is Ireland – Highlights from Census 2011 Part 2', press release <www. cso.ie/en/newsandevents/pressreleases/2012pressreleases/pressreleasethisisireland-highlightsfromcensus2011part2> accessed 20 September 2012.

— (2011d) *Statistical Yearbook of Ireland 2011* <www.cso.ie/en/media/csoie/ releasespublications/documents/statisticalyearbook/2011/webversion2011yearbook. pdf> accessed 20 September 2012.

— (2011e) 'Census 2011 Reports' <www.cso.ie/en/census/census2011reports/>; religious affiliation <www.cso.ie/px/pxeirestat/Statire/SelectVarVal/Define. asp?maintable=CDD36> accessed 25 September 2012.

— [website] Population figures 1901–2006 <www.cso.ie/Quicktables/ GetQuickTables.aspx?FileName=CNA13.asp&TableName=Population+1901+- +2006&StatisticalProduct=DB_CN> accessed 23 September 2012.

Cherrytree (2007a) *Marriage Celebrations*. London: Cherrytree Books, Evans.

— (2007b) *End of Life Rituals*. London: Cherrytree Books, Evans.

Child, Ben (2010) 'Dev Patel attacks Hollywood over lack of roles for Asian actors', *The Guardian* 11 August 2011 <www.guardian.co.uk/film/2010/aug/11/dev-patel-asian-roles-slumdog> accessed 8 October 2012.

Chiriyankandath, J. (2007) 'Colonialism and Post-colonial Development' in P. Burnell, V. Randall and L. Rakner, *Politics in the Developing World*. Available at <www.oup. com/uk/orc/bin/9780199296088/burnell_ch02.pdf> accessed 6 October 2012.

Citizens Information [website] <www.citizensinformation.ie>

Cloyne Report (2010) *Commission of Investigation Report into the Catholic Diocese of Cloyne* <www.justice.ie/en/JELR/Cloyne_Rpt.pdf/Files/Cloyne_Rpt.pdf> accessed 14 September 2012.

Colombo, G., Cullen, R. and Lisle, B. (eds) (2001) *Rereading America: Cultural Contexts for Critical Thinking and Writing* (5th edn). Boston, MA: Bedford/St Martins.

Commission to Inquire into Child Abuse (CICA) (2009) *Final Report* <www.childabusecommission.com/rpt/pdfs> accessed 14 September 2012.

Cortes, C. (1987) 'A long way to go: minorities and the media' in *Media and Values* Issue 38 <www.medialit.org/reading-room/long-way-go-minorities-and-media> accessed 4 October 2012.

Council of Europe (1995) *All Different, All Equal*: Youth Directorate education pack <http://eycb.coe.int/edupack/contents.html> accessed 23 September 2012.

— (2008) *Living Together as Equals in Dignity*: White Paper on Intercultural Dialogue <www.coe.int/t/dg4/intercultural/source/white%20paper_final_revised_en.pdf> accessed 23 September 2012.

— [website] 'The concept of intercultural dialogue' <www.coe.int/t/dg4/intercultural/concept_EN.asp> accessed 23 September 2012.

Curry, T., Jiobu, R. and Schwirian, K. (2005) *Sociology for the Twenty-first Century* (4th edn). New Jersey: Pearson/Prentice Hall.

Darwin, J. (2008) 'Britain's Empires' in S. Stockwell (ed.), *The British Empire: Themes and Perspectives*. Oxford: Blackwell.

Davies, J. and Smith, Carol R. (1997) *Gender, Ethnicity and Sexuality in Contemporary American Film*. Edinburgh: Keele University Press.

Davies, L. (2010) 'Election candidate in headscarf causes uproar in France' <www.guardian.co.uk/world/2010/feb/10/french-election-headscarf-candidate> accessed 20th September 2012.

Delaney, B. (n.d.) 'Rural Electrification and Network Renewal' <www.birrstageguild.com/ESB%20RE.htm> accessed 23 December 2012.

Department of Communications, Marine and Natural Resources (DCMNR) (2004), Public Service Broadcasting Charter, available from <www.rte.ie/documents/about/psb.pdf> accessed 2 October 2012.

Department of Social Protection (2012) 'Exceptional needs payments' <www.welfare.ie/EN/OperationalGuidelines/Pages/swa_exneeds.aspx> accessed 19 September 2012.

Dilley, A.R. (2008) 'The Economics of Empire' in S. Stockwell (ed.) *The British Empire: Themes and Perspectives*. Oxford: Blackwell.

Dominell, L. (2008) *Anti-racist Social Work* (3rd edn). New York: Palgrave Macmillan.

Dorning, A. (2007) 'Black hair dos and don'ts', ABC News 10 October <http://abcnews.go.com/US/story?id=3710971&page=1> accessed 4 October 2012.

Dunne, Paul (2001) *A History of Ireland in Song*, available from <http://ireland.dyndns.org/A_History_of_Ireland_in_Song.html> accessed 4 October 2012.

Earp, B.D. (2010) 'Automaticity in the classroom: unconscious mental processes and the racial achievement gap', *Journal of Multiculturalism in Education* 6(1), 1–22 <http://oxford.academia.edu/BrianEarp/papers/484912/unconscious_mental_processes_and_the _racial_achievement_gap> accessed 30 April 2012.

Ebert, R. (2005) 'Crash' (film review) <http://rogerebert.suntimes.com/apps/pbcs.dll/article?AID=/20050505/REVIEWS/50502001/1023> accessed 8 October 2012.

Elyrics.net [website] 'Strange Fruit' lyrics <www.elyrics.net/read/b/billie-holiday-lyrics/strange-fruit-lyrics.html> accessed 9 October 2012.

Encyclopaedia Britannica (1982) (15th edn) Macropaedia, Vols 4 and 18. William Benton.

Equality Tribunal [website] <www.equalitytribunal.ie/ > accessed 18 September 2012.

European Court of Human Rights [website] <www.echr.coe.int/ECHR/Homepage_En/> accessed 4 October 2012.

European Network Against Racism (ENAR) Ireland [website] <www.enarireland.org> accessed 14 September 2012.

Eurostat (2011) 'Final decisions on (non-EU-27) asylum applications, 2010' <http://epp.eurostat.ec.europa.eu/statistics_explained/index.php?title=File:Final_decisions_on_(non-EU-27)_asylum_applications,_2010_(number).png&filetimestamp=20111118152029> accessed 3 October 2012.

Fáilte Isteach [website] <www.thirdageireland.ie/what-we-do/15/failte-isteach/> accessed 10 September 2012.

Fairtrade Ireland (2011) *Newsletter* <www.fairtrade.ie/assets/files/Fairtrade_Newsletter_2011.pdf> accessed 4 October 2012.

— [website] <www.fairtrade.ie/what_is_fairtrade.html> accessed 4 October 2012.

Fanning, B. (ed.) (2007) *Immigration and Social Change in the Republic of Ireland.* Manchester: Manchester University Press.

— (2012) *Racism and Social Change in the Republic of Ireland* (2nd edn). Manchester: Manchester University Press.

Farley, John E. (1982) *Majority–Minority Relations.* New Jersey: Prentice Hall.

Fedorowich, K. (2008) 'The British Empire on the Move, 1760–1914' in S. Stockwell (ed.), *The British Empire: Themes and Perspectives.* Oxford: Blackwell.

Fisk, R. (2005) *The Great War for Civilisation: The Conquest of the Middle East.* London: Fourth Estate.

Giddens, A. (2001) *Sociology* (4th edn). UK: Polity Press.

Goldberg, Stephanie (2012) '"Hunger Games" and Hollywood's racial casting issue', CNN 28 March <http://edition.cnn.com/2012/03/28/showbiz/movies/hunger-games-black-actors/index.html> accessed 8 October 2012.

Gombrich, E.H. (2005) *A Little History of the World*, trans. Caroline Mustill (first published 1936). Yale University Press.

Halilovic-Pastuovic, M. (2007) 'The "Bosnian Project" in Ireland: A "Vision of Divisions"' in B. Fanning (ed.), *Immigration and Social Change in the Republic of Ireland.* Manchester: Manchester University Press.

Hall, C. (2008) 'Culture and Identity in Imperial Britain' in S. Stockwell (ed.), *The British Empire: Themes and Perspectives.* Oxford: Blackwell.

Haralambos, Michael and Holborn, Martin (2004) *Sociology Themes and Perspectives* (6th edn). London: HarperCollins.

Harley, D. (2005) 'Family and Society' in C. Partridge (ed.), *The World's Religions* (3rd edn). Oxford: Lion Hudson.

History.com [website] <www.history.com> accessed 23 September 2012.

Hoggard, Liz (2005) 'Colour code', *The Observer* 7 August <www.guardian.co.uk/film/2005/aug/07/features.review> accessed 15 September 2012.

Holmes, Anna (2012) 'White until proven black: imagining race in *Hunger Games*', *New Yorker* 30 March <www.newyorker.com/online/blogs/books/2012/03/hunger-games-and-trayvon-martin.html> accessed 8 October 2012.

Holocaust Memorial Day Trust [website] 'The Holocaust' <http://hmd.org.uk/genocides/the-holocaust> accessed 9 September; 'Victims of Nazi Persecution' <http://hmd.org.uk/genocides/victims-of-nazi-persecution/> accessed 9 September 2012.

Hornaday, Ann (2011) 'Black and white, and not enough "Help"', *Washington Post* 10 August.

Human Rights Watch (1999) 'Leave None to Tell the Story' <www.hrw.org/legacy/reports/1999/rwanda/rwanda0399.htm> accessed 9 September 2012.

Immigrant Council of Ireland (ICI) [website] <www. immigrantcouncil.ie> accessed 14 September 2012.

Independent News and Media (INM) [website] <www.inmplc.com/operations/ireland> accessed 4 October 2012.

International Court of Justice [website] <www.icj-cij.org/court/index.php?p1=1> accessed 3 October 2012.

Ireland-information.com [website] 'Irish Songs' <http://www.ireland-information.com/irishmusic/irishsongs-music-lyrics-midis.htm> accessed 12 September 2012.

Irish Aid [website] <www.irishaid.gov.ie/about.html> accessed 6 October 2012.

Irishbarrister.com [website] 'Defamation law in Ireland' <http://irishbarrister.com/defamation.html> accessed 2 October 2012.

Irish Examiner (2012) 'Media control – dominance not good for democracy', 22 August <www.irishexaminer.com/archives/2012/0822/opinion/media-control-dominance-not-good-for-democracy-204887.html> accessed 5 October 2012.

Irish Independent (2012) 'We're losing our faith faster than most countries as only 47pc say they are religious', 8 August <http://www.independent.ie/national-news/were-losing-our-faith-faster-than-most-countries-as-only-47pc-say-they-are-religious-3194317.html> accessed 1 October 2012.

Irish Statute Book (1963) Official Secrets Act <www.irishstatutebook.ie/1963/en/act/pub/0001/print.html#sec1> accessed 2 October 2012.

— (1989) Prohibition of Incitement To Hatred Act <www.irishstatutebook.ie/1989/en/act/pub/0019/index.html> accessed 2 October 2012.

— (2004) Irish Nationality and Citizenship Act <www.irishstatutebook.ie/2004/en/act/pub/0038/print.html> accessed 2 October 2004.

Jandt, Fred E. (2004) *An Introduction to Intercultural Communication – Identities in a Global Community* (4th edn). Thousand Oaks, CA: Sage.

Jandt, Fred E. and Taberski, Derrick J. (1998) *Intercultural Communication Workbook* (2nd edn). Thousand Oaks, CA: Sage.

Jensen, Robert and Wosnitzer, Robert (2007) '*Crash* and the self-indulgence of white America', *Dissident Voice* 21 March <www.dissidentvoice.org/Mar06/Jensen-Wosnitzer21.htm> acccessed 8 October 2012.

Kane, E. (1983) *Doing Your Own Research: How to do Basic Descriptive Research in the Social Sciences and Humanities*. Dublin: Turoe Press.

Kenyon, P. (2010) 'Tabloid treatment of asylum seekers under fire', *The Guardian* 7 June 2010 <www.guardian.co.uk/media/2010/jun/07/tabloids-treatment-asylum-seekers> accessed 4 October 2012.

King-O'Riain, R. C. (2008) 'Miss China Ireland 2006' in Mary P. Corcoran and Perry Share (eds), *Belongings: Shaping Identity in Modern Ireland*. Dublin: Institute of Public Administration.

Krings, Torben (2006) 'Irish Ferries, Labour Migration and the Spectre of Displacement' in Mary P. Corcoran and Perry Share (eds), *Belongings: Shaping Identity in Modern Ireland* (2008). Dublin: Institute of Public Administration.

Lally, C. (2012) 'Crime statistics Ireland', *Irish Times* 18 August <www.irishtimes.com/newspaper/weekend/2012/0818/1224322378674.html> accessed 19 September 2012.

Leigh, Danny (2010) '*Essential Killing* and *The Last Airbender*: the race row returns to film', *The Guardian* 9 July <http://www.guardian.co.uk/film/filmblog/2010/jul/09/essential-killing-last-airbender> accessed 8 October 2012.

Lodge, Tom (2006) 'An 'boks amach: the Irish anti-apartheid movement', *History Ireland*, 14(4), 35–9 <www.historyireland.com/volumes/volume14/issue4/features/?id=330> accessed 24 September 2012.

Longworth, Karina (2011) 'Civil rights through a soft focus lens in *The Help*', *Village Voice* 10 August <www.villagevoice.com/2011-08-10/film/the-help-mean-girls-vs-the-maids/> accessed 8 October 2012.

Lyricsmode.com [website] 'Blind' Lemon Jefferson lyrics <www.lyricsmode.com/lyrics/b/blind_lemon_jefferson/> accessed 9 October 2012.

MacGreil, M. (1996) *Prejudice in Ireland Revisited*. Maynooth: St Patrick's College.

Macintyre, J. (2012) 'The "leftwing bias" charge is distracting the BBC', *The Guardian* 15 May <www.guardian.co.uk/commentisfree/2012/may/15/leftwing-bias-bbc-myth> accessed 2 October 2012.

Macionis, J. and Plummer, K. (1997, 2002) *Sociology: a Global Introduction* (1st edn, 2nd edn). Prentice Hall.

Marsh, I. and Keating, M. (2000) *Sociology: Making Sense of Society* (2nd edn). Pearson Education.

McCann James, C., de Róiste, Á. and McHugh, J. (2009) *Social Care Practice in Ireland: An Integrated Perspective*. Dublin: Gill & Macmillan.

McDonald, B. (2009) *An Introduction to Sociology in Ireland* (2nd edn). Dublin: Gill & Macmillan.

Meagher, J. (2006) 'Was this the most wicked man in Irish history?' *Irish Independent* 30 September <http://www.independent.ie/opinion/analysis/was-this-the-most-wicked-man-in-irish-history-80792.html> accessed 9 September 2012.

Metro Éireann (2007) 'RTÉ – ethnic minorities not programmed out' <http:// metroeireann.com/article/rte-ethnic-minorities-not-programmed-,21> accessed 12 September 2012.

Migrant Rights Centre Ireland (MRCI) [website] <www.mrci.ie> accessed 10 September 2012.

Mitchell, Rodney (1987) 'And the company president is a black woman', *Media and Values* Issue 38 <www.medialit.org/reading-room/and-company-president-black-woman> accessed 12 September 2012.

Morris, Jan (1968) *Pax Britannica: The Climax of an Empire*. Faber & Faber.

National Archives [website]. Census of Ireland 1901/1911 <www.census. nationalarchives.ie/search> accessed 20 September 2012.

National Consultative Committee on Racism and Interculturalism (NCCRI) [website] 'Refugees and asylum seekers' <www.nccri.ie/cdsu-refugees.html> accessed 18 September 2012.

National Consultative Committee on Racism and Interculturalism (NCCRI) and Equality Authority (2003) *Media Coverage of Refugees and Asylum Seekers in Ireland* <www.nccri.ie/pdf/ireland_case_study.pdf> accessed 4 October 2012.

National Council for Curriculum and Assessment (NCCA) (2006) *Intercultural Education in the Post-Primary School* <www.ncca.ie/uploadedfiles/publications/ Interc%20Guide_Eng.pdf> accessed 10 September 2012.

National Council for Curriculum and Assessment and Integrate Ireland Language and Training (NCCA/IILT) (2003: revised 2005) *Integrating Non-English Speaking Pupils into the School and Curriculum: Handbook for Primary Schools* <www.ncca. ie/uploadedfiles/Curriculum/inclusion/Handbook_primary.pdf> accessed 10 September 2012.

National Union of Journalists (NUJ) (2007) 'Guidelines on race reporting'. London: NUJ. Available at <www.dochas.ie/Shared/Files/7/Guidelines_on_Race_Reporting. pdf> accessed 4 October 2012.

Neill, K. (1975) *Our Changing Times: Ireland, Europe and the Modern World since 1890*. Dublin: Gill & Macmillan.

O'Brien, E. (1995) *Modern Ireland 1868 to 1966: History Essays for Leaving Cert.* Dublin: Mentor.

O'Donnell, G. (2002) *Mastering Sociology* (4th edn). Basingstoke: Palgrave.

Office of the Press Ombudsman [website] <http://www.presscouncil.ie/office-of-the-press-ombudsman.167.html> accessed 2 October 2012.

Office of the Refugee Applications Commissioner (ORAC) [website] 'Criteria for the Grant of Refugee Status' <www.orac.ie/pages/Blue/Criteria.htm> accessed 22 September 2012.

— 'Legal and administrative framework for decision making' <www.orac.ie/pages/Blue/Frame_Work.htm> accessed 18 September 2012.

— (2011) *Annual Report 2011* <www.orac.ie/pages/CorpOff/publications.htm> accessed 18 September 2012.

Onanuga, Tola (2011) '*Wuthering Heights* realises Brontë's vision with its dark-skinned Heathcliff', *The Guardian* 21 October <http://www.guardian.co.uk/film/filmblog/2011/oct/21/wuthering-heights-film-heathcliff> accessed 12 September 2012.

O'Riordan, Tómas (n.d.) 'Charles Edward Trevelyan', University College Cork (UCC) Multitext Project in Irish History: Emancipation, Famine and Religion: Ireland under the Union, 1815–1870 <http://multitext.ucc.ie/d/Charles_Edward_Trevelyan> accessed 9 October 2012.

O'Toole, F. (1997) *The Ex-Isle of Erin: Images of a Global Ireland.* Dublin: New Island.

Owen Sound (2004) *Owen Sound's Black History.* Lyrics of 'Follow the Drinking Gourd' <www.osblackhistory.com/drinkinggourd.php> accessed 9 October 2012.

Padgett, T. (2007) 'Ethnic hairstyles can cause uneasiness in the workplace', *Chicago Tribune* 12 December <http://articles.chicagotribune.com/2007-12-12/features/0712100189_1_hair-glamour-dreadlocks> accessed 4 October 2012.

Patterson, O. (1998) *Rituals of Blood: Consequences of Slavery in Two American Centuries.* New York: Basic Civitas.

Peters, W. (1987) *A Class Divided: Then and Now* (expanded edn). New Haven, CT: Yale University Press.

Pols, Mary (2012) 'The bold, the beautiful and yes, occasionally boring new *Wuthering Heights*', *Time* 5 October <http://entertainment.time.com/2012/10/05/the-bold-the-beautiful-and-yes-occasionally-boring-new-wuthering-heights> accessed 8 October 2012.

Poole, S. (2006) *Unspeak.* Little, Brown.

Press Council of Ireland [website] <www.presscouncil.ie/> accessed 2 October 2012.

Princeton University [website] 'Primary and secondary sources outlined' <www.princeton.edu/~refdesk/primary2.html> accessed 8 October 2012.

Reception and Integration Agency (RIA) (2011) 'Direct provision house rules' <www.ria.gov.ie/en/RIA/> accessed 3 October 2012.

Reilly, C. (2012) 'RTÉ "stuck in the past"' *Metro Éireann* 1 July <http://metroeireann. com/article/rt-stuck-in-the-past,3393> accessed 15 September 2012.

Rhem, J. (1999) 'Pygmalion in the classroom', National Teaching and Learning Forum February, 8(2), 1–4 <www.ntlf.com/html/pi/9902/v8n2smpl.pdf> accessed 30 April 2012.

Rifkin, I. (1988) 'Covering conflict: how the news media handles ethnic controversy', *Media and Values* Issue 43, available from <www.medialit.org/reading-room/ covering-conflict-how-news-media-handles-ethnic-controversy> accessed 8 October 2012.

Rose, Steve (2011) 'How Heathcliff got a "racelift"', *The Guardian* 13 November <www. guardian.co.uk/film/2011/nov/13/how-heathcliff-got-a-racelift?intcmp=239> accessed 3 October 2012.

RTÉ (2005) *Scannal: Boycott: The Story of the Dunnes Stores South Africa Strike* <www.rte. ie/tv/scannal/Dunnes.html> accessed 25 September 2012.

RTÉ News (2011) Enda Kenny's speech on the Cloyne Report <www.rte.ie/ news/2011/0720/cloyne1.html> accessed 14 September 2012.

— (2012) 'New CSO figures show 1.8% drop in employment numbers' <www.rte. ie/news/2012/0919/unemployment-rate-steady-at-14-8-in-q2-business.html> accessed 19 September 2012.

Ruckenstein, L. and O'Malley, J.A. (eds) (2004) *Everything Irish: The History, Literature, Art, Music, People and Places of Ireland from A–Z*. Cork: Mercier Press.

Ryan, D., Benson, C. and Dooley, B. (2007) 'Forced Migration and Psychological Stress' in B. Fanning (ed.), *Immigration and Social Change in the Republic of Ireland*. Manchester: Manchester University Press.

St John, Pete (1979) 'The Fields of Athenry'. Lyrics available at <www.athenry.net/ lyrics.html> accessed 9 October 2012.

Schueler, Eva H.L. (2012) '*Hunger Games* casting: why Jennifer Lawrence shouldn't play Katniss', *The Communicator: A Student Voice* 3 January. Available at <www. huffingtonpost.com/2012/03/01/hunger-games-movie_n_1314053.html> accessed 8 October 2012.

Share, P., Tovey, H. and Corcoran, M.P. (2007) *A Sociology of Ireland* (3rd edn). Dublin: Gill & Macmillan.

Sharp, R. (2008) 'Fashion is racist: insider lifts lid on "ethnic exclusion"', *The Independent*, 16 February <http://www.independent.co.uk/news/uk/home-news/ fashion-is-racist-insider-lifts-lid-on-ethnic-exclusion-782974.html> accessed 4 October 2012.

Sheridan, V. (2007) 'Tuyen Pham: Caught between Two Cultures' in B. Fanning (ed.), *Immigration and Social Change in the Republic of Ireland*. Manchester: Manchester University Press.

Show Racism the Red Card Ireland [website] <www.theredcard.ie> accessed 10
    September 2012; 'Travellers and racism' <www.theredcard.ie/travellers_racism.
    php> accessed 9 September.
Somerville-Large, P. (2000) *Irish Voices: An Informal History 1916–1966*. London:
    Random House.
Sparknotes [website] Summary of *Birth of a Nation* <www.sparknotes.com/film/
    birthofanation/summary.html> accessed 8 October 2012.
SPIRASI [website] <www.spirasi.ie> accessed 10 September 2012.
Steinhorn, L. and Diggs-Brown, B. (1999) 'Virtual Integration: How the Integration of
    Mass Media Undermines Integration' in Gary Colombo, Robert Cullen and Bonnie
    Lisle (eds), *Rereading America: Cultural Contexts for Critical Thinking and Writing*
    (2001) (5th edn). Boston, MA: Bedford/St Martins.
Summerfield, E. and Lee, S. (2001) *Seeing the Big Picture: Exploring American Cultures
    on Film*. Maine: Intercultural Press.
Tapia, A. (2010) '*Dora the Explorer*, cultural change agent?', *The Inclusion Paradox*
    9 October <http://inclusionparadox.com/dora-the-explorer-cultural-change-agent/>
    accessed 12 September 2012.
Third Age [website] <www.thirdageireland.ie> accessed 10 September 2012.
Thompson, A. (2008) 'Empire and the British State' in S. Stockwell (ed.), *The British
    Empire: Themes and Perspectives*. Oxford: Blackwell.
Thorne, F. (2011) 'Child migrants sent "halfway across the world" for better life', Mail
    Online 14 June <www.dailymail.co.uk/news/article-2003422/British-child-slaves-
    launch-legal-action-Australian-government.html> accessed 5 October 2012.
Tour Egypt [website] 'Culture, customs and conduct' <www.touregypt.net/culture.
    htm> accessed 2 October 2012.
Tralee International Resource Centre (TIRC) [website] <www.tirc.ie> accessed
    10 September 2012.
United Against Racism [website] <www.unitedagainstracism.org/pages/infoARW_12.
    htm> accessed 14 September 2012.
United Nations (UN) [website] <www.un.org>.
— 'Rwanda: Unity in Diversity' available at <http://rw.one.un.org> accessed 2 October
    2012.
Varma, Meena (2009) 'India's elephant in the room', *The Guardian*, 11 February <www.
    guardian.co.uk/commentisfree/2009/feb/10/india-slumdog-millionaire-caste>
    accessed 8 October 2012.
Ward, T. (2002) *Asylum Seekers in Adult Education: A Study of Language and Literacy
    Needs*. Dublin: City of Dublin VEC and County Dublin VEC.
Waterford Area Partnership, Men's Development Network and RAPID (2006) *The
    Needs of Asylum Seeker Men living in Viking House Direct Provision Centre Waterford*

<www.wap.ie/Publications/Viking%20House%20Research%20Report%20Nov%20
06.pdf> accessed 19 September 2012.

Webb, R. and Tossell, D. (1999) Social Issues for Carers: Towards Positive Practice
(2nd edn). London: Hodder Arnold.

Whitaker, B. (2012) 'Record number of people fleeing Syria, UN reports', The
Guardian, 4 September 2012 <http://www.guardian.co.uk/world/2012/sep/04/
syria-refugees-asylum-un> accessed 25 September 2012.

Whiting, Beatrice B. (ed.) (1963) Six Cultures: Studies of Child Rearing. New York and
London: Wiley .

Whiting, Beatrice B. and Edwards, Carolyn P. (1988) Children of Different Worlds:
The Formation of Social Behavior. Cambridge, MA: Harvard University Press.

Williamson, N. (2007) Rough Guide to the Blues. London: Rough Guides.

Wolf, N. (2012) 'This global financial fraud and its gatekeepers', The Guardian
14 July <www.guardian.co.uk/commentisfree/2012/jul/14/global-financial-fraud-
gatekeepers> accessed 2 October 2012.

Woll, A. (1988) 'Century of abuse: ethnic images on the big screen', Media and Values
Issue 43 <http://www.medialit.org/reading-room/century-abuse-ethnic-images-big-
screen> accessed 12 September 2012.

Wright, Charlie (2010) 'Tesco adds seven ranges to ethnic line', The Grocer 30
November <www.thegrocer.co.uk/companies/tesco-adds-seven-ranges-to-ethnic-
line-up/214320.article> accessed 10 September 2012.

Wright, Richard (1938) 'The Ethics of Living Jim Crow' in Uncle Tom's Children.
Harper.

Wuthering-heights.co.uk [website] 'Was Heathcliff black?' <http://wuthering-heights.
co.uk/faq.htm> accessed 8 October 2012.

Index

INDEX 187

India
  caste system, 19, 21, 50, 146
  child rearing, 35, 36
  death rituals, 53–4
  weddings, 50–1
Industrial Revolution, 106, 109
inequalities
  and globalisation, 39
  wealth, 23
institutional racism, 18, 78–9, 112, 147
integration, 2–3
  as function of religion, 42
  Great Britain, 112
  language barriers, 76, 101
  organisations promoting, 80–3
  USA, 120, 143
  see also migrants, organisations
    promoting integration
interculturalism
  dialogue, 1, 2–3, 9
  education, 78, 79, 83
  events, 75
  National Consultative Committee
    on Racism and Interculturalism
    (NCCRI), 79, 83, 134–5
  television programmes, 139–40
International Court of Justice, 167, 168
International Day Against Racism, 83
internationalism, 8–9
internment, 59
interviews, 74
IRA (Irish Republican Army), 58, 59
Ireland
  1937 Constitution, 61
  asylum seekers and refugees, 134–5
    see also asylum seekers; refugees
  citizenship, 166–7
  colonisation, 108
  independence, 57
  Irish identity, 14

migration, 10–11, 14, 99–100, 152–3,
  159–60
nationalism, 8
prejudice against ethnic minorities, 25
rebellions, 153
recession and boom, 11
religious make-up, 47–8
secularism, 61–3
songs and ballads, 151–3
Irish Aid, 112
Irish Constitution, 125
The Irish Emigrant, 152
Irish Famine see Great Famine
Irish Ferries dispute, 90, 100
Irish Human Rights Commission (IHRC),
  84
Irish Orphan Scheme, 110
Irish Republican Army (IRA), 58, 59
Irish Rugby Union Players Association, 83
Islam
  death rituals, 53–4
  dietary requirements, 77
  Five Pillars, 44
  fundamentalism, 54
  hijab, 63–5
  history, 43–5
  in Ireland, 49
  persecution, 56
  Qu'ran, 44, 47, 51, 52
  Sharia law, 86–7
  similarities to Judaism and Christianity,
    47
  weddings, 51–2
Israel, 45, 56, 111

J
Jackson, Andrew, 116
Jandt, Fred, E., 24
Japan, 36
Jerusalem, 56